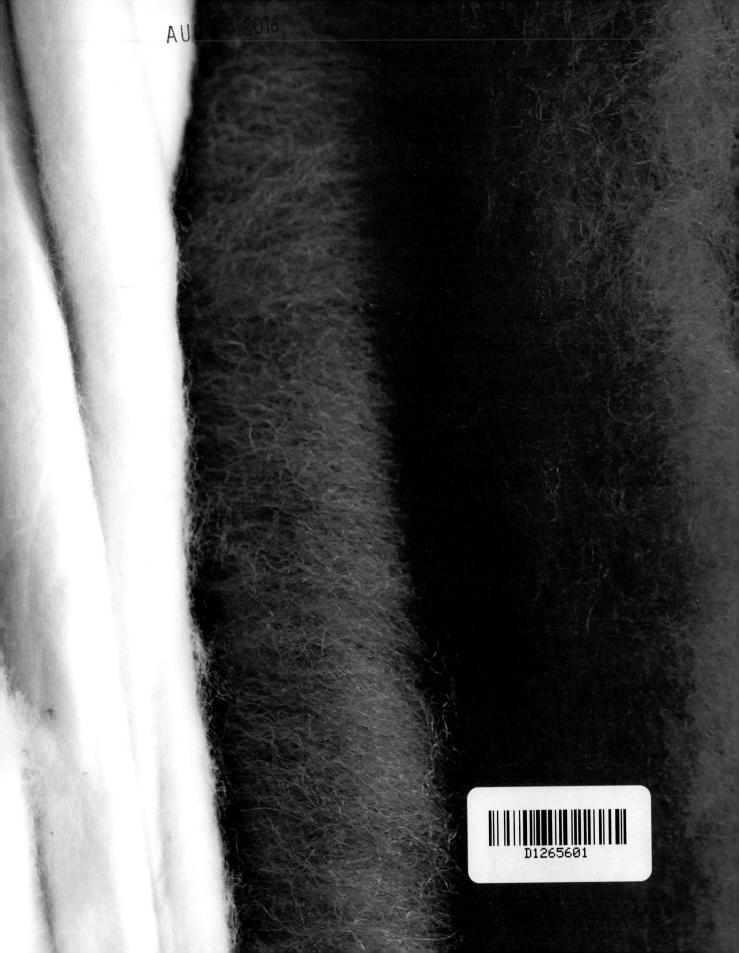

D1265601

yarn·i·tec·ture

yarn·i·tec·ture

A Knitter's Guide to Spinning:
Building Exactly the Yarn You Want

JILLIAN MORENO

Storey Publishing

*The mission of Storey Publishing is to serve our customers by
publishing practical information that encourages
personal independence in harmony with the environment.*

Edited by GWEN STEEGE
Art direction and book design by CAROLYN ECKERT
Indexed by NANCY D. WOOD

Cover photography by MARS VILAUBI,
except for: JOHN POLAK, back (bottom & author);
© RYANN FORD: back (all except top right & bottom)

Interior photography by:
JOHN POLAK: Inside front and back covers; 1–9, 14–24,
26 top, 28–35, 38, 42, 43 bottom, 44, 45, 47–48, 50 bottom, 51–53, 54 top, 55, 57–62, 64, 65, 69–74, 75 top, 76,
77 inset, 78 left, 79–81, 82 top & bottom right, 83, 84 top
& bottom right, 85, 86, 88–90, 93–96, 97 inset, 98–124,
126–133, 135, 136, 138, 140–142, 147, 151, 153, 154, 156 left,
157, 159, 160, 162, 165 right, 168, 171, 173, 174, 176–177, 179,
183, 185, 186, 187 bottom, 188, 191, 193 middle, 195-198,
201, 203, 204, 206 right, 207, 209, 211, 212, 213 bottom
left, 214–215, 217, 218, 221

MARS VILAUBI: 10, 13, 37, 40, 46, 50 top, 56, 82
bottom left, 84 bottom left, 87 top, 92, 97 top, 125, 134,
166, 169, 170, 200

© RYANN FORD: Opposite half title page, 148–150, 152,
155, 156 right, 158, 161, 163, 164, 165 left, 172, 175, 178, 181,
182, 184, 187 top, 190, 193 top & bottom, 194, 202, 205,
206 left, 208, 210, 213 top right, 216, 219, 220, 239

Additional photographs by: © dem10/Getty Images:
26 bottom, 41, 54 bottom, 63, 75 bottom, 87 bottom, 137,
143; © Joe Coca, Lendrum: 66 top left; © photo courtesy of HansenCrafts LLC: 66 bottom right; © LOUET:
66 bottom left; © Michael Lichter, Michael Lichter
Photography LLC, Schacht: 66 top right; © Science Photo
Library/Getty Images: 43 top; © wdstock/Getty Images:
32, 42 bottom, 50 bottom (background), 67, 77 (background), 78 (background), 97 (background)

How-to illustrations by ALISON KOLESAR
Charts and pattern illustrations by ILONA SHERRATT

© 2016 BY JILLIAN MORENO

STOREY PUBLISHING
210 MASS MoCA Way
North Adams, MA 01247
storey.com

Printed in China by R.R. Donnelley
10 9 8 7 6 5 4 3 2 1

Library of Congress Cataloging-in-Publication Data
Names: Moreno, Jillian, author.
  Title: Yarnitecture : a knitter's guide to spinning :
    building exactly the yarn you want / Jillian Moreno.
  Description: North Adams, Massachusetts :
    Storey Publishing, [2016] |
Includes bibliographical references and index.
  Identifiers: LCCN 2016005996 (print) |
    LCCN 2016015983 (ebook) |
    ISBN 9781612125213 (hardcover : alk. paper) |
    ISBN 9781612125220 (ebook)
Subjects: LCSH: Hand spinning. | Yarn.
Classification: LCC TT847 .M67 2016 (print) |
LCC TT847 (ebook) | DDC
746.1/2--dc23
LC record available at https://lccn.loc.gov/2016005996

DEDICATION

To my loves, Andy, Isobel, and Henry,
for keeping me laughing

con·tents

foreword · clara parkes 11

foreword · jacey boggs 13

introduction · why this book? 15

1 | the blueprint

Yarn Vision 25

Why Am I Spinning? 25

The Advantage of Keeping Track 26

Getting Motivated to Spin with
    Intention 27

Keeping Your Yarn Vision on Track 29

2 | the foundation

Sheep Breeds and Beyond 31

Wool: The Backbone of Spinning 31

Angora: A Class of Its Own 35

Camelids: Warmer than Wool 36

The Big Beasts: Yak, Bison,
    and Musk Ox 36

Get My Goats 36

Seductive Silk 39

Other Natural Fibers 39

Synthetic Fiber: Nylon Can
    Be a Spinner's Friend 39

3 | the frame

Fiber Preparations 41

Woolen vs. Worsted Fiber Preparation 41

Silk Preparations: Beyond Top and Roving 47

4 | the walls

Drafting 49

A Few Words about Twist 49

Drafting Triangle: The Sweet Spot in Drafting 50

Drafting against Type: What Happens 55

Drafting Fiber Blends: Dealing with Mismatched
Staple Lengths 56

Thick or Thin: Controlling Yarn Size while
Drafting 59

Don't Fight It! Your Wheel Is Your Friend:
Work Together 60

Predrafting 60

Ratios and Whorls (Pulleys): The Basics 63

Drive Systems: They Can Make
Spinning Easier 64

How to Draft Consistently 68

Semi-Worsted and Semi-Woolen Throwdown!
Or, a Plea for Sanity 68

con·tents

5 | the roof

Plying 71

What Is Ply and Why Do It? 71

The Basics of Equipment and Setup 77

How to Ply 77

Resting and Rewinding Singles:
    Pros and Cons 79

How Twist Affects Knitting 79

How Ply Affects Knitting 81

Plying Mistakes and What to Do 87

6 | the paint

Color 91

How Dyers Dye 91

What Affects Color on Fiber 91

Digging into Your Stash 98

The Secret to Plying to Match 101

Mixing It Up within a Braid 101

Combining Variegated Colors 109

Working with Batts 111

7 | the front door

Finishing 117

Steaming 117

Soaking 117

Snapping 118

Centripetal Force (Lasso) 118

Whacking 119

Fulling 119

Menacing 119

8 | the landscaping

Knitting with Your Handspun 127

A Word on Mill-Spun Yarns 127

Measuring Handspun Yarn 130

Sampling and Keeping Track 144

Planning Knitting Projects 145

Twist and Knitting Style 146

9 | housewarming

12 Patterns Using Handspun Yarn 149

SWEET OMEGA MÖBIUS
Designed by Lynne Vogel 150

MAYA CARDIGAN
Designed by Kirsten Kapur 158

JILLIAN SHAWL
Designed by Rosemary (Romi) Hill 166

LINA TOE-UP SOCKS
Designed by Kate Atherley 172

BUMP IN THE NIGHT
Designed by Amy King 178

TETRIS PULLOVER
Designed by Julia Farwell-Clay 182

WENNY SHAWL
Designed by Amy King 190

LA CUERDA
Designed by Laura Nelkin 194

WINTER LIBRARY SHAWL
Designed by Jillian Moreno 198

RIGBY CARDIGAN
Designed by Bristol Ivy 202

HIVE MIND
Designed by Adrian Bizilia 210

DYE GODDESS PULLOVER
Designed by Jillian Moreno 216

Appendixes 222

suggested reading 222

glossary of techniques 223

abbreviations 231

resources 232

acknowledgments 233

index 234

foreword

CLARA PARKES

I STILL REMEMBER MY FIRST SKEIN. Lumpy and overtwisted, it was hardly enough "yarn" to be useful in any way. But it marked the beginning of my journey toward understanding how, with just a little bit of work, you could transform almost any jumble of fibers into *yarn*.

Like riding a bike, I gradually got better at keeping my spindle (and, soon, wheel) in steady motion while managing an even draft and twist. It seemed absurdly hard at first, but I kept going, and then one day, it clicked.

My fiber consumption slowly increased from a few ounces to a few pounds to a sheep's worth of fleece. Now that I deal in flocks, my currency is the bale. I have someone else do the scouring and spinning and plying and skeining for me. But if I hadn't begun as a handspinner, I'd be completely lost. Learning to spin is the very best way to understand how yarn really works — and in that regard, I wish every knitter would learn how to do it.

Only after I tried knitting with my handspun did I discover another problem: it turns out spinning yarn is rather easy, but spinning a yarn that serves a purpose, that fulfills your hopes and dreams for a specific knitted project? That's where the journey toward wisdom really begins — and that's where this book begins as well. It assumes you already understand the basics of spinning and are ready to go further.

A masterful explainer of things, Jillian walks you through all the tiny but vital variables that come into play when you're creating a lovely and useful yarn. She touches on choosing your fibers and fiber preparations, working with solid and multicolored fibers, and even juggling the nuances of drafting and plying and finishing. Best of all, Jillian makes it abundantly clear what beautiful rewards await you at the end.

How I wish Jillian had written this book when I was first learning to spin. It would've saved me a lot of trial and error . . . okay, mostly error.

Lucky for you, the book is now here, and it's in your hands. Use it well.

foreword

JACEY BOGGS

THE HUMAN BRAIN is an amazing and confounding instrument, isn't it? When I started spinning, I read everything I could get my hands on that dealt with this craft. I perused and then pored over text after tome after magazine.

Some of it sank in, but much seemed beyond my understanding, presented in a way that didn't fit precisely into my brain. It's one of the reasons I started *PLY* magazine, because what I wanted wasn't out there yet. My brain style — nimble at times, lumbering at others — wasn't well represented. I wanted spinning laid out before me like a magnificent feast of hows, whys, and what-ifs. I wanted a clear map from start to finish but one that was smart and open-minded with lots of scenic routes and off-road adventures. I wanted Jillian — I just didn't know it yet.

Spinning, with its endless options and differing opinions, can be overwhelming. This is not news to you, I bet. Sometimes it can feel like you have to know everything, to get each thing exactly right, or you might as well give up and go commercial. I felt this many times as I tried to find a way to force all the spinning facts into my strange-shaped brain. Jillian's house-building metaphor slides perfectly into my brain, like a key in a lock. It was made for a mind like mine, where the tumblers sometimes jam and require clear and precise instructions or a swift kick. There are a million different ways to build a house, but they all have the same basic elements, and what you choose to spotlight is up to you. Your house might have the brightest front door on the block (look at that colorway), her house might have the sturdiest foundation (great-grandchildren will inherit it), his house sure has nice windows (no cold getting in there); they're all different and they all bring their inhabitants joy, but you can bet the builder learned from each one.

You are an adventurer, a traveler, a builder. Go explore and build. Learn as you go, pay attention, make alterations, grow and change, and embrace the journey. You don't have to know it all right now. You just have to have a good map, nimble fingers, and an open mind. You're holding one of the best maps I've seen, so stretch out your fingers and mind and get started!

introduction:
WHY THIS BOOK?

HAVE YOU NOTICED how many more spinners there are nowadays? What was once a cozy, tiny group of weirdos has become a loud, brash family. Have you also noticed how many more fibers there are to buy and how many more places to buy it? I never thought I could walk into a knitting store and find beautiful fiber, much less take spinning classes there.

The spinning world is growing, and the spinning world is changing. More spinners are coming from the knitting world. Some come to spinning because they want to create their own yarn, exactly how they want it, choosing every aspect from color to feel to gauge. Some come because they have fallen in love with the braids and batts dyed by one of the hundreds of talented dyers around the world.

Many spinners aren't interested in buying a fleece or doing their own preparation — they want to spin from the ready-made beauties they buy at the Maryland Sheep and Wool Festival, New York Sheep and Wool Festival (a.k.a. Rhinebeck), Black Sheep Gathering in Oregon, and Madrona Fiber Arts retreat in Washington, as well as from online sites such as Etsy or at their local knitting stores. It's not even just new spinners who fall into that category of spinners — I am proudly one of them. I've been spinning off and on for almost 20 years, and I don't like to process my own fiber. I know how to do it, and I know the upside to choosing and processing, but I am thoroughly in love with handdyed, commercially processed fiber.

Commercially processed fiber has had a bad reputation in the spinning world as overprocessed and compacted, hard to spin and not as worthy as hand-processed fibers. Like the rest of the fiber world, however, commercial processing has grown and matured, developing nuances beyond compacted, scoured fiber. Fibers are being processed in smaller batches, many locally sourced and processed. And the color — that's where the magic lies. That's what draws me across the shop, room, or fairground, keeps me coming back to websites and keeps me spinning. Gone are the days of hobby handdyers who dyed a few braids or batts with Kool-Aid for a local guild sale or fiber fair. The women and men who are dyeing now are artists with full-time businesses. The variety and beauty of their work is astonishing, and my overflowing stash is testament to that.

Many spinners are coming from a knitting background, as I know I did. I spin to use my yarn for knitting. These spinners know about yarn, know what they want in a yarn, and want to know how to make it. They want something unique, something they can't find in a shop. For a long time, the yarn was the end product, the whole point of the activity, and it still is for some spinners. I consider myself a spinning knitter, and my point is to use the yarn, whether I'm spinning for a particular project or spinning for the joy of it and then finding a project to use it for.

I love knitting with handspun. I love knitting period, but handspun takes it to a different level, even if it's handspun I didn't spin. Handspun yarn is lively and has so much to say about how it wants to be. Most mill-spun yarns are passive, but handspun wants a say in the knitting process. I've thought long and hard about why I love knitting with handspun, and I came up with five reasons: choice, control, craft, creativity, and connection.

CHOICE

I love having choices. Sometimes I choose a commercial yarn because it's just right, but nothing looks and feels like handspun yarn. I have yet to knit with a commercial yarn that feels like handspun. Commercial yarn is prepped and spun by machines that hold it under a lot more tension than most spinners would. That tension stretches a little bit of the life, the spring, out of the yarn. Then it's wound by machine and stacked in boxes, stretching and compressing the fibers more. All this machinery gives a mill an easily repeatable and predictable yarn.

To me, commercial yarns seem a little limp, whereas handspun yarn seems alive, almost as though it breathes. It's brash and energetic. It can be uneven and sometimes a little unpredictable, but for me that adds to the excitement of knitting with it; it's never boring.

Because fiber processed specifically for handspinning is usually dyed before it's spun, the colors in handspun are deeper, and I'm able to manipulate how they fall from variegated tops and rovings into the yarn. Sometimes I want very clear-cut colors; sometimes I want them muddied or blended or in a different order.

The finished fabric is somehow different, too. It looks vibrant and feels lively. It has personality and attitude. Even when I spin just to spin, with nothing particular in mind, I always knit a little with my handspun. It never feels quite done until I hold that little swatch.

CONTROL

I won't deny that one of the things I love about knitting with handspun is the control I have over creating the yarn. Sometimes it feels like there are a million different options when it comes to spinning yarn. I narrow it down to seven things and ask myself lots of questions.

What am I spinning for? Am I interpreting a commercial or handspun yarn for a pattern? Am I spinning yarn first, then finding a pattern? Am I just spinning to spin? What type of yarn do I want to end up with?

Breed and fiber. Because of the work of Clara Parkes, Deb Robson, and Beth Smith, most spinners and knitters know that there are different sheep breeds and that the wool from each has different properties that lend themselves to particular yarns. Non-wool fibers, whether animal, plant, or man-made, all help yarn feel and look a

One braid, five completely different yarns. **FROM THE TOP,** yarns and knitted swatches: (A) fractal spun 2-ply; (B) chain plied; (C) plied as it came; (D) flipped 2-ply; (E) singles

A

B

C

D

E

particular way, too. What am I looking for in my yarn? What will I use it for? Does a kernel of it lie in breed or fiber choice?

Prep. Am I starting with a fleece or commercially prepared fiber? How will I prepare the fleece? How was the commercial fiber prepared? Each preparation method, no matter the fiber, influences the finished yarn. What do I need for the yarn in my mind?

Color. Am I dyeing my fiber? What colors? Will I dye before or after I prepare my fiber? Before or after the yarn is spun? If I'm using gorgeously dyed top or roving or batts, will I spin the colors as they are or manipulate the color flow somehow? Will I combine the colors with another dyed fiber? Will I combine colors in the draft or ply?

Draft. Do I want compact or lofty yarn? Smooth or textured yarn? Somewhere in between? Am I blending colors here? Am I working with or against the preparation? How much twist do I want?

Ply. Am I plying? How many plies? Am I blending colors here? Do I want a textured or art ply? How much ply twist do I want?

Finish. How will I finish it? Will I full or felt? Will I whack it, snap it, or just hang it? Is there any reason to block the yarn?

Whew! It seems like a lot, but I mostly do all of this in my head in a minute or two. When I'm planning a big or very specific project, I sit and write it all out.

CRAFT

This is the making part, the hands-on part. This is the part where I grow as a spinner *and* as a knitter by spinning the yarn I knit with. For me, it's an ongoing conversation back and forth, round and round, between the starting fiber, the finished knitted fabric, and all of the steps in between. My craft is constantly evolving based on curiosity, experience, obsession, and trial and error.

The learning, the questing, and questioning — this might be my favorite part. I am perpetually asking questions like these:

- I want to make a yarn like this commercial yarn; how do I reverse-engineer it?

- I tried to make a yarn for a particular knitting pattern and it's a disaster; what went wrong?

- I hate one of the colors in this variegated roving; what can I do to save it?

- I love this dyed fiber in the braid. I spun and knit it, but it's gross and the colors pool; what should I have done differently?

- I want to spin a particular type of yarn; how do I learn? Who do I talk to? Who do I take a lesson from? What do I read?

CREATIVITY

The originality of handspun yarn is astonishing. No two spinners will spin an identical yarn given the same wheel, fiber, and parameters. It can have the same twist, wraps per inch (wpi; see pages 26 and 130), and gauge, but somehow it won't look the same. It's just something that each spinner breathes into his or her yarn when spinning it.

Once I take control of fiber with some intention, my creative mind explodes. It might be the opposite of what works for you, but for me, giving myself even a small parameter, such as "spin yarn for a shawl," guides my thinking to be more creative. It plucks my brain out of all the overwhelming things and infinity of ideas and settles it into "shawl yarn." (Well, that's just 650 ideas for shawls to sort through.)

CONNECTION

I love being part of something that reaches forward and back and that has a vibrant "now." I may not always be in the thick of it posting on Ravelry (I'm shy that way), but I love the underground rumble I always feel. I love that when I have an idea or question I can look at old books and magazines and search online and find a variety of answers and opinions. I love that when new magazines, books, or conversations come up, there is always something new, a new twist, a new process.

In-person spinning energy is crazy. When I spin with friends or go to a fiber sale, class, retreat, or one of the big events, I am always full and exhausted afterward. It takes me a while to work through the things I learned and even longer to try them out. There is such a feeling of process and liveliness when spinners get together; it's the best, really.

IS THIS BOOK FOR YOU?

This book is for spinning knitters and for spinners who are interested in creating yarns that would be good for knitting (and other things, too). Chances are that if you picked up this book you are a spinner *and* a knitter — or you are one and about to become the other. I assume that you already know how to spin. This isn't a beginner's learn-to-spin book. Rather, it's about how to spin to get a specific yarn as well as a spruce-up-your-spinning book.

I came to spinning after first being a weaver, then a knitter. I thought I knew about commercial yarns, but spinning taught me things about how yarns work, why they do so, and how to get them to behave. Spinning taught me why some of my early knitting efforts were abject failures, and the reasons included using the wrong yarn or yarn structure.

It's safe to say that most spinners who pick up this book are knitters, too. This makes you an educated spinner, because you know about yarn. In fact, you know a lot about how yarn is constructed, how it behaves, and (mostly) what you find unique: something in colors that you can't find or that commemorate a trip, a yarn with more or fewer plies, a yarn that stripes differently. The possibilities are vast. You want to spin to make something you want to see come from that gorgeous braid you fell in love with.

WHAT IS YARNITECTURE?

Yarnitecture is simply the concept that all of the component parts of spinning a yarn build on each

Spinning your own yarn gives you control, for example, over how many plies to use for a specific project.

Spinning is a craft that can help you grow not only as a spinner but as a knitter.

other to create the yarn you envision. It is the idea of exploring connections, and then learning how to get the parts to work together (or against each other) to create exactly the yarn you want. It's like creating a building or a home. In this book, I hope to save you a few steps by pointing you in a direction without dictating a must-do.

Sometimes my ideas are as concrete as a specific pattern, while at other times they are rather general: "I think I'll knit a sweater . . . or maybe a shawl." In the past, I spun without really thinking too much, hoping that the thoughts in my brain would convey that certain need-to-know to my hands, fiber, and wheel, and that I would

magically spin exactly the yarn that would work for my dream project. I would say that 90 percent of the time I failed miserably. I failed on so many levels. Most of the time I didn't even have enough fiber!

I like to pick at things, however, to poke things with a stick and figure out why and how to do things better. So I started thinking and reading. What I found was that there are so many possibilities for what can go into spinning for a knitting project that it's a wonder anyone does it at all. It's paralyzing. But when I spun, I started with an idea, and then, by taking all of the component parts and actions, with their million variables,

I arrived at a plan. Yes. Then I let it all stew for a while, doing more spinning and thinking about all of the parts that go into making and building yarn. I was still a little overwhelmed, but it was a focused overwhelmed — like when I clean out my closet, get everything out, and then think, holy crap, that is a lot of stuff — but there's no turning back now. I continued to spin, made lists, and talked to all of the spinning people I know.

One day I was reading a book, not about spinning or yarn or knitting, and an idea politely tapped me on the shoulder: "It's like building a house." So I decided to break down the project I was working on into these parts: an idea, the fiber, the preparation of the fiber, how I spin the fiber, how I finish the fiber, and how I knit with the fiber — because handspun is a different beast from commercial yarn. Spinning includes drafting and plying, and then there's the complex and frustrating and fabulous idea of color.

Next, I started wondering how someone building a house would describe this. I often find that if I take something that confuses or overwhelms me and cloak it in a different context, it takes the scariness, the panic, the overwhelmingness out of it. I went through the parts of a house and the rudimentary parts of the building process in my head. I have never built a house or studied architecture, but I came up with components: the blueprint, the foundation, the frame, the walls, the roof, the door, the paint, and the landscaping. I was envisioning and building yarns for a specific use — I was a yarnitect.

I came up with a method that made sense to me based on what (little) I know about house building and what I know about getting from idea to finished project. I started making very conscious decisions at each step in the process. At first, it took a great deal of time because I did a lot of research and sampling in order to make my decisions, but now that I've been following this process for a while, it takes less time — or it *can* take much less time. I still am a sucker for experimenting.

This process first became a proposal for this book, then the outline, and now it serves as the table of contents.

Blueprint = Yarn vision or idea

Foundation = Fiber

Frame = Fiber preparation

Walls = Drafting

Roof = Plying

Paint = Color

Front door = Finishing

Landscaping = Knitting

Housewarming = Patterns

For this book, I contacted designers to create things from handspun. Some of these knitting designers are also spinners, and some just appreciate and really love to knit with handspun yarn. Each one is an amazing designer; each one I have admired for years. They have created beautiful patterns for you to knit with your handspun.

In this book, I offer guidance based on my spinning and my research, and I show lots of samples. This book is a shortcut for spinning knitters, a little education and a lot of tips and tricks. Most of all, it's a heaping helping of "just get in there and do it."

RIGBY CARDIGAN SCHEMATIC PAGE 202

MAIN MEASUREMENTS:

bust circumference, with front bands overlapping:
33½ (37½, 41½, 45½, 48¾, 52¾, 56¾, 60¾)"

waist circumference, with front bands overlapping:
27¼ (31¼, 35½, 39¼, 42½, 46½, 50½, 54½)"

hip circumference, with front bands overlapping:
35¼ (39¼, 43¼, 47¼, 50½, 54½, 58½, 62½)"

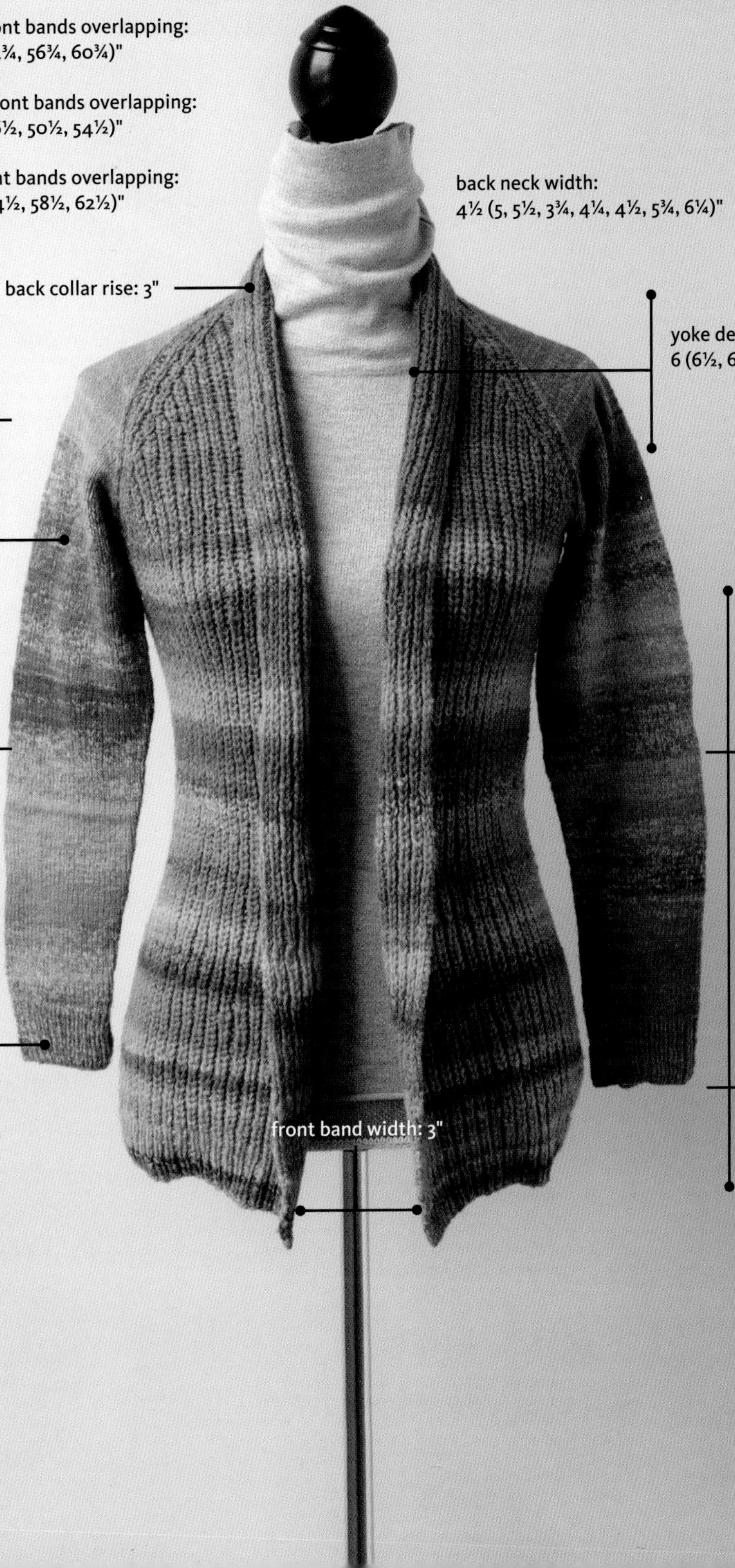

back neck width:
4½ (5, 5½, 3¾, 4¼, 4½, 5¾, 6¼)"

back collar rise: 3"

yoke depth:
6 (6½, 6¾, 7¼, 7½, 8, 8½, 9)"

total sleeve length:
19 (19, 19½, 19½, 20, 20, 20½, 20½)"

upper arm circumference:
10¾ (11¾, 12½, 13½, 14¾, 16¼, 17¼, 18½)"

stockinette sleeve length:
17 (17, 17½, 17½, 18, 18, 18½, 18½)"

cuff circumference:
7½ (7½, 8, 8, 8¼, 8¼, 9, 9)"

cuff ribbing:
2"

total body length:
16¾ (16¾, 17¼, 17¼, 17¼, 18, 18, 18)"

waist to underarm length:
5 (5, 5½, 5½, 5½, 6¼, 6¼, 6¼)"

hip to waist length:
9¾"

hem ribbing:
3"

front band width: 3"

1 | the blueprint:
YARN VISION

WHEN YOU SIT AT YOUR WHEEL to create yarn, do you know what you want to spin? If you are spinning for something other than just the spin of it, do you know how to get there? Can you see the finished yarn in your mind's eye, feel it running through your hands as you knit? Can you see the beautiful finished project created from your yarn?

Do you ever take more than a second to think about the yarn you want to make, to use, even before you sample, and before you buy or shop your stash for fiber?

Taking time to really describe the yarn you want to use can be the difference between loving your final yarn and project, and disappointment. When I express all of the details of a future yarn, I call it a *yarn vision*. I do it when I am spinning for a specific project, and I do it just to stretch my creativity in spinning. I started doing it because I would spend most of my time just spinning aimlessly, and even when I had a project or yarn in mind, I would sit at my wheel and hope for the best. Needless to say, I was disappointed most of the time!

So now I dream part of the time and plan part of the time to make a yarn vison, and I spin with clearer ideas and intent. I find I spin more because my time is better balanced between dreaming and spinning. I also find I spin with more creativity because my best creative moments come from veering from a path (what if I do it the way everyone says you can't?) or combining paths that I've never put together before.

My planning usually consists of asking myself questions. I love questions, I love lists, and I'm a visual person, so my yarn vision frequently looks like an explosion of fiber, paper, tags, markers, and photos. In this chapter, I describe some of the ways I get motivated.

WHY AM I SPINNING?

That's always my big question, the perfect place to start. Here are a bunch of reasons I might be spinning.

- To just spin or relax. Sometimes I set myself a time each day just to spin at my wheel if I feel I haven't been spinning enough or to unwind without a spinning have-to.

- To learn something new

- To practice a technique from a class or spin along with a class

- To get to know a wheel or to try a new setup.

- To be creative. I try to match yarn with something: a photo, movie, book, or abstract idea.

- To experiment — to try out the "what if this comes up" when I'm spinning, teaching, or reading; I need time and space to sort ideas out

- For a project. Am I spinning for a specific project or something general, like some sort of a sweater?

THE ADVANTAGE OF KEEPING TRACK

I'm not great at following this principle, and I'm always unhappy when I don't. Decide how you will keep track of your spinning. Use a method that works for you that is easy. Mine is low tech and unsexy; I use zip-top plastic bags, index cards, and Tyvek wristbands. It works for me. I've tried to use fancier systems, but I love keeping my yarn samples on Tyvek wristbands, and I can't work without zip-top bags — I can stuff everything in them. Here's what I keep track of:

- The yarn I am trying to make. I describe it in detail technically, but also how I want it to look and feel.

- Fiber type

- Colorway

- Dyer

- Label that came with the fiber (if I have it)

- Wheel and setup

- Predrafting or splitting of fiber

- Color manipulation

- Drafting method

Label Tyvek wristbands with information about the skein, such as fiber, spinning method, and grist.

- Wraps per inch (wpi; see below and page 130)

- Singles (wpi and twist direction)

- Ply (number of plies, wpi, and twist direction)

- Twist angle (see below and page 133)

- Ply

- Twists per inch (tpi; see below and page 135)

- Grist or yards per pound (ypp; see below and page 137)

Spinning Speak

The fiber world has a whole vocabulary of its own. You'll find more in-depth discussions of many of these terms in other sections of the book, but here's a quick reference to some that you'll encounter early on.

wpi (wraps per inch)	A unit measure of yarn width, measured with a wpi gauge or a ruler
twist angle	A unit measure of the angle of the fibers in a yarn, measured with a protractor in degrees
tpi (twists per inch)	A unit of measure of number of rotations (twists) per 1" of yarn
grist	A unit of measure combining the length and weight of a yarn; its density, expressed as ypp (yards per pound)

GETTING MOTIVATED TO SPIN WITH INTENTION

Here are some ideas for spinning with intention. When I'm interested in learning something new, I pick a skill or challenge, such as one of these:

- Spinning a longwool fiber with a woolen draft or draw

- Spinning and knitting something to wear with less than 2 ounces of fiber

- Spinning 8 ounces of fiber with a less favorite drafting method

- Reading a chapter in a spinning book or an article in a magazine and spinning the fiber as the author recommends

- Having a friend teach me his or her favorite method of spinning

- Practicing. This is the one I was happy adding to my spinning intentions. After I've taken or watched a class, there are always things I want to practice. I mark these things in my notes or keep a list as I'm watching. Then I go back and practice. When I practice, I do it as closely as possible to the instructor's method. After I feel like I understand the crux of it (not looking for perfection or conversion), I move to experimenting with how to do it my way if the instructor's way doesn't seem a good fit for me.

IS YOUR WHEEL KEEPING YOU FROM SPINNING?

One of the things that surprised me when I started focusing on my spinning process was that sometimes I don't spin, or spin efficiently, or spin with joy, because of my wheel. I would sit at my wheel, and something wouldn't be right, either mechanically or with me relating to my wheel.

I admit that sometimes I let my wheels languish. I also get into system ruts by always spinning Scotch or double drive. Or I get the idea into my head that I want a new wheel or that I should sell one of mine. (I confess that I always fall back in love with a wheel I'm thinking of selling, or I realize that the actual problem is that something needs fixing or adjusting.) To settle myself down when I realize I'm going down that path, I use the following strategies:

- I get a wheel out and put her through her paces, or I borrow a wheel that I think I want to buy.

- If the wheel I'm using has more than one drive system, I consciously change from the one I typically use.

- I switch out the kind of yarn I'm spinning, going from woolen to worsted, fat to thin, and back again, plying, stopping, starting. I spin my default yarn, then spin both fatter and thinner yarns.

- Sometimes I do a wheel spa: dusting, oiling, changing the drive band, cleaning my WooLee Winder.

USING CREATIVE SPINNING TO DEVELOP YOUR VISION

Sometimes when I just want to spin, I need a little prompt. I call this creative spinning. I let myself be inspired by something and aim to create a yarn that represents it. Here are some of my inspirations:

- A word

- A phrase

- An idea

- A book, movie, person, or song

- A photo

This type of spinning usually has a preparation component to it: fibers and colors get combined, commercially prepped fibers are reprepped, sometimes the dye pots come out. I'm open to other kinds of experimentation, as well, and all of my questions are the prompts — anything that starts with a "what if." I try spinning a fiber against its type, for example, spinning a longer longwool with a woolen draft, when many spinners would spin it worsted draft only. I experiment with color, I test just how low low-twist can go. I base my yarn on something non-fibery, like a song or a photo.

If I'm spinning for a specific project, I ask myself:

- Is there a deadline?

- Is it a gift? If so, does the person I'm knitting for have favorite colors or fiber allergies? Do I have all of the measurements I need? How carefully will he or she follow care instructions?

- What type of fiber, and how much, do I need?

- How much extra do I need for sampling?

- What type of yarn does the pattern call for, especially if I'm spinning for a pattern that calls for mill-spun yarn? This description might include aspects of the pattern that will influence your yarn making, like whether it's a drapey lace or it features crisp cables.

- How might I want to make changes to the recommended yarn, for example, using a different fiber or a different drafting method or number of plies, and so on?

- What yardage do I need?

- What are the yarn particulars that I know; for example, wpi (see page 130), knitted gauge, number of plies?

If I spin the yarn first and then decide on the project, my questions are different:

- How do I want the yarn to look and feel? I try to describe the yarn, even if very vaguely, with a first impression of its size, hand, and ply.

- Do I have even a slight idea of what my project might be? Even better, what is the stitch pattern likely to be (for example, cables)?

Find a comfortable spot, concentrate, and go with the flow of your yarn vision.

KEEPING YOUR YARN VISION ON TRACK

Once you start spinning, make sure you're following your unique blueprint. Keeping your vision in mind as you get through your project, practice, or intention is easy. It's equal parts of concentration and flow. The flow part is just spinning within the parameters of how your ideas, pictures, thoughts, and inspirations move you. The concentration part comes down to sampling, then sampling again, taking notes, and checking back as you work. You can change your vision at any time, but don't throw away your original work or samples, as they always come in handy for other projects. Remember, this is your yarn and your spinning party, so have fun!

SHEEP BREEDS AND BEYOND

WHY SHOULD YOU CARE about the fibers that you spin and knit? Have you ever fallen in love with a braid of fiber because of the color, then spun it and knit it, yet it became something you were not expecting? Droopy or stiff, scratchy, hairy, shedding everywhere? It could be because of the fiber. I will admit to being seduced by color and colorways of many talented dyers without realizing until I got home and started spinning that even though the colors are indeed beautiful, the fiber or fiber blend is completely inappropriate for what I want to make.

This is because fiber is the backbone, the essence of what your yarn is. It's the foundation that your yarn will stand on. If the foundation isn't right, frequently there's nothing to be done to make it right, other than use it for a different project.

The choice of fiber is fundamental to yarn. The characteristics of the fiber translate directly into characteristics of the yarn you make with it. (See Characteristics to Consider before Spinning a Fiber, page 32.) Fiber also comes into play if you have allergies and when you're thinking about stitch patterns. It affects the weight and softness of your finished piece. Everything about a fiber is relevant to the yarn you spin.

When you use blends, aspects of all fibers in the blend inform your yarn, and some overshadow others. Every fiber, be it wool, synthetic, or silk, affects the finished yarn. Some spinners work only with wool, but more and more are branching out to fiber blends and different varieties of fiber. I didn't include cotton or cellulose fibers, because commercially prepared and dyed options for them are not as readily available to a spinner as wool and wool blends are. However, more and more commercial fibers are available to the spinner, especially different wools. Let's explore some of the most popular types of fibers commercially available to spinners and what their properties mean to yarn and knitting.

WOOL:
The Backbone of Spinning

There is nothing I love more than to shop at a fiber festival and be faced with a booth overflowing with choices of braids of fiber to spin. It used to be that the selection was only about color. I'd find mountains of braids in every variation of color that a dyer could think of in Merino or Bluefaced Leicester (BFL) top. Now, if you are a wool spinner, you have no doubt noticed that the choices are growing beyond color. More breeds are available as commercially prepared fiber, ready to spin, than ever before. You don't have to buy a fleece and process it yourself to be able to spin fiber from different breeds of sheep.

With the advent of more choices, however, come more decisions. Now a spinner has to decide not only on the "purple and orange" or the "green and gold" but also BFL, Polwarth, or Teeswater. The fleece from each breed of sheep, whether processed by hand or machine, has unique properties that will contribute to your final yarn and whatever it is you make with it.

Wool is the backbone of spinning, and most spinners spin wool or wool blends. Sheep breeds are so versatile and varied that a spinner could spin only wool for his or her entire spinning life and never get bored. It used to be that unless spinners started with fleece, they would get only a generic wool to spin a blend of middle-of-the-road wools. But things have changed, and there has never been a better time than now to be a wool spinner. At the last fiber show I attended, I counted 20 different breeds and fiber blends in commercially processed and handdyed top.

For my experiments in this book, I chose to explore three breed categories that are easy to find at fiber shows. These categories show a range of characteristics that make a difference to your yarn and knitting. For each category, I've chosen three breeds to use as examples. Although this is general information, you can find many other books that go into great detail about sheep breeds if you are interested. (See Suggested Reading, page 222.)

FINE WOOLS:
Merino, Cormo, Rambouillet

Fine wools are short-stapled and crimpy, and they spin into elastic yarns. They have a matte appearance, so they don't reflect light well. Dyed colors look lighter on fine wool. Fine wools are the standard of soft by which most spinners judge other fibers. They are so soft that they can be spun and knit into camisoles and worn all winter without a

Characteristics to Consider before Spinning a Fiber

- **Staple length.** How long is a single staple of fiber? Knowing this helps when you are drafting your fiber. A fiber drafts more easily if you keep your hands about a staple length apart.

- **Crimp.** The natural waves in a fiber contribute to the yarn's elasticity. Elasticity is important if you want memory in your yarn so that your knitted socks will stay up and your sweaters will keep their shape.

- **Strong or tender.** How strong and prone to pilling is it? Fiber diameter contributes to this; the larger the diameter, the stronger the fiber and the less it may pill.

- **Shine or matte.** Will the fiber reflect or absorb light?

- **Elasticity or drape.** Does this fiber tend to spin into a yarn that's elastic and springy, or something more supple, with drape?

- **Spin.** For an intermediate spinner, how easy is this fiber to spin? Is there a particular way it is inclined to be spun? What type of drafting will bring out the best in the fiber?

- **Skin.** What does this fiber feel like on your skin? Neck soft? Sock soft? On your head or hands? Do you need a layer of some other fabric between you and the finished piece?

- **Knit.** If you spin it the way it inclines to be spun, how does it knit up, crisp or drapey?

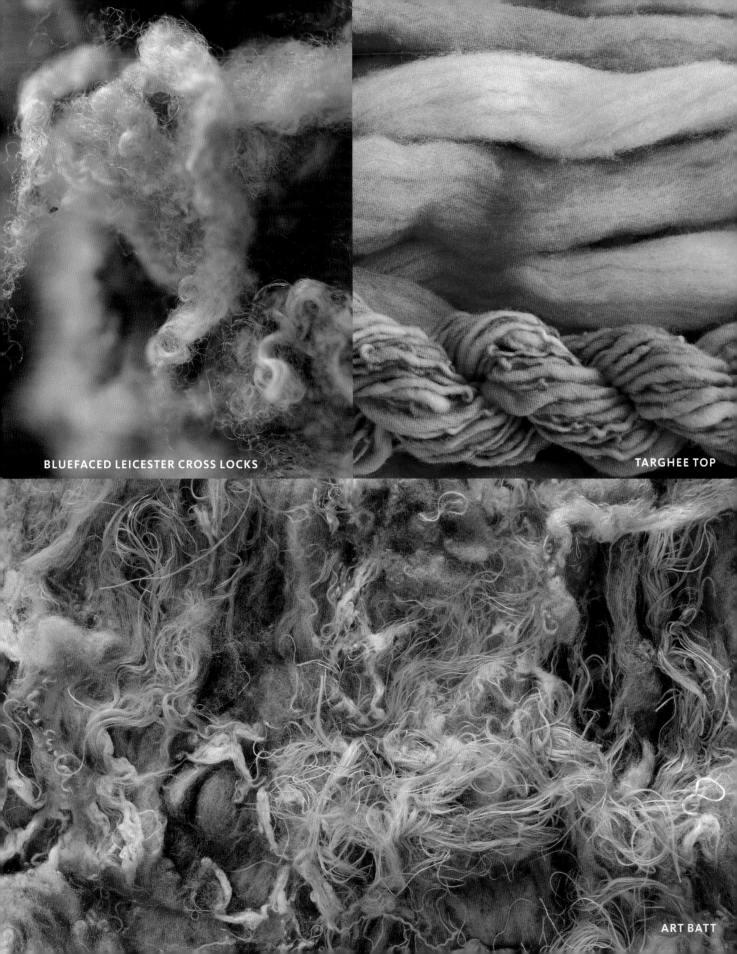

BLUEFACED LEICESTER CROSS LOCKS

TARGHEE TOP

ART BATT

WOOL TOP AND ROVING

tickle or scratch. They are frequently used when knitting for babies. Because the individual fibers are fine, however, the yarns are inclined to be tender — they easily pill and felt. To counteract this, look for one of the many fine-wool blends, frequently with silk or nylon for a great sock yarn.

Fine wools can be spun with a high or low twist, though low twist exacerbates their less-than-durable quality if knit into something that will get a lot of abrasion. Also, because of their short staple, fine wools can be tricky for a new spinner. On the other hand, fine wools make a gorgeous, fine laceweight yarn. Merino is a favorite of lace master Margaret Stove.

MEDIUM WOOLS:
Corriedale, Columbia, Falkland
Medium wools are the go-to fibers of the spinning world. They are easy to spin, knit, and wear. They are excellent fibers for beginning spinners and for any spinner who's learning something new. Medium wools balance durability and elasticity beautifully: they are not as elastic as crimpy fine wools, but they have enough well-defined crimp and spring to spin and knit into garments that hold any stitch. Medium wools have the greatest range of softness. Most people can wear something knit of medium wool next to their skin — maybe not on their necks, but as hats, mittens, gloves, and socks. They also make a great sweater yarn. Medium-wool yarns have excellent stitch definition when drafted either woolen or worsted.

LONGWOOLS:
Wensleydale, Romney, BFL
Longwools have big personalities: they are bold, shiny, and drapey. The range of characteristics of fleeces in this category varies dramatically. I

TEESWATER LOCKS

can barely wrap my head around the idea that BFL and Wensleydale are in the same category. All longwools have a delicious luster, even when spun with a woolen draft. They all also have a long staple length, from 4 to 12 inches. I often find myself fighting to draft a longwool, only to realize my hands are spaced to spin Merino, not a longwool, and as soon as I separate my hands a bit, drafting is a breeze.

Choosing which of the longwools works for different kinds of wearables is an interesting thought process. BFL is neck-soft and wonderfully durable, so it's no wonder that, for many, it's a favorite fiber to spin. Wensleydale is sometimes referred to as rug wool, but that's not the case! Wensleydale makes beautiful lace, and a Wensleydale lace shawl is a thing of beauty. Longwools don't need as much twist as their shorter-stapled sisters. Extra twist is what leads a longer longwool, like Wensleydale, to become hard and wiry.

ANGORA:
A Class of Its Own
Angora is the down combed or clipped from the angora rabbit. Short-stapled with no crimp, it makes a soft and very fuzzy yarn. Warmer than

wool, it's mostly used in a blend. Angora can be tricky for new spinners to spin, as it has short, slippery fibers that need a fair amount of twist. Knit into garments, it is next-to-the-skin soft but may be tickly because of the halo. Angora yarn doesn't have much elasticity. Spin it with more twist than you think it needs, and when you finish it, full it if you want the halo to come up right away (for fulling, see page 119). An entire sweater made from angora may be too warm for many, but it's excellent for accessories and in a blended yarn.

CAMELIDS:
Warmer than Wool

Camelids have been domesticated for thousands of years, used both for their fiber and as pack animals. Their fiber is fine, light, and multiple times warmer than wool.

ALPACA AND LLAMA

Alpaca is soft and lustrous, it has beautiful drape, and it is extremely durable and warm. Alpaca has little to no memory and is often blended with wool or silk. It can be spun with a woolen draft to give yarn a small amount of loft, or worsted to showcase the shine. It knits into beautiful garments, but keep in mind that alpaca is not springy and it is warmer than wool. Beware the sweater that grows to your knees and is too hot to wear except when there's a blizzard.

Llama is related to alpaca, but llama has a dual coat: a soft, downy undercoat and a wiry, water-resistant outercoat. If the coats are spun together, the yarn will be incredibly durable but not skin friendly. On the other hand, llama's undercoat is warm and soft enough to wear next to the skin. It's well worth looking for dehaired llama fleece.

CAMEL

Two-humped camels are the best fiber-bearing camels. They have three coats, all used for different purposes. Spinners look for the downy undercoat that is short and fluffy, with crimp. In spite of this crimp, however, it still isn't very elastic to knit with. Spinning it fine with a woolen draft and a little extra ply twist can help add a little spring.

THE BIG BEASTS:
Yak, Bison, and Musk Ox

All three of these big beasts have multiple coats, with the downiest undercoat being the fiber that spinners clamor to spin. If you buy raw yak, bison, or qiviut (from the musk ox), the down needs to be dehaired before spinning to preserve its luscious softness. The fibers of all three are short and elastic. Bison, especially, has very elastic down. Spinning woolen and giving your yarn a hard finish, à la Judith MacKenzie, will result in a beautiful matte, fuzzy yarn that is a pleasure to knit with and wear because of its over-the-top softness. Do keep in mind that all of these beastly down fibers are much warmer than wool. Those fibers are what keep these big animals warm in subzero temperatures.

GET MY GOATS

Goats have some of the most wide-ranging and sexy fibers. From the strong and shimmery ringlets of the angora goat to the luxurious down of cashmere, goat fiber can stand alone or work beautifully blended with other fibers. It always brings a little something special to the spinning party.

CASHMERE

Cashmere is the gold standard in luxury fiber, and it's easy to find. It behaves like the big-beast

CASHMERE

BOMBYX MORI/YAK

BISON

QIVIUT

ALPACA

PYGORA

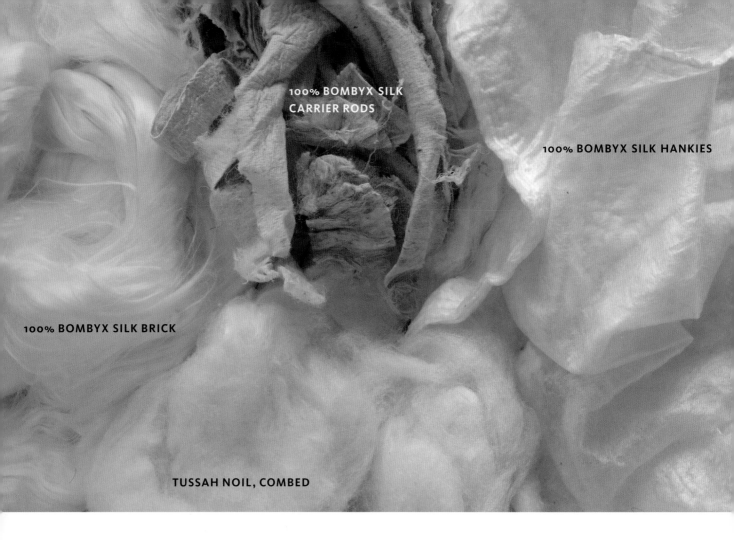

100% BOMBYX SILK
CARRIER RODS

100% BOMBYX SILK HANKIES

100% BOMBYX SILK BRICK

TUSSAH NOIL, COMBED

fibers (yak, bison, and qiviut) because of its incredibly warm, downy undercoat, which is short-stapled with crimp. When spun, fulled, and knit, cashmere has a soft matte appearance. It makes gorgeous accessories and can be blended with many other fibers.

ANGORA GOAT

Mohair is the fiber from the angora goat. The fiber is long, strong, and shiny. Mohair is often added to fiber blends and commercial yarns to give strength. After it's spun or knit, mohair can be brushed to create a fabric with an amazing fuzzy halo. Kid mohair is softer and finer than adult mohair but still strong and glossy. Dyed mohair has intense color. Mohair locks are a favorite of textured- and art-yarn spinners. Like fiber from the longwools, mohair doesn't need much twist and will turn wiry if overtwisted. When you knit with mohair yarn, especially yarn that has been, or will be, brushed in the fabric, go up a needle size or two. The mohair fuzz takes up a lot of space!

GOAT HYBRIDS:
Cashgora and Pygora

Cashgora is a crossbreed of a cashmere and an angora goat. The fiber is not as soft as cashmere, but it's longer than cashmere and lustrous. Pygora is a cross between a pygmy and an angora goat. The fiber is as soft as kid mohair, even on adult animals.

SEDUCTIVE SILK

The options for preparation, blend, and type in the world of silk seem to have exploded lately. The two most common silks used for spinning are bombyx and tussah. (For examples of various preparations, see chapter 3.)

Silk is soft and light. It retains warmth in the cold, and it "breathes" to keep a wearer cool in warm weather. It can be shiny or matte, takes dye like a duck to water, is crazy strong, and blends well with nearly every fiber on the planet.

For a new spinner, silk can be intimidating to spin. Tussah is a better choice for a newbie or the silk intimidated. Tussah is silk fiber gathered from silk cocoons after the moth has eaten its way out. The fibers are textured, shorter, and not as slippery or fine as bombyx silk. Tussah can be spun with a woolen or worsted draft.

Bombyx silk is reeled from whole cocoons of the *Bombyx mori* moth and is luminous and bright white, with a long, fine fiber. For the most shine from bombyx silk, spin it worsted. If the long staple length is troublesome for you, spin from the fold — from the flat, not the tip. It will help control the fiber and still encourage shine. When knitting with silk, remember that it is not a very elastic fiber.

OTHER NATURAL FIBERS

The fibers in this category are manufactured using scientific techniques, but they are based on natural products, not synthetics. These fibers include rayon and bamboo (both plant based), casein (milk based), soy (tofu), and Tencel (wood pulp based). Used rarely by themselves, they are first pulped and extruded into long, thin strands (think of a Play-Doh Fun Factory or a pasta maker). (Some bamboo is not lab processed, so read product descriptions closely if this is important to you.) If spun by themselves, they act similar to bombyx silk — long, strong, and shiny. When blended with other fibers, usually wool, they impart lovely shimmer, drape, and strength.

BAMBOO

Bamboo is absorbent and breathable, and it has sheen and drape. It spins similarly to bombyx silk, and it blends beautifully with other fibers. There are two kinds of bamboo in the fiber world; both are made from the same bamboo plant, but they are processed into spinnable fiber in two ways with different environmental impacts. The type most readily available to spinners is the chemically pulped-and-extruded bamboo fiber. Harder to find but lighter on the environment is bamboo processed into spinning fiber by retting (a natural way of separating fiber from stem) and combing.

TENCEL

Tencel, made from wood pulp, is soft and strong, and it, too, has sheen and drape. It works well in blends, but it has no elasticity.

SYNTHETIC FIBER:
Nylon Can Be a Spinner's Friend

Lab-grown and manufactured, nylon is used in blends to give strength, durability, and elasticity to fine natural fibers; for example, Merino/nylon is a popular blend for sock yarn. Nylon also brings the party to spinning: Firestar, the brightly colored and sparkly glitz that is added to fiber blends and batts, is made from nylon.

Rolags and a batt
made from the
braid at the top

3 | the frame:

FIBER PREPARATIONS

NOW THAT WE HAVE DIPPED INTO TYPES OF FIBER, what kind of preparation do you want to spin? How fibers are aligned in one of those braided lengths you purchase has an influence on yarn and knitting. Are the fibers aligned straight and smooth, or are they fluffy and going every which way?

Is the silk you have your eye on a handkerchief ("hankies"; see page 47) or roving? What exactly is "cloud"? Many commercially prepared fibers, most of them gorgeously handdyed, are available for spinners. Some spinners are disinclined to spin anything that they haven't prepared themselves, and other spinners don't really want to take the time to hand-prepare fiber and are happy with the commercially prepared fiber that is available. I fall into the latter camp. I can hand-prepare my fibers, and sometimes I do, but there is so much lovely commercially prepared and handdyed fiber around that I almost always reach for that when I spin.

WOOLEN vs. WORSTED FIBER PREPARATION

Woolen and worsted are both types of fiber preparations as well as types of drafting styles, which can make talking about them confusing. In "ye olde times" of spinning, woolen preparations were spun with a woolen draft, and worsted preparations were spun with a worsted draft. That is no longer the case. Spinners freely spin any preparation with any draft they choose. The key is to know what type of yarn you'll get from each type of preparation-and-spin combo. When you throw in the *semi* phrases (semi-worsted and semi-woolen), the confuse-o-meter goes up another notch.

Commercially Prepared vs. Hand-Prepared

I feel that I have to interject a bit about the glory of hand-prepared fiber. There is nothing like spinning hand-prepared fiber: it is the ultimate in spinning; nothing drafts like it. But for me, it's also a luxury. I often don't like to take the time to hand-prepare my fiber, and I like the variety in fiber, fiber blends, and color that commercially prepared fibers bring me.

It's not the washing of the fleece that stops me. Even if someone handed me a clean fleece to prepare, I still wouldn't be inclined to do so most of the time. There are days that combing a little and spinning a little is the perfect thing — exactly what I want to do — but right now it's not my thing, though I do admit the fiber is amazing.

At their most basic, all preparations begin with fibers that are neither uniform nor varied: it's the way that they are prepped that makes them either woolen or worsted:

- *Worsted preparation.* To prep worsted, the fleece is combed to remove uneven fibers and stray bits of vegetable matter. The result tends to be compact and smooth, with the fibers parallel, aligned, and of similar length.

- *Woolen preparation.* For a woolen prep, the fleece is carded, causing the fibers to go in different directions and also adding air to the mixture. The result is a fiber package that is lofty, with an uneven surface.

Worsted preparation spun worsted and woolen preparation spun woolen emphasize the characteristics of the preparation. Woolen and worsted preparations spun using the opposite technique create a lovely mixture of both. (For information about spinning worsted and spinning woolen, see chapter 4.)

You can find all of the following types of fiber preparation in commercial fibers. I've split them into worsted and woolen preparations and given silk its own category.

WORSTED PREP: TOP

A worsted preparation results in top, the most commonly available commercially prepared fiber.

You'll find it in wools, wool blends, alpaca, rayon, Tencel, yak, camel, angora, and silk. In fact, many fibers and fiber blends are combed into top. Here are some characteristics of commercial top:

- The machine combing removes short fibers and inconsistencies and leaves the fibers parallel. The combing process also removes most of the air between fibers, making the top dense and smooth.

- Top is said to have a direction. If you find yourself spinning a top that seems to be particularly feisty, you may be spinning against the

Braided top (worsted preparation)

More Spinning Speak

- COMBING is a fiber-preparation technique that straightens and aligns fibers, while removing fibers of uneven length. The goal of combed preparation is to have the fibers parallel and of uniform length.

- CARDING is a fiber preparation technique that encourages fibers to lie in multiple directions; it keeps all lengths of fibers, including very short and broken fibers. The goal of a carded preparation is to have fibers that are lofty and aligned like mesh.

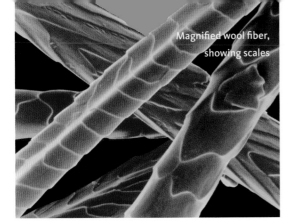

Magnified wool fiber, showing scales

smooth direction of the nap (surface grain or surface flow created by the combing machine) of the top. Try turning the top around and spinning from the other end.

- Top spun with a worsted drafting style is lustrous and smooth, and when used in knitting, the yarn has amazing stitch definition.

- Commercial top spun with a woolen draft takes on a bit of air, becoming smooth and lofty. It creates a lighter yarn than top spun worsted. When the yarn is used in knitting, a bit of stitch definition is lost, but warmth and lightness are gained.

WOOLEN PREPS

You will find several different types of woolen preparations, including roving and its subcategories sliver, pin roving, and pencil roving. (Other woolen preparations include batts, rolags, puni, and clouds, described on pages 44 and 45. Roving is the most common commercial woolen spinning preparation. Commercial roving is made on carding machines that process fiber like a giant handcard or brush. The fibers in roving are disorganized, going in lots of different directions rather than lying parallel. Roving looks puffier than top, with a matte and uneven surface. When roving comes off the machine, a slight twist is put into it. Roving that is spun with a woolen draft makes yarn that is warm and light. Roving spun with a worsted draft is more compressed, not as light, but more durable over time.

- **Sliver** is a thinner version of roving with no twist. It is often used to prepare plant fibers.

Fiber preparations *from left to right:* Sliver, top (a worsted prep), roving, and pencil roving

- **Pin roving** is thinner than both roving and sliver, with fibers a bit more aligned but still carded. It is often used when preparing fine wools.

- **Pencil roving** is the thinnest of all rovings. The width of a pencil, it is excellent for beginning spinners.

Batts

Batts are giant sheets of carded fiber. They can be made on a commercial carding machine or a drum carder. Batts are frequently blends of fiber and run the gamut from mild and smooth to wild and chunky. Batts, especially fresh batts, are amazingly airy and can be spun in two directions: if spun with the grain of the batt (the direction it was carded in), the yarn is lofty; if spun against the grain, the yarn becomes super lofty.

Spinning a batt with a woolen draft emphasizes the loft. The yarn is spongy and light, but it can be quite delicate. Spinning a batt with a worsted draft removes the signature air, creating a more compact yarn. Smooth batts made of slick, lustrous fibers are lovely spun worsted, as that method brings out the most shine possible in the fiber. Spinning a chunky, wild batt with a worsted draft, however, can be an exercise in frustration. This is a batt that won't make a smooth yarn.

Batts, which are large sheets of carded fiber, offer many options for spinners.

Rolags

Rolags are made with handcards or a blending board, and then rolled loosely into a tube. They spin like smaller versions of batts. Rolags made on handcards frequently contain only one fiber, or perhaps a blend of two or three fibers. Rolags made on blending boards rival art batts for their variety of content and color. (See page 33 for a photograph of an art batt.)

Fauxlags

Fauxlags are made from portions of batts, top, or roving wound into a tube around a dowel, knitting needle, chopstick, or ruler. They are usually not as lofty as rolags.

Puni

A puni is a smaller version of a rolag, rolled tightly when taken off handcards or a blending board. These are often used for cotton and other short-stapled fibers.

Cloud

A cloud is an airy handful of fiber, usually pygora, cashmere, camel, or yak. After the coarse fibers have been removed (dehaired) and what remains has been washed, it is left as a mass of fiber that looks a lot like a cloud. The fiber is not directional, so it is simply spun from the little nest of fiber. Cloud spun woolen preserves the airiness in the preparation and the downy fibers; cloud

Rolags and punis, which are loosely rolled tubes made from carded fiber, spin much like batts.

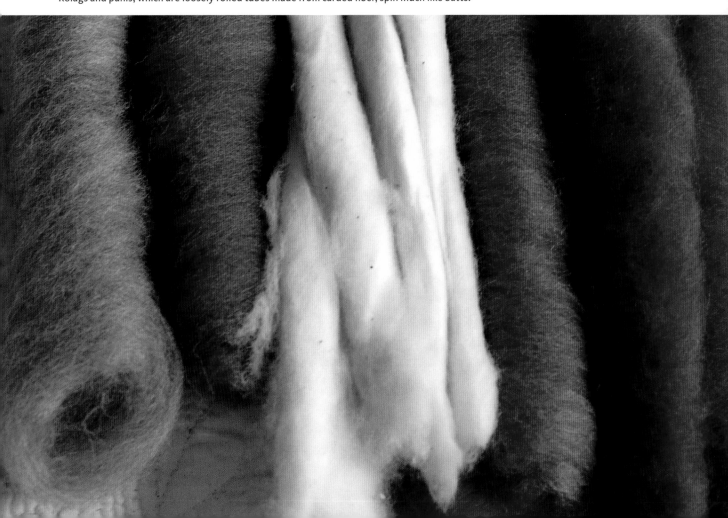

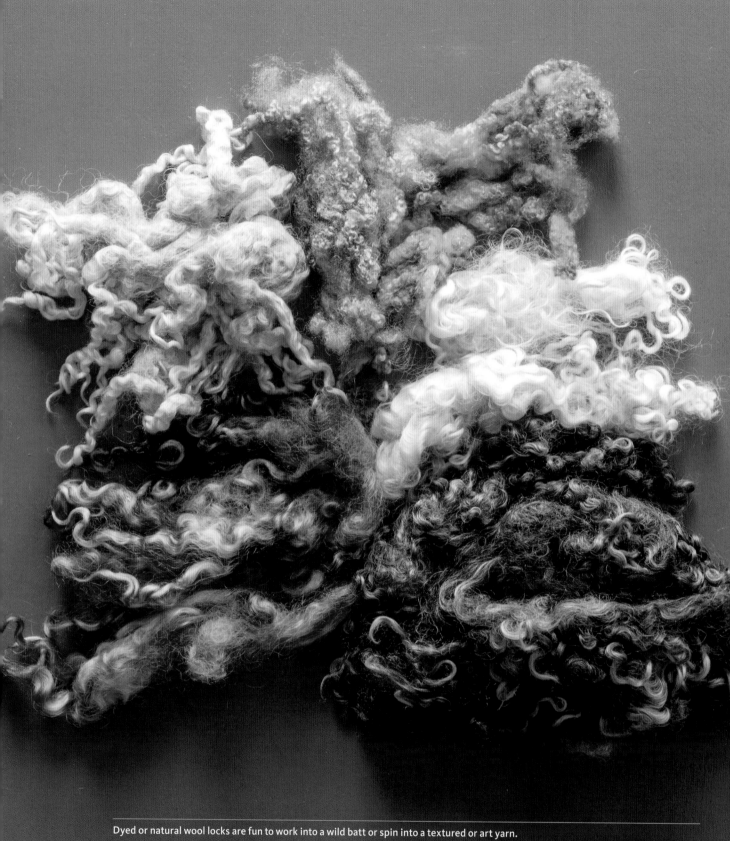

Dyed or natural wool locks are fun to work into a wild batt or spin into a textured or art yarn.

spun worsted makes a more durable, less lofty yarn.

Wool Locks

The fiber of longwool sheep is washed and frequently dyed without further preparation, or it may be added to wild batts and spun into textured and art yarns. These locks are gorgeous and very textural.

SILK PREPARATIONS:
Beyond Top and Roving

Silk seems to come in the biggest variety of preparations. While it is available as top and roving, here is a quick look at some other preparations you might find when fiber shopping.

- **Hankies, bells, and caps.** These are all made from degummed silk cocoons stretched over a frame in layers. The hankie frame is square, the bell frame is bell shaped, and the cap frame is cap shaped (that is, rounder than the bell).

- **Silk brick** is a by-product of the silk reeling process (the process of unwinding cocoons into thread). The fiber is folded into brick shapes. Silk brick can be spun like top, but the silk fibers are not as uniform and aligned as top.

- **Silk noil, throwsters, and carrier rods** are all remnants of the silk-production process. They are used to blend into fiber or as big chunky add-ins for wild batts and textured yarns.

- **Sari silk.** Silk waste threads from the commercial sari-making process may be spun alone or blended into other fibers.

One silk preparation that is easy to spin is known as a hanky.

Sari silk can be a colorful addition when blended with other fibers.

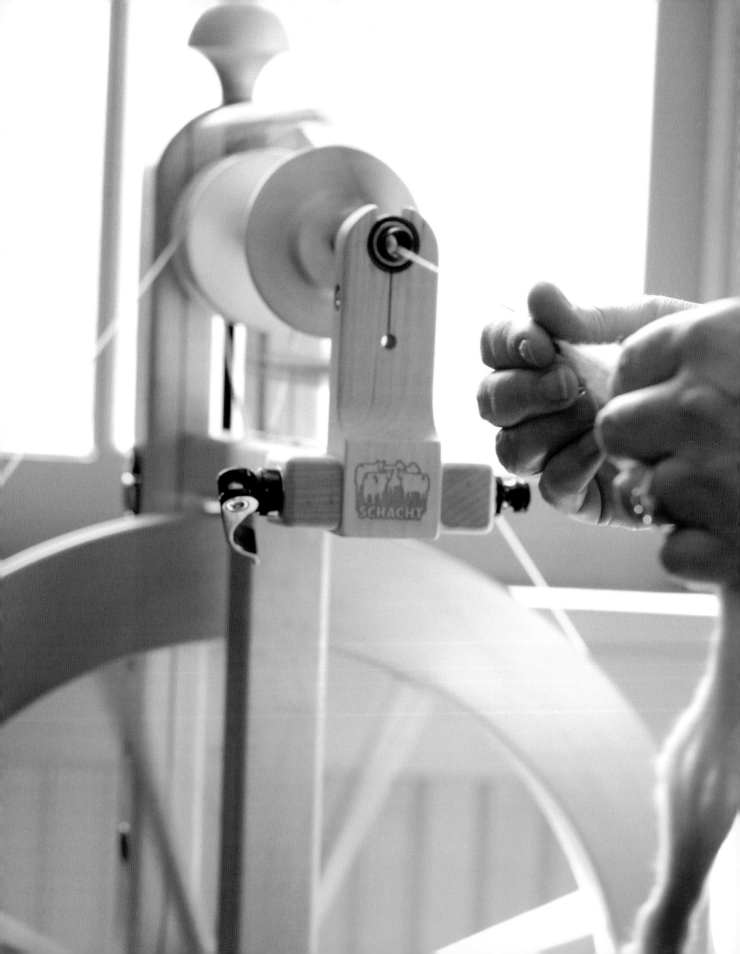

DRAFTING

WOOLEN, WORSTED, OR SOMEWHERE IN BETWEEN? Which drafting method makes a soft yarn and which one makes a yarn that is hard-wearing? Drafting either woolen or worsted is the act of attenuating fiber so that twist can enter and make yarn. Drafting, along with twist and fiber, creates yarn. There can be no yarn without all three. How and where the twist gets into your fiber determines whether the draft is woolen or worsted.

Drafting is a fundamental technique that can make or break your yarn. The specific drafting technique you choose can make fiber warm and lofty or sleek and hard-wearing, or a little bit of each. But what exactly does drafting do? How does it work? How does it affect finished yarn? Drafting is the mediator between fiber and twist. How big do you want the singles that you're spinning, and how much, if any, air do you want in it? What kind of yarn do you need for what you want to knit? Of course, there are other factors, such as fiber and preparation, to consider, but when all things are equal, draft is the spinning taskmaster. (Remember, we are talking about commercially prepared fibers only in this book. There is no talk of the one true worsted or the one true woolen yarn, hand-processed to the highest degree of perfection.)

The ultimate goal of drafting is a continuous flow, of finding the perfect wheel setup and the perfect balance between hands and feet to control the twist in the fiber of your choice to make a specific yarn. Most spinners' default yarns are usually somewhere between woolen and worsted.

A FEW WORDS ABOUT TWIST

Twist is the energy that makes yarn. You, as the spinner, put it there, and you give it as much as you need with the fiber you have to make the yarn you want. You manipulate it in your draft, in your ply, and in your finish. Twist then shines in your knitting. Like anything full of energy (puppies, toddlers, or over-caffeinated coworkers), twist sometimes needs a firm hand to get it to cooperate. It's easy to be intimated by twist or to be excited by twist. You risk not adding enough and having your yarn fall apart, or adding too much and ending up with something closer to wire than yarn.

To me, twist is magic. It's what holds everything together, what makes yarn soft and strong at the same time, what makes yarn utterly unique. If you can understand and control twist, you can make any yarn. The balance between twist and drafting is exactly how to get twist to do what you want.

The drafting triangle

DRAFTING TRIANGLE:
The Sweet Spot in Drafting

No matter which style of drafting is your go-to way to spin, worsted or woolen, they both have this sweet spot in common: the drafting triangle. Learn to recognize it, learn to love it, buy it gifts, and sing it sweet lullabies; this is where all of the drafting action happens and where your yarn decision is made. Do you let twist into the triangle or do you keep it out? That is the big difference between the two styles of drafting: woolen lets the twist in, and worsted doesn't. There are several ways to do both styles of drafting, and of course, there are many, many opinions about all of them.

WORSTED DRAFTING

Worsted yarns are smooth, sleek, and strong. If your fiber has an inclination to be shiny, a worsted draft will make it luminous. Worsted yarns are dense and drapey, durable, and less prone to pilling than woolen yarns. Worsted-spun yarns are also less elastic and not as warm as woolen-spun yarns.

Worsted-style drafting is frequently the style that is taught to brand-new spinners, and for a very good reason: control. Not because it's the *best* reason; there are no best reasons, just the best one for the yarn you are making. I never feel more in control of my yarn construction than when I draft worsted. This is the style of drafting that does not let twist into the draft triangle. New spinners learn what is called the "inchworm style" of worsted drafting — short forward pulls of fiber. The photos on the facing page show how it's done.

Getting Started: Leaders

Used to help you get started spinning or plying yarn, a leader is a length of multi-ply yarn that is attached with a lark's head knot to the bobbin and threaded through the orifice. You attach the fleece or singles yarn to this leader when you start to spin or ply.

Notice that when drafting worsted-style, the twist enters the fiber after it has been drafted out but while it is still under tension. No matter how your fiber is prepared, this style of drafting will align the fibers as much as they can be aligned before locking it into yarn. Any air or loft in the fiber is removed. I think of worsted drafting as exhaling compared to woolen's inhaling: two sides of the same coin.

1. Pinch an amount of fiber tightly enough that you don't let any twist through to the drafting triangle, but not so tight to change the color of your fingers.

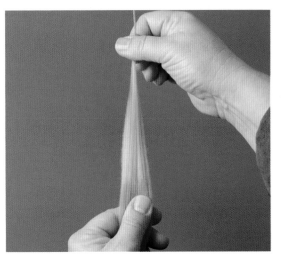

2. Pull this bit of fiber forward toward the orifice.

3. Slide your finger back along the freshly made yarn.

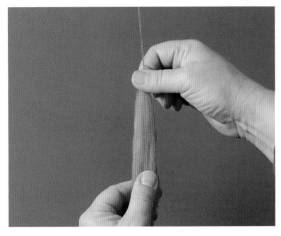

4. Pinch again in front of the drafting triangle.

Continue to repeat this action. As worsted drafting gets more comfortable, your hands get faster. Some spinners work a backward draft, in which the general idea and motions are the same: pinch, pull, slide, repeat, allowing no twist into the drafting triangle.

JOINING FOR WORSTED-STYLE

The best style of join for worsted drafting is a side join, in which you add just a few fibers at a time to keep from adding air and to keep the join smooth, not lumpy.

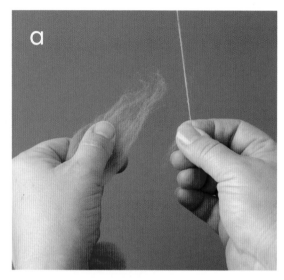 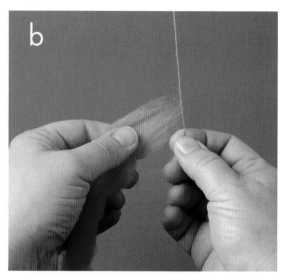

Fluff out the end of your top so that you have a couple of inches of thin fiber (a), then hold the fiber at a right angle to the yarn as you continue to spin and allow the fiber wisps to catch on (b). Once the fibers attach, continue to draft as before.

CORRIEDALE TOP SPUN WORSTED. When knit, worsted yarns have excellent stitch definition. They make crisp cables and textural stitches, and they highlight the movement of lace stitches. When you plan to knit an heirloom project that can be worn and passed down for generations, look no further than a worsted yarn.

WOOLEN DRAFTING

Woolen yarns are light and fluffy — or as light and fluffy as their fiber allows them to be. They bloom when they are finished after spinning, achieving their loftiest state. They are elastic and hold warmth. On the other hand, they are not as consistent as worsted yarns, and it's easy for noils (small pieces of loose fiber — think the tweedy bits in tweed yarn) and neps (small tangles of fiber) to get drafted into woolen yarn. Woolen-spun yarns, especially when you use short-stapled fiber, are prone to pilling.

Woolen yarns make warm, lightweight sweaters and socks, but because these yarns abrade easily, you can use extra plies, higher ply twist, and/or a fiber blend that includes silk or nylon to help offset (though not eliminate)

pilling. Woolen yarns are excellent for felted knitwear.

Woolen drafting takes a little confidence and willingness to let go: confidence that the twist is going to do what it's supposed to, and literal letting go, allowing the twist to enter the drafting triangle. There are many more styles of drafting woolen, including forward, backward, long draw, sliding long draw, supported long draw, and double drafting, to name a few.

When drafting woolen, twist enters the fiber before and during drafting. As twist enters the fiber, it swirls the fiber like a tornado. This swirl traps air as the fiber is spun, creating the ubiquitous loft of woolen-spun yarn. Most woolen-style drafters pull backward, long or short, which is what's described here.

DRAFTING WOOLEN-STYLE

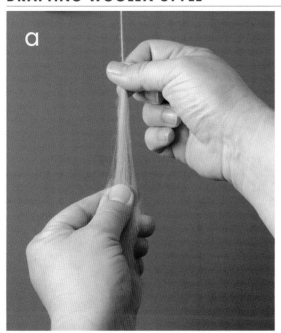
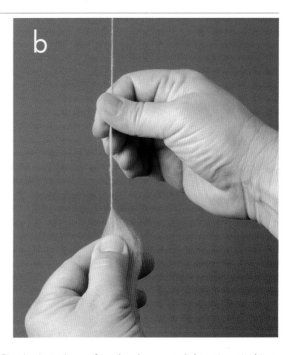

DRAFTING WOOLEN-STYLE. While your fiber hand pulls the fiber backward, your front hand opens and closes in a pinching motion (a). This pinching action supplies the bit of extra tension needed to draft against, while also allowing the twist to run into the drafting triangle (b). Using the front hand in this manner makes this method more like a supported woolen draft; for the long-draw method, a front hand is used less frequently.

JOINING FOR WOOLEN-STYLE

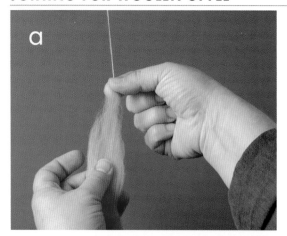

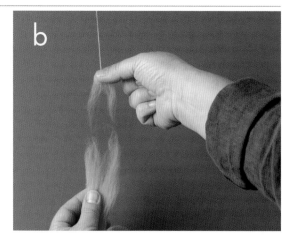

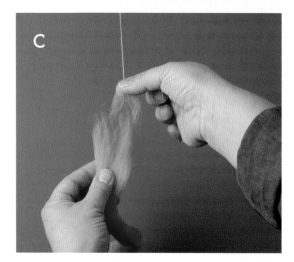

Joining. The best type of join for woolen drafting is a mattress or a sandwich join. Either lay the new fiber on top of the old (like lying on a mattress) (a), or split the existing fiber (b) and insert the new fiber in between (c). Let the twist travel from the old to the new fiber.

It's a Matter of Trust

Many new woolen spinners worry and let the twist run all the way into their fiber supply. The most common reason for this (and I've been guilty of it myself) is that they don't trust the twist. If I don't trust that the twist I have set up between the wheel and my treadling rhythm will flow in my fiber to create a happy woolen yarn, I treadle faster, creating more twist. Everything else about my draft is set up for the original amount of twist to work, and when I let this new, more energetic twist zip down my fiber, it bursts right through my drafting zone and into my fiber supply, locking it up. Trust the twist, and trust your spin. Spend an evening just practicing, not to make a particular yarn but to watch the twist and control it.

DRAFTING AGAINST TYPE:
What Happens

Top is the most popular commercially available fiber preparation, but what if you want to spin it woolen? Do it! You won't get as lofty a yarn as you would with a woolen preparation like roving or a batt, but it will add air and spring.

The same is true for a woolen preparation. Using a worsted draft for a fiber prepared woolen smooths and aligns the fibers under drafting, squeezing out the air and creating a yarn that, if not sleek, is compact and sturdy. In the photo below, roving is being spun with a worsted draft. Though the yarn won't be perfectly smooth and lustrous, it will be a more controlled and consistent yarn with better stitch definition when knitting.

When top is spun woolen, air is allowed into the drafting triangle and fibers, forcing fibers to misalign and trap air as the fibers become yarn.

When roving is spun worsted, some of the air is squeezed out, creating a compact, sturdy yarn.

Corriedale top spun woolen

Roving spun worsted

DRAFTING FIBER BLENDS:
Dealing with Mismatched Staple Lengths

With so many commercially prepared fiber blends on the market, how do you choose how to draft a blend with wildly different staple lengths, especially if keeping your hands close to a staple length apart is part of the draft? For example, I love silk mixed with anything. But I will admit to some frustration when spinning silk, which is a long fiber, blended with something soft, sexy, and short like Merino, Polwarth, or cashmere. Here are a few tips about spinning fiber blends with different staple lengths.

- **Plan for drafting.** Rarely do the staple lengths match in a blended or combined fiber. When spinning blended fibers of different staple lengths, take the time to get your hand positioning right. If you sit down with a Merino/silk blend and try to draft with your hands spaced closely for Merino, you might find it hard to draft because of the silk in the mix. Spacing your hands for silk would be too far apart for the Merino, so finding that sweet spot between the two is worth taking the time to discover.

- **Be ready to go.** Make sure your fiber is ready to draft — in other words, that the fibers slide by each other easily. If they don't, shake out your fiber or predraft in another way, fluffing (page 61) or attenuating (page 62) slightly.

- **Prepare manageable-size pieces.** Work with fiber pieces that you feel comfortable with sizewise. A full top's width of fiber isn't always easy to control, and adding varied staple lengths makes it even harder. If a piece of fiber feels too big or unmanageable, split it lengthwise and try again to spin it. I know that when I start fretting about spinning a particular fiber, my hands start to sweat, which makes the fiber even harder to draft.

- **Keep a goal in mind.** Know what you want from your fiber. Do you want the silk literally

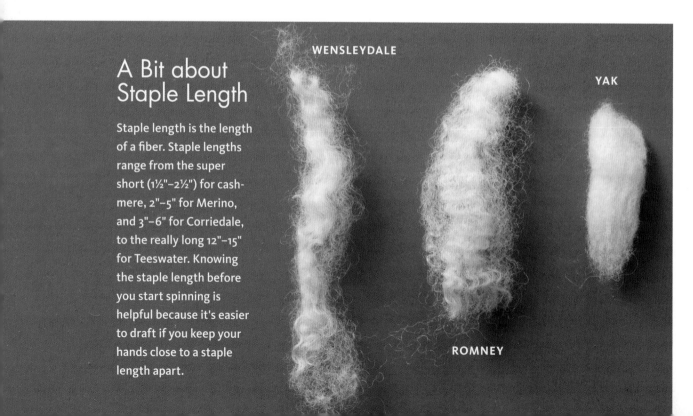

A Bit about Staple Length

Staple length is the length of a fiber. Staple lengths range from the super short (1½"–2½") for cashmere, 2"–5" for Merino, and 3"–6" for Corriedale, to the really long 12"–15" for Teeswater. Knowing the staple length before you start spinning is helpful because it's easier to draft if you keep your hands close to a staple length apart.

WENSLEYDALE

YAK

ROMNEY

A Good Tool in Your Spinning Arsenal

SPINNING FROM THE FOLD is a good way to feel in control of drafting rambunctious fibers, slippery fibers, and fibers with mismatched staple lengths in a blend. Spinning from the fold can also add elasticity to long fibers.

1. Pull out a length of fiber (a) and fold it in half over your finger (b).

2. Draft either from the tip off the end of your finger (a), or from the flat off the top of your finger (b).

Both approaches add air to a worsted prep, extra air to a woolen prep, or spring to a long-stapled fiber. Folding and holding the fiber gives you more control when drafting, and there are no rules

about how to draft from the fold: woolen and worsted both work. In fact, the only rule about spinning from the fold is the folding part: you don't have to keep your finger in the fiber when you start spinning; you can spin with your finger in or out of the fiber.

The downside to spinning a long, lustrous fiber from the fold is that bending the long staple in half reduces its shine and its resistance to abrasion. These may be the reasons you chose a long fiber in the first place! Spinning from the flat rather than the tip, however, helps preserve some of that shine, especially in silk, because the fibers are more aligned when you use that technique, rather than spinning from the tip.

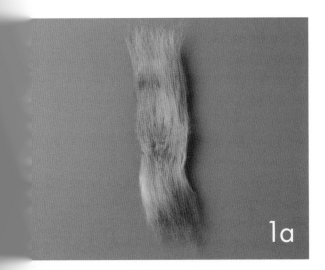

1a

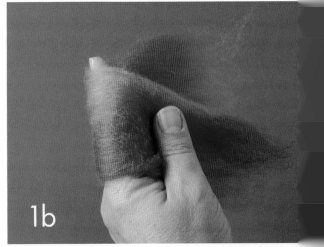

1b

2a

2b

to shine? In that case, spin your fiber worsted. If you're going for a loftier yarn with silk that glints, spin woolen.

- **Spin from the fold.** If spinning from the tip doesn't work, try spinning from the fold. Spinning from the fold can help control uneven stapled fiber blends or slippery fibers. (For information about spinning from the fold, see A Good Tool in Your Spinning Arsenal, page 57.)

THICK OR THIN:
Controlling Yarn Size while Drafting

Drafting is one way to control the size of your yarn. I hear spinners say, "The more I spin, the thinner my yarn gets, and I can't go back." It's not magic, however, and once you get the thick-and-thin facts down, it's pretty easy to go back and forth between thick and thin. It gets down to the amount of fiber and the amount of twist. That's it. Your wheel, hands, and feet adjust to help make it happen, but fiber and twist are the heart of it.

Another thing to keep in mind is the relationship between twist and yarn size. Although you can make a yarn finer by adding more twist, more twist squeezes all the air out and compresses the fiber into a smaller space. If you use this method for making a smaller yarn, your yarn will be denser and heavier, and you are thus changing the yards-per-pound measurement (the *grist* of the yarn; for information about grist, see page 137).

TO SPIN FINE YARN

For spinning fine, you need less fiber and more twist. It makes sense, doesn't it? It would be hard to make a laceweight yarn by twisting an inch-wide strip of fiber. And if you have four individual fibers you'd like to spin into thread, it's going to take more than two twists per inch to hold it together.

- **Your wheel.** Use a smaller whorl, and use less takeup. A smaller whorl makes your bobbin or flyer spin more times for each revolution of your drive wheel. Less takeup allows your yarn to wind on more slowly, gathering more twist before it winds onto the bobbin.

- **Your hands.** Slow down the drafting speed of your hands; by letting the yarn hang out before you let it go through the orifice, it gathers more twist. When you draft, whether woolen or worsted, draft fewer fibers, and watch the drafting triangle while you're finding your rhythm so that you can see how much fiber you're drafting. Keep the amount of fiber and the distance you draft out consistent, and your yarn will be more consistent, too.

- **Your feet.** Treadle faster.

Remember: Less fiber, more twist, fast feet, and slow hands = Fine yarn.

TO SPIN THICK YARN

To spin thick yarn, do the opposite. You need more fiber and less twist. A fat chunk of fiber doesn't need much twist to hold it together, and using lots of twist with a wide piece of fiber makes a dense, heavy yarn.

- **Your wheel.** Use a bigger whorl and use more takeup. A bigger whorl makes your bobbin or flyer spin more slowly, putting less twist into your fiber. More takeup winds your yarn onto the bobbin faster, zipping it onto the bobbin before too much twist can gather in the yarn.

- **Your hands.** Speed up your hands. You'll get less twist by getting the yarn onto the bobbin faster, rather than hanging out gathering twist. When you draft, take bigger bites of fiber, and again watch the drafting triangle. Keep your fiber grab and drafting distance consistent.

- **Your feet.** Treadle slower.

Remember: More fiber, less twist, slow feet, and fast hands = Thick yarn.

DON'T FIGHT IT! YOUR WHEEL IS YOUR FRIEND: Work Together

I've seen lots of spinners in my classes fighting their wheel. In extreme cases, it looks like the spinner is deep-sea fishing and has hooked a particularly feisty marlin. Usually they have their takeup (how quickly the yarn winds onto the bobbin) turned as high as it will go. They are treadling out of control to keep up with the takeup, trying to draft yarn before the wheel rips it from their hands. When I ask why they set their takeup so high, I get one of two answers, and sometimes both: "I like a lot of takeup" and "It makes me spin faster." They may like a lot of takeup, but it probably doesn't make them spin faster, and it can hurt their body. You only want as much takeup as your yarn needs. Don't set yourself up to have your yarn ripped from your hands — just like in kindergarten, that's not friendly!

Bad things can happen when you wrestle with your wheel. When you have your wheel pulling hard and you're treadling like crazy, and drafting your yarn is more about pushing and pulling in a less-than-smooth motion, there's a lot of extra tension and stress on your fiber, yarn, and wheel, as well as on your body. You can develop pain from your fingers and hands to your neck, spine, and elbows. Your yarn isn't too happy with all of that extra tension either. Fighting with your wheel and fiber leads to an uneven yarn, lots of breaks, and a less controlled yarn overall. You aren't really spinning faster, because you are expending lots of energy fighting your wheel and yarn and, in the end, probably not getting the yarn you want.

PREDRAFTING

I've noticed that a big area of contention among spinners and spinning teachers centers around predrafting. Predrafting includes stripping,

The photo at the left shows braided top as it comes packaged; the same fiber has been unbraided at the right.

fluffing, or attenuating commercially prepared fiber to spin just a regular yarn, not a textured, fancy, or art yarn. When it comes to predrafting, most of the time the sides line up as either "always" or "never." My thoughts lie somewhere in between with "it depends."

I spin mostly commercially prepared fibers that are dyed by fiber artists in small batches. There's nothing I love more than spinning a fluffy, "just-shake-and-spin" roving or top. Shake-and-spin fibers are ones where I can do just that: pull them out of their braid or bag, give them a shake, and spin away without a hitch or a clump. I would say 30 to 40 percent of the fibers I spin are shake-and-spin worthy. Many factors go into the fluffiness of a roving or top, including the quality of the roving or top before it's dyed, how the fiber is handled when it's dyed and dried, how the dyer stores it, and how long it sits around as stash. Other features come into play as well: sometimes fiber gets compacted, sometimes the fiber seems just too big, sometimes I want to alter the color, sometimes I just want to touch it before I spin it. Depending on the fiber, the yarn I want, and my mood, I almost always fluff, usually strip, and occasionally attenuate. I want my spinning to be easy, if not effortless, and, if my fiber isn't loose enough to draft, it can make spinning miserable, so I predraft in one of several ways.

FLUFFING

I love to fluff my fiber. Fluffing is pulling the top or roving horizontally, just a little, enough to tease it open. I fluff fiber when it seems closed, perhaps because it sat squashed in my stash. I also fluff to get to know my fiber. As I fluff along the top or roving, I notice any lumps, bumps, or vegetable matter (VM) in the fiber and remove them as I go. I also study the color changes and decide if I want to strip the fiber.

A fluffed section of the top on the facing page

The same top stripped in half lengthwise

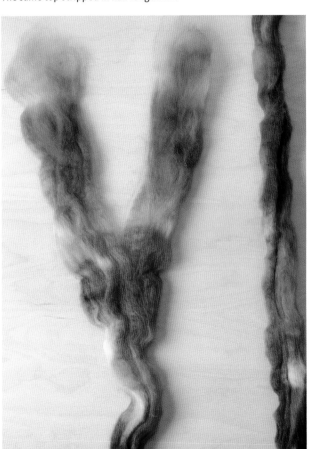

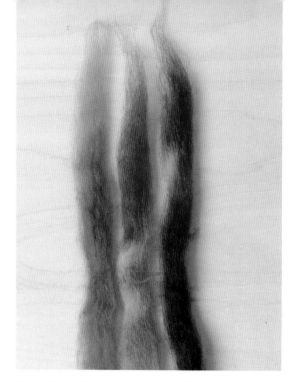

Three pieces of top stripped to the width required when spinning the three together

The top at the right has been attenuated. Compare the length of the green section to the same section of unattenuated top at the left.

STRIPPING

Stripping is the process of dividing the top or roving fiber lengthwise. First, let me say that I never strip my fiber to the size I want my yarn. Yes, I said "never." If I were to strip to size, there would be no time or space to draft my fiber. If you strip to size, the only thing you can do with the fiber is to add twist. Drafting is what makes my yarn what I want it to be. I have to draft it forward to get the smoothness of worsted and draft it back to trap the air for woolen. I couldn't do either if I stripped fiber to the size I wanted my yarn.

On the other hand, I do usually strip my fiber to control bulk or color. I may reduce the bulk simply because I don't want to hold the whole roving or top in my hand. Sometimes it just feels unwieldy; sometimes it makes my hands sweat. So I divide the fiber in half lengthwise and carry on.

Another reason I might strip a top or roving is if it's variegated. I can control color by stripping (or not stripping) in a couple of ways. If I want long color runs, I don't strip, and I do my best to draft the fiber back and forth across the tip of the fiber, like typing along the carriage of an old-fashioned typewriter. If I want shorter runs of color, I divide the fiber at least in half lengthwise, and sometimes into more lengths. (For more about this technique, see page 96.)

I also like to combine colored tops and rovings by drafting two or three (or more) together at one time. To do this without losing my grip (or mind), I strip each top or roving thin enough so the whole fiber bundle is one or two fingers wide.

ATTENUATING

I don't attenuate often. I do this only when a fiber is compacted and fluffing alone won't turn it into a lovely, lofty fiber. For me, attenuating top or roving is a lot like stripping to finished yarn size;

it removes the space for drafting. But when a fiber is compacted, it can make the difference between fighting the fiber and happily spinning.

The photo at the bottom of page 62 shows a before and after. On the left is the "before" fiber. If I had tried to spin this fiber as is, I would have said a lot of words, none of them nice. The fiber isn't felted, but it's compacted, and there would have been pushing and pulling and overtwisting while I tried to spin it. The fiber on the right has been fluffed and attenuated slightly. It looks like it's taken a big breath of air. The predrafted top is fluffy and smooth, a dream to spin, and rescued from the wrath of a frustrated spinner.

RATIOS AND WHORLS (PULLEYS):
The Basics

I admit that when I first read a description in a spinning magazine that threw around numbers, like 10:1, I kind of freaked out. I don't do much math, and I don't feel comfortable with math things. But really, all those numbers are doing is describing the whorls (also called pulleys)

available for your wheel. Here's the thing: you don't have to live by the numbers if you don't want to. Whorls (pulleys) impart twist into your yarn. The smaller they are, the more twist goes into your yarn each time you treadle. That's it. To make yarn, you need fiber, twist, and pull, so I say, "Yay, twist!"

The numbers in a ratio refer to how many times the flyer (or bobbin) spins with one rotation of the drive wheel. So 10:1 means that every time the drive wheel goes around once, the flyer spins 10 times. Ratios for wheels have a big range. For example, the range of standard whorls for a Schacht Matchless is 9:1 to 15:1, and extra whorls are available, taking the range from 4:1 to 21:1. The second number is always *1*, referring to the single rotation of the drive wheel. The larger the first number, the smaller the whorl and the more twist you get in your yarn.

Why should you care, or even want, to change your ratios when spinning? Because they make spinning easier. They let you adjust the amount of twist in your yarn while treadling at the same rate you always do. I know I can change how slow

Treadling Is Not like Driving a Car

When I was a new spinner, I made a mistake regarding twist and takeup — one that I still make many years later when I'm in a hurry or not relaxed when I spin. The mistake is to think that treadling faster makes you spin faster. I learned to spin after I learned to drive a car. Deep in my brain I think that if I push those treadles, which look like huge accelerators to me, the yarn will get on the wheel faster. Treadling faster does not make you spin faster, however; treadling affects twist more than it affects pull (see page 54).

Don't know your ratio numbers and want to? Here's a quick way to figure it out. Mark your drive wheel with a piece of tape. Mark one arm of your flyer with a piece of tape. Start with the tape on the drive wheel and flyer at 12 o'clock. Rotate the drive wheel and count how many times the flyer rotates during one rotation of the drive wheel. If you are trying to determine a very high ratio, you could record it with a video camera or your phone and slow the recording down to count the rotations. Do this with all of your whorls and you'll know all of the ratios possible with your wheel.

If you don't mind writing on your equipment, write the ratio on each of your whorls with a fine-point permanent marker.

or fast I treadle when I start making a yarn, but I almost always fall back into my standard treadling rhythm unless I am 100 percent focused on what I'm doing. So instead of having laserlike focus while spinning a bobbin of fat yarn, I think to myself that fat yarn needs less twist, so I use a lower ratio, like 6:1. When I want to spin fine, fine yarn, I need more twist, so I move to a higher ratio of 15:1. Some wheels have different whorls or pulleys to change out, whereas other wheels have multiple ratios built in; some, such as electric spinners, just have a knob to twist.

DRIVE SYSTEMS:
They Can Make Spinning Easier

If you are having trouble drafting the type of yarn at the size you want, even after you have adjusted your wheel as much as you can, the issue may be your wheel's drive system. Wheels are tools; they are machines, and like most machines, some are better at some things and some are just better than others. You wouldn't use a chain saw to fine-cut a piece of wood to make a violin. It's the same with wheels. Generally, a particular kind of drive system makes spinning a certain type of yarn easier. It's not that it can't be done with another drive system; any spinner can learn the skills to make almost any yarn on almost any wheel. Depending on the wheel, it may have only one drive system or it may be able to be converted to any of the three.

A double-drive system uses one long drive band that goes around the drive-wheel flyer and bobbin. There is no fine-tuning between flyer and brake; they are adjusted with a single knob within the same range. The flyer and bobbin spin at different rates to allow twist and wind-on, because the bobbin and whorl are different sizes. The bobbin is smaller, so the bobbin spins faster

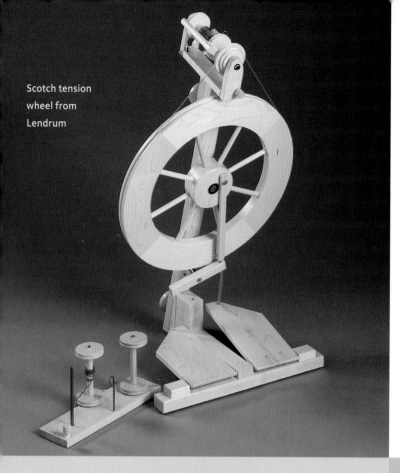

Scotch tension
wheel from
Lendrum

Double-drive
system from
Schacht

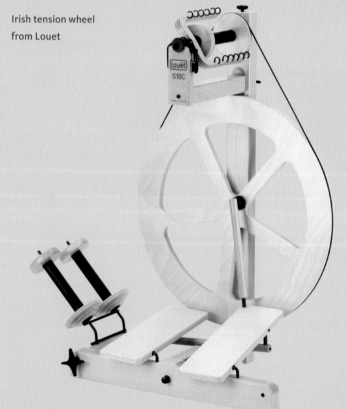

Irish tension wheel
from Louet

miniSpinner from
from HansenCrafts

than the flyer. Double drive is good for medium to fine yarns and high-twist yarns.

Scotch tension is flyer led with a single-drive setup. The drive band is on the flyer, and a separate brake band is on the bobbin. When yarn winds onto the bobbin, the bobbin slows and the flyer keeps spinning for the windon. The most adjustable drive system, Scotch tension can be very finely tuned. The brake band is controlled by a tension peg. The looser the brake band, the lighter the takeup, which means more twist in your yarn before it winds on. The tighter the brake band, the stronger the takeup, which mean less twist before it winds on. Scotch tension is a great all-around drive system. With it, I find I have the most control between twist and wind-on, so I especially like it when I have a yarn that needs manipulation — like a bouclé or when I'm

learning a new technique or trying a new fiber or fiber blend. Electric spinners have Scotch tension.

Irish tension is bobbin led, also with a single-drive wheel. The drive band is on the bobbin, and the brake band is on the flyer. When yarn winds onto the bobbin, the flyer stops and the bobbin keeps spinning to wind on the yarn. This tensioning system has a strong pull and is great for big yarns, low-twist yarns, textured yarns, and plying; in other words, it's good for any type of yarn that needs to get onto the bobbin quickly. As the bobbin fills, its weight may slow down the bobbin so that it fills more slowly. To compensate, turn up the brake tension slightly and you'll be back to your regular pull. You'll notice that the treadles will be a little harder to push as the brake band is tightened.

Counting Treadles

Counting treadles is a technique that some spinners use all the time and some never use. I use it to help keep my singles and plied yarns consistent. Here's how I do it:

The treadle part. I count with one foot (my right foot, even when I use a double-treadle wheel). Every time I push down with my right foot, I count up from one.

The hand part. Hold them still — that's it. While you count, an amount of twist is gathering in a length of fiber. If your hand moves, that changes, thus changing the consistency.

Putting it all together. I start counting right after I wind on my last length. My feet never stop treadling at the same rate. My pull back is usually 1, then I keep counting for the number I've set, say 2 or 3, then I wind on for another 3 or 4. Then I start again with 1 as I pull back. I repeat this two or three times before I do a ply-back test to see if my singles or ply is where I want it twistwise. If my yarn needs more twist, I add treadles; if it needs less, I treadle less, then check with a ply-back test again.

When I have my magic treadle number, and I've written it down, I use it until I feel like I have the rhythm. I then stop counting and just spin with the rhythm. Some spinners count the whole time they're spinning. If I get up from my wheel for any length of time, when I return to spinning, I count for a minute or two to find my rhythm again.

HOW TO DRAFT CONSISTENTLY

My best advice for drafting consistency is to find your groove. Do sampling with some different wheel adjustments. Try different treadle counts, different lengths of draft, different amounts of twist and fiber. Play with purpose for a bit and find what it takes to make the yarn you want to spin. Make sure to write down your experiments, or at least the ones you decide to use to spin. Remember, the goal is flow, constant relaxed motion. If you feel like you're fighting your wheel to get the yarn you want, something isn't right.

The key to consistency is to do the same thing the same way every time, or as close to every time as you can. Pinch the same amount of fiber, while drafting the same distance, while treadling the same amount, with your wheel set up the same way for all the yarn for a particular project. That's it. It's as easy or complicated as you want to make it. Check your yarn every so often with a ply-back sample (see sidebar on the facing page) or another way of measuring. You can stress the minutiae, or you can find your groove and flow.

SEMI-WORSTED AND SEMI-WOOLEN THROWDOWN!
Or, a Plea for Sanity

What do *semi-worsted* and *semi-woolen* mean? I hear these terms used all the time, and I always ask the spinner to explain what he or she means. Yes, even if it's in an article or a book, I look for a detailed explanation. I've decided that they mean something different to every spinner. Both start out with the spinner drafting in a style different from the preparation; for example, taking top, which is a worsted preparation, and drafting it woolen-style by letting twist into the drafting triangle. Is this semi-woolen or semi-worsted? I've heard it emphatically called both. Similarly, taking a woolen preparation, such as a roving or batt, and drafting it worsted, with no twist in the drafting triangle, may be called either semi-woolen or semi-worsted.

My advice is to just say what you're doing, and don't confuse the issue. For instance, say, "I'm spinning top woolen" or "I'm spinning roving worsted." Then there is no confusion — none.

I have a dastardly plan to confuse things even more by making up abbreviations like WLN/WST (a woolen draft on a worsted prep) and WST/WLN (a worsted draft on a woolen prep). No? More confusing, or is it genius?

How to Make a Ply-Back Sample

A ply-back sample is an easy way to spot-check that your spinning is consistent. Simply put, it's a length of fresh yarn pulled from the active bobbin that is allowed to twist (ply) back on itself. Here's how to do it:

After spinning for two or three minutes, stop and pull about 12 inches of yarn off the bobbin, double it, and let it twist on itself. This little length of yarn approximates what the singles you are spinning would look like as a balanced 2-ply. Do you like it? If yes, break off your sample, knot the two loose ends together, and save it. You can hang it on an easy-to-access knob on your wheel, or attach it to your wheel on a piece of card stock or index card.

Get back to your spinning, and then, two or three times while you're spinning a bobbin full of yarn, check your singles by doing a ply-back sample (without breaking it off) against the plyback sample you've saved. If you don't want to break off your original sample, you can measure the bumps per inch (see page 135) and instead jot down that information to check against later.

If you don't like the bit of yarn your ply-back sample makes, first check what it would look like with both more and less ply twist, by manually adding or subtracting twist to the sample in your hand. Still don't like it? Spin more yarn with a different amount of twist, and try the ply-back sample again, until you have a sample you like.

5 | the roof:
PLYING

TO SOME SPINNERS, ply is an afterthought, something they'd like to skip or rush through, something they do the same way every time for every project and yarn. I see these spinners disappointed with their yarns and knitting. Their knitted stitches don't look quite right. They question their fiber, their draft, their wheel, their ability to spin. The fix, however, can be as simple as changing their ply. Or just thinking about their ply.

WHAT IS PLY AND WHY DO IT?

Plying is combining two or more singles in the opposite direction that they were spun in. The singles are twisted (not drafted) while they are held under identical tension, so that the twist enters both (or all) the singles at the same time. (The exception is textured and art yarns, which you may purposely hold under different tensions to get special effects.) Sounds simple doesn't it? It *is* simple, and there is huge potential for creating particular types of yarns that will enhance your knitting, not fight against it. Plying is one of the magical skills of spinning. It can make singles that are just okay into yarn that is amazing. It offers more design possibilities than you may have thought imaginable, such as the following:

- Plying evens out singles. No matter how hard I try, my singles are rarely uniform. In fact, it seems that the harder I try, the more uneven my singles get. Plying comes to my rescue every time. With two or three (or more) singles, thin and fat spots snuggle up to each other, evening out thick and thin spots and creating a more uniform yarn.

- Plying makes a stronger yarn. The more plies, the stronger the yarn. My hands tell me this every time I try to break a 3-ply, thinking it will pull apart as easily as a singles.

The singles on the right may look a bit uneven, but plying it, as shown on the left, evens out the thin and fat spots.

The plied yarn on the right is about the same size as the thick singles on the left.

- Plying can make huge yarns. Instead of spinning a thick singles yarn, consider spinning six or more plies of a finer singles, and then plying them together. It's easy to control and fine-tune the size of your yarn by playing with the size, as well as the number, of singles.

- Plied yarns are less susceptible to pilling. Think about how much surface is exposed in a singles yarn in contrast to the surface of each singles in a plied yarn. The plies protect each other from abrasion, so there is less pilling. This is especially good if you are a fan of short-stapled fibers, like Merino.

- Plying is fast. It's silly, maybe, but on those days I feel like my spinning project is never ending, I do a little plying and am so satisfied with how quickly I end up with beautiful yarn.

- Plying can create new and combined colors. In fact, a crazy number of color combinations are possible with plied yarn, limited only to the colors available and your own imagination.

- Plying can create new fiber blends. Think about a ply of bombyx silk with a ply of the same-color Merino, rather than two plies of a silk/Merino blend: there will be lots more sheen, speckles, and dots of shine, rather than a uniform glow.

Ply to create a new fiber blend. This yarn is a combination of a 50 Merino/50 Tencel blend plied with Bluefaced Leicester.

The yarn on the left has one silk ply and one Tencel ply; the 2-ply yarn on the right is a Merino/Tencel blend. The roving at the top is Merino/Tencel; the fiber at the bottom is silk. All the fiber was dyed the same variegated colorway.

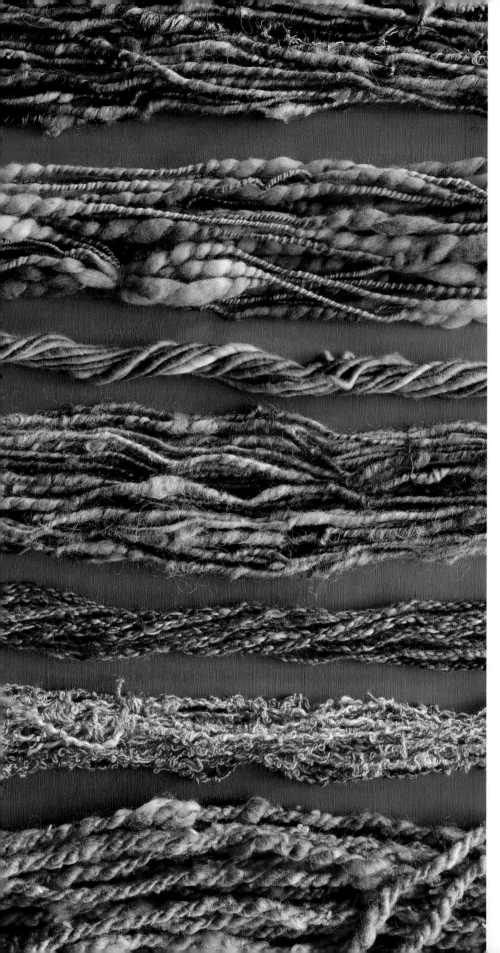

- Plying can create interestingly textured yarn. Start with a plied yarn with singles of different diameters, and let your mind wander around all of the coils, spirals, loops, and cables you can create.

- Plied yarns are lighter than a singles of the same diameter. Consider a worsted-weight singles silk yarn and the same worsted-weight silk as a 2-ply. Whether woolen or worsted spun, the plied yarn contains air in the space between the plies and in the small amount of space the singles untwists as it becomes a plied yarn.

- Plying can affect the clarity or softness of knitting stitches. You can control how your knitting will look, especially with particular knit stitches, with plying. (For more information about the effect of plying on knit stitches, see page 81.)

Create interestingly textured yarns by experimenting with different plying or singles techniques.

FROM LEFT TO RIGHT: (a) A finished 2-ply yarn spun from singles originally spun to be used as singles; (b) an unfinished singles spun to remain singles; (c) an unfinished singles spun to be plied; (d) a finished 2-ply spun from singles spun with enough twist to ply. The twist angle difference between the two singles is approximately 30 percent.

Singles to Stay Singles

The basic theory about why a singles that will be plied needs more twist than a singles that will stand alone is this: because of the plying! When a singles is plied, the yarn is twisted in the opposite direction from the way you spun it into singles, thus untwisting some of the singles twist.

Sometimes my 2-ply yarns look softer than I expect. The singles look untwisted and not very substantial. I've always wondered how much twist is lost in plying. I knew that some was, but how much? Using the same fiber, I spun some samples, leaving some of the yarn as singles and plying another part of it. When I measured and compared the twist in the singles and in the plied yarn, I found that the twist angle was 27 percent higher in the singles than in the plied yarn. That's a lot of twist to lose. Now I know to pay more attention to my singles' twist angles. (For more information on twist and bias, see pages 98 and 124.)

DETAIL

THE BASICS OF EQUIPMENT AND SETUP

To ply, you need some basic equipment: a wheel or spindle, singles to ply, and something to hold the singles. That's it. Of course, there are many tools to help you ply, but I've made good plied yarn with two hand-wound balls of singles, each in its own bowl, and a handspindle. The tools I usually use, however, are a wheel, the bobbins holding the singles, a lazy kate to hold the bobbins, measuring equipment, and a control card (for information about control cards, see page 99). Other tools I find useful are storage bobbins and a bobbin winder, a ball winder or nostepinder, a niddy noddy, tags or bands, and a permanent marker.

SETTING UP YOUR WHEEL

Plying goes faster than spinning singles, so I set my wheel with a little extra pull. When I ply a yarn spun worsted in the singles, I use a little less twist in the ply than I do with a woolen-spun singles; when I ply a yarn spun woolen in the singles, I use a little more twist than I do with a worsted-spun singles to help build the structure. (The exception to adding extra pull is if you are manipulating your yarn in some way, especially with textured and art yarns, such as coils, spirals, and bouclés.)

LAZY KATE SETUP

I place my lazy kate to the side and in back of me on the fiber-supply side. Make sure the yarn is coming off all of the bobbins in the same direction (that is, all clockwise or all counter-clockwise). How much distance and how much tension I use depends on my singles and the yarn I want to make. I like an angled lazy kate because the 45-degree angle puts enough tension on my bobbins to keep them spinning freely but without backspin (and subsequent tangles). If my singles are particularly unevenly twisted, I move my kate farther away from me. This gives extra space for the twist to travel and even out in the singles before it gets plied.

HOW TO PLY

Twist and tension: The right tension is everything to plying. To get an evenly plied yarn, the tension of all the singles you are plying together should be the same, and the twist should enter all of the singles at the same time.

There is tension between the wheel and your hands, just as in drafting, but instead of working with a mass or strip of fiber, you are working with already-spun yarn — singles or to be combined. There is tension between your hands, between

Three (or More) Is a Crowd

Plying templates are an excellent tool to have on hand if you plan on working with more than three plies. I get fumble-fingered holding more than three singles. A plying template looks like a biggish button with four or more holes. You can find beautiful handmade ones, or a button with the right number of holes works fine. The plastic tops on shakable spice jars work wonderfully. You can find those with any number of holes ranging from 3 to as many as 12. You can also make your own custom template for a plying project with a piece of cardboard and a hole punch. If you are using a found or homemade plying template, make sure that the inside edges of the holes are smooth. You don't want to fray your singles as it passes through on its way to be plied.

the wheel and the singles, between the singles themselves, and between the bobbins (or ball) holding the singles and your plying motion. It seems like a lot of things to think about, but it all works seamlessly, and when it doesn't, it's easy to check where in the plying tension something has gone wrong.

The little tension supplied by a lazy kate that holds bobbins at a 45-degree angle is almost always enough tension for me. As mentioned above, if my singles are particularly lively, I move the kate farther away, giving those happy singles more room to expel energy before getting plied. Still snarly? If neither of those options gives me enough tension, I add a tensioning band. Several angled lazy kates come with the option of adding a tensioning band.

When I first was learning to ply, it took several tries for me to get to the best plying motion. I used to use a hand-over-hand style of motion, but I found I wasn't able to catch those little tiny pigtails in my singles, and it was hard to get an even ply. I switched to the hip-lock style of plying a couple of years ago, and it works great for me. I call it hip-lock because I lock my fiber-supply hand at my hip: it doesn't move forward or back. I make sure that each of the singles I'm plying remains separated by keeping a finger of that hand between each one. This helps me control

the tension and catch pigtails or other inconsistencies that may try to creep through. If I have more plies than fingers, I use a plying template. You can buy one or they are easy to make out of cardboard or the top of a spice jar. (See Three (or More) Is a Crowd, on page 77.)

The hand I use for drafting when I spin is also my plying hand, the one that moves when I ply. It feeds plied yarn into the orifice at regular intervals. I regularly slide my plying hand back down the singles I'm plying. I do this lightly so I don't disturb or fuzz up the fiber, but I do it to feel if there are any tiny pigtails or pieces of vegetable matter (VM) that I might want to remove. I let as much twist enter my yarn as I want, and then I pinch off the twist with my drafting hand and feed the yarn into the orifice.

I regularly check my ply twist by pulling a length off the bobbin and letting it hang in a loop. If I'm going for a balanced ply in my finished yarn (that is, a yarn that will hang in a mostly open loop after finishing), I don't want my test sample to hang in an open loop. This is because twist escapes when the yarn is finished, so if your test yarn hangs in an open loop, it will likely seem underplied rather than plied to balance when it's finished. As I check my ply, I'm looking for the balance I want in my yarn as well as consistency in the ply. (For how to finish yarn, see chapter 7.)

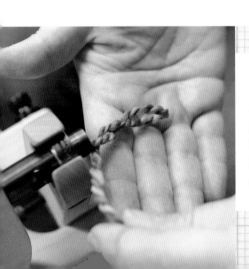

Finding Balance

Just what is a balanced yarn? A balanced yarn is one that hangs in an open loop after finishing with no extra twist in either direction. This is the holy grail of yarns for some spinners, but others like their yarns a bit over- or undertwisted, depending on what they will use the yarn for.

TO COUNT OR NOT TO COUNT

I usually count treadles to get a feel for the rhythm when I'm just getting started plying, and then I stop counting. I make note of how many times I treadle between winding the last plied yarn onto the bobbin and winding on the next to get the ply I want, and I write this number down on a tag hanging on my wheel. If I get up from my wheel for any reason, when I come back, I count again to get myself started. My advice is to pick a way to count that works for you. I count with the downstroke of my right foot, but then I stop counting as my yarn winds on. If you're using a double-treadle wheel, you may want to count with both of your feet — or not. Whatever option you choose in both of these instances, count the same way every time. (See also Counting Treadles, page 67.)

RESTING AND REWINDING SINGLES:
Pros and Cons

Both resting and rewinding singles helps with twist control. Resting lets the fresh twist settle a little, and rewinding helps even out the twist in a singles. I rarely rest my yarn on purpose. I'm usually so excited that I want to ply right away. What I probably wouldn't do is ply a freshly spun bobbin to a well-rested (on the bobbin for more than a day or two) bobbin, because the twist will be different in each of the singles and then the twist will change again after it's finished. So what you see when you ply may not be what you get in the finished yarn. If I had to ply a well-rested and a fresh single, I would do a sample all the way through to finishing the yarn to minimize surprises.

I rewind my bobbins a lot. I like using cardboard storage bobbins for big projects, because I can write on them and it keeps my spinning bobbins free. For me it makes plying easier because I can rewind the bobbins evenly, unlike when I'm spinning. (I'm not always great at moving hooks as often as I should when I spin, so I get a few hills and valleys on my bobbins.) Unevenly spun bobbins don't spool as smoothly, and that can interfere with the tension when plying. Rewinding bobbins also helps even out the twist in a singles by moving the twist through the yarn.

To rewind bobbins you need storage bobbins and a bobbin winder. There are many kinds of both on the market — the choice is yours. Storage bobbins come in wood, plastic, and cardboard; many of them are made for weaving, but spinners borrow them. Bobbin winders can be manual or electric. Some spinners adapt an electric drill as a bobbin winder; some use a quill attachment for their electric spinner.

Rewinding bobbins does not add or subtract twist to your singles because the winding is done as a side-to-side feed. If, however, you wound a bobbin into a center-pull ball and pulled the yarn from the center and wound it onto a bobbin, you would add or subtract twist depending on how the singles was spun. Yes, this happens to any yarn you knit from the center of a center-pull ball, too.

HOW TWIST AFFECTS KNITTING

A major question for knitters is, "How much ply twist do you need for knitting?" I use different amounts of ply twist for different yarns. I will admit that much of it has to do with how I like the look. On the next page are a few samples of top drafted woolen and also drafted worsted. For each, I spun a balanced-ply yarn, a slightly under-plied yarn, and a slightly overplied yarn.

Sampling Twist in Plied Yarns

Woolen-Spun

BALANCE	TWIST PER INCH (TPI)	COMMENTS
Balanced	4 tpi/ 8 bumps	The benchmark ply; best all-around ply for all knitting.
Undertwisted	1.5 tpi/ 3 bumps	This seems too soft for me. My needle tips slipped between the plies and once or twice split the singles. I don't feel like this yarn would hold up well when knit.
Overtwisted	6 tpi/ 12 bumps	This has been my go-to yarn for a while. I love the spring that the extra twist gives the yarn. It also starts to get rounder with more ply twist and to cheat to some properties of a 3-ply. An overtwisted 2-ply yarn behaves a little like a 3-ply, it has a little more durability and a little more stitch definition — not as much as a 3-ply, but more than a 2-ply.

Worsted-Spun

BALANCE	TWIST PER INCH (TPI)	COMMENTS
Balanced	4 tpi/ 8 bumps	The benchmark ply; best all-around ply for all knitting.
Undertwisted	1.5 tpi/ 3 bumps	I love this one. It's soft looking but still seems like it will hold together. It has wonderful drape. I would use this to knit lace or a loose-gauge garment.
Overtwisted	6 tpi/ 12 bumps	This starts to look and feel harder, a little stiff. It would be durable. I would use it for outerwear sweaters and mittens that would keep you warm and shed some moisture.

SAMPLING SINGLES

STOCKINETTE

LACE

CABLE

VARIEGATED

HOW PLY AFFECTS KNITTING

Singles

Singles do their own thing because they are full of twist energy. Knitted stitches look fluid — they have movement. Knitted singles block wonderfully, and stitches stay where you put them. Singles, especially short, soft wools, are prone to pilling (see page 53).

WHAT TO USE THEM FOR

Lace. Singles yarns are pliant and compliant. When blocked, singles yarn stays where you put it and gives a softer look to the lace.

WHAT THEY'RE NOT SO GREAT FOR

Stockinette stitch. Often the swatch biases. Notice also its uneven surface and strong vertical line.
Cables or Texture. I find a singles cable limp and soft looking, not what I want in a cable.

WHAT HAPPENS WITH VARIEGATED YARN

Singles yarns maintain long color runs and can be used for most smaller-patterned stitches without much visual distortion.

STOCKINETTE **LACE** **CABLE**

2-Ply Yarn

A 2-ply yarn is oval in shape and tends to roll out. A knitters' favorite, 2-ply yarn is easy to make and extremely versatile.

WHAT TO USE IT FOR

Stockinette stitch. I was surprised at how textured the surface of the 2-ply swatch above looks. The bias is gone, and the stitches have a lot of visual movement as they push apart from each other.

Lace. A 2-ply yarn is more oval than round. The visual motion in the stockinette sample works to great advantage in lace. The stitches roll away from each other, opening the lace holes. It makes a fantastic open-lace yarn.

Soft colorwork. With its oblong shape, 2-ply yarn creates soft lines between colors, making it a good fit for the flow of soft colorwork designs, such as Fair Isle and other stranded knitting (below right).

Intarsia

Stranded knitting

SEED STITCH   LACE   CABLE

WHAT IT'S NOT SO GREAT FOR

Cables. The 2-ply cable is better than the singles cable. There are times I would like the extra visual motion the 2-ply gives the cable, but it is still a flattish cable with some, but not great, substance.

Hard-edged colorwork. The lines between colors are softer and visually blend, which means this yarn is not a good choice for hard-edged colorwork like intarsia (facing page, bottom left).

WHAT HAPPENS WITH VARIEGATED YARN

When you spin a variegated yarn as it comes from the roving or top, it usually marls or barber poles, and if this marling has high contrast, it interrupts most patterns. You'll see the color patterning of the yarn and have to hunt for the stitch patterns. This can work for simple texture patterns but doesn't work well for lace and cables.

SAMPLING 3-PLY YARNS

STOCKINETTE   LACE   CABLE

3-Ply Yarn

A 3-ply yarn is round and rolls in when knit. Yarns with three or more plies are the least prone to pilling.

WHAT TO USE IT FOR

Stockinette stitch. The 3-ply swatch looks so smooth next to the 2-ply. The stitches line up and lean in, and the roundness of the yarn settles them.

Cables. Attention! This cable stands up. The rolling in that makes a 3-ply not the perfect lace yarn makes it a fab yarn for cables. The stitches press together and stand up. It's the perfect yarn for a cable.

Hard-edged colorwork. A 3-ply yarn creates a crisp edge that makes the shapes in intarsia stand out (see below, left).

Intarsia

Stranded knitting

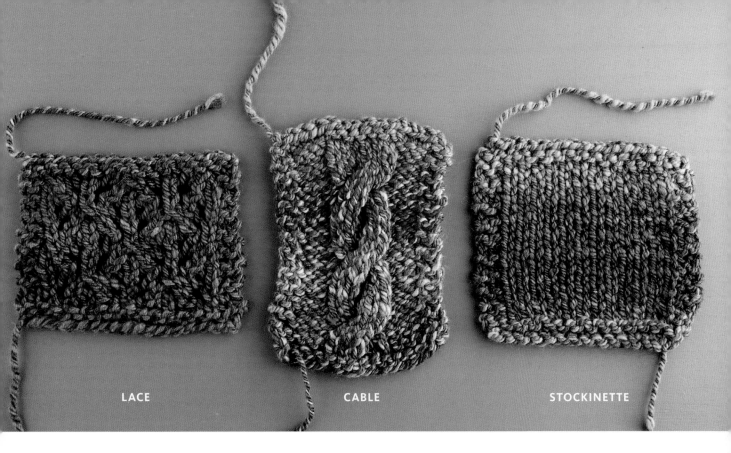

LACE   CABLE   STOCKINETTE

WHAT IT'S NOT SO GOOD FOR

Lace. A 3-ply yarn is round and rolls into the stitch; it wants those yarnovers to close. It's much more interested in making the decreases pop. Even a firm blocking yielded a not-so-very-lacy lace.

Soft colorwork. The roundness of the 3-ply yarn keeps colors from blending visually (see facing page, bottom right).

WHAT HAPPENS WITH VARIEGATED FIBER

The 3-ply yarn moves color dots from spots to speckles, smaller and able to more easily blend visually. A 3-ply works better for many pattern stitches. Keep pattern stitches small, and swatch before starting a project, though I like a variegated 3-ply for cables.

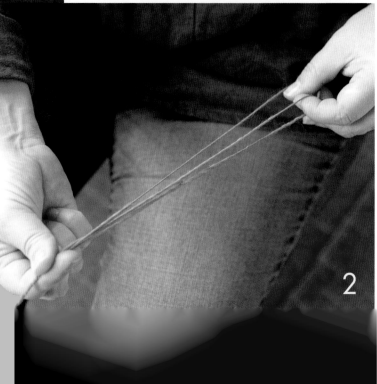

There are as many ways to chain ply as there are spinners. But the basics are the same: pull a loop of yarn through another loop of yarn, like making a crochet chain. Here's how to chain ply:

1. Make a large slip knot (the loop is the size of an orange) with a long (4 inches) tail. Tie the tail to your leader. The yarn coming from the bobbin runs under the loop. Position your hands so your drafting hand (front hand) is holding the tail just under where it is tied to the leader; this will help tension the yarn while creating loops. Your fiber hand (back hand) should have your thumb and first two fingers inside the loop, ready to grab the singles spooling from the bobbin and pull it through as a new loop.

2. Start spinning slowly in the opposite direction your singles was spun. Use your fiber fingers to grab the singles through the loop and pull it through, creating a new loop. Don't pull your fingers out of the new loop! Open your front hand and let twist travel back into the looped yarns and let the plied yarn wind on.

   Repeat from grabbing the singles through the loop (step 2).

It sounds like a lot to think about, but it happens almost simultaneously once you get used to it. It helps at first to practice with a commercial yarn; a sock yarn is great. Remember to slow down. Chain plying doesn't go as fast as plying a 3-ply yarn; manipulating the yarn into the chain takes extra time. As you get comfortable with chain plying, practice working with different-size loops. This will help when you're working with a variegated single, using bigger loops within a single color length and smaller loops when colors change to help keep the colors as clear as possible.

Chain Ply

When it's knitted, chain ply behaves like a 3-ply. All of the knitting factors are the same with one difference: done with a variegated fiber, the colors blend smoothly from one to another more like a singles yarn, keeping the colors intact rather than blending them. When you knit with a variegated chain-ply yarn, structurally it will behave like a 3-ply, but the color play will be like a singles, where there is the possibility of pooling: make sure to swatch.

Chain-plied yarn and swatch

PLYING MISTAKES AND WHAT TO DO

It is as inevitable as rain at a summer family reunion that you will make mistakes when you ply. Most mistakes are easy to fix! Plied yarn can be unplied and re-plied until you like the yarn you have. If your yarn feels too stiff, run it back through your wheel, unplying it slightly. If your yarn feels too floppy, run it back through your wheel, adding twist. Here are some other common problems and what to do when they happen.

One of your singles breaks while plying. Stop and unply your yarn until you get to the broken singles. Splice the broken ends of the single together (I spit splice [see below] just to be sure), and then resume plying.

You've twisted the ply in the wrong direction. I've done this so many times, even taken the yarn through finishing. I just thought my yarn looked weird and would be fine after it dried. It wasn't.

- If you notice this while you are still plying, just reverse. Pull out the yarn you've plied and ply it in the right direction.

Spit Splice

First, let me say that for this technique you don't have to use spit — water works just fine. Spit splicing is a nearly seamless way to attach two pieces of wool yarn. It can be used to fix broken singles when plying, and it can also be used in knitting when starting a new yarn, therefore avoiding having ends to weave in.

What you do is basically felt the two ends of yarn together.

Taking the two singles you want to splice together, fluff open the ends and wet them. How much and how wet? I wet about an inch's worth of yarn, making it a little more than damp but not dripping wet. Stack the ends on each other so that the tip of one damp end overlaps the dry part of the other yarn by ¼ inch to ½ inch. Now, place the stacked yarns between your palms and

rub your hands back and forth to create heat and friction. I do this for 20 seconds before checking the splice. The splice should be felted enough to just hold and not be hard felted. The length of time it takes to splice this way will depend on the fiber and fiber blends you use. Some portion of your blend must be regular wool; superwash won't work.

If you make a center-pull ball with a nostepinder, you can ply from both ends of the ball.

- If you have a full bobbin of misplied yarn, put your bobbin on a lazy kate and re-ply the way you want it.

- If you have already wound it into a skein or even finished it, put your misplied skein on a swift and re-ply from there.

One of your bobbins runs out and the other still has yarn. Break the singles that is still attached to the bobbin with yarn. Ply from both ends of the yarn that's left in one of a couple of ways. In both cases, you will have to splice the ends of the newly rewound singles to the ends of the singles waiting on your wheel.

- Wind the leftover singles into a center-pull ball by hand, with a ball winder, or onto a nostepinder.

- Andean ply from your hand. Here's how (see photos on facing page).

1. Lay one yarn end across your palm, and secure it with your thumb.

2. Take the yarn across the back of your hand to its base below your little finger, across your wrist on the palm side, then up between your ring and middle fingers.

3. Loop the yarn around your middle finger clockwise.

4 and 5. Take the yarn down to the base of your hand on the thumb side, around your wrist, then between your middle and index fingers. Loop the yarn around your middle finger counterclockwise, then down to the base of your hand on the outside. Wrap the yarn across the palm-side of your wrist. You are now at the point where you started in step 1.

6. Repeat steps 2–4 until you have used up all your yarn.

7 and 8. Take hold of both ends of yarn, and hold them out on the palm side of your hand.

9 and 10. Still holding the ends of yarn, wriggle the bundle of yarns up to the base of your fingers just enough so that you can draw your middle finger out of its wraps.

11. Slide the bundle back onto your wrist. Tie the ends to a leader or other plied yarn, and ply the strands together as you allow the yarn to release from your yarn "bracelet."

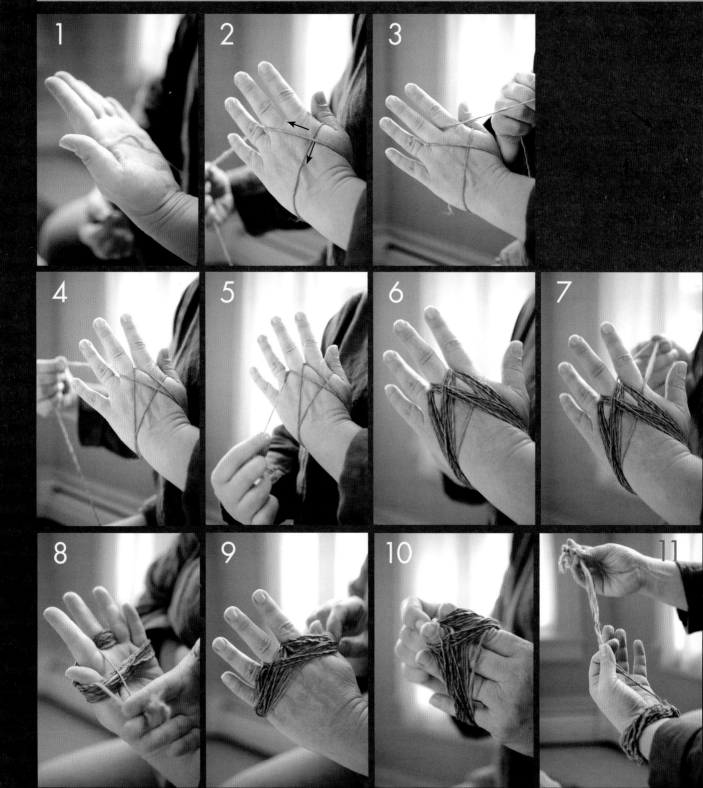

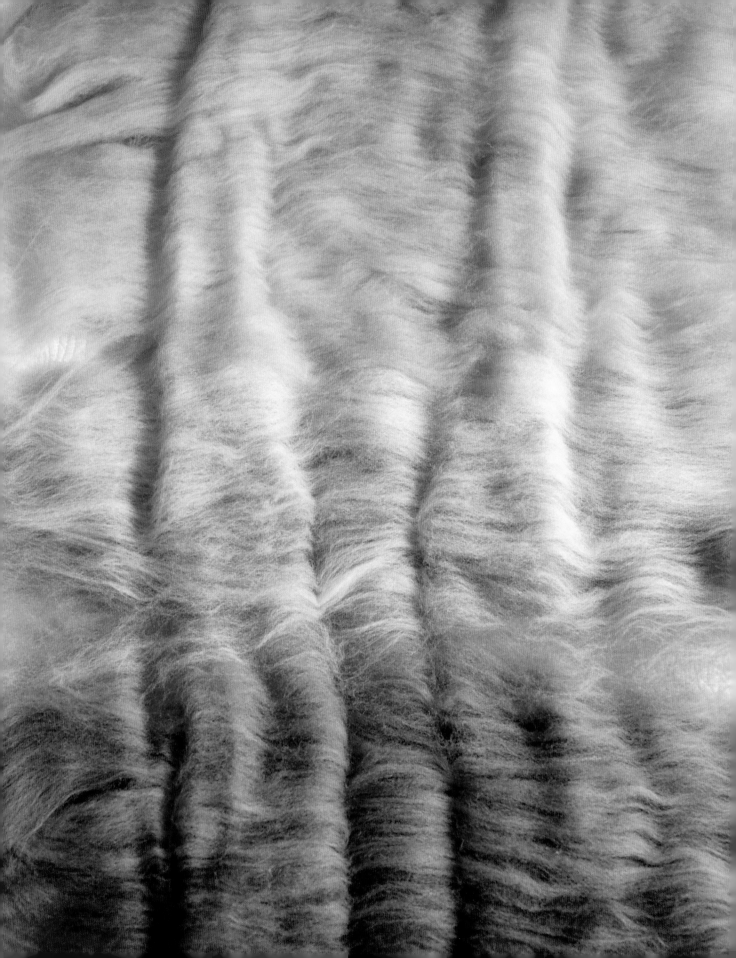

6 | the paint:

COLOR

MOST SPINNERS I KNOW ARE INTRIGUED, smitten, and captivated by color, and almost as many are perplexed and nearly paralyzed when it comes to working with it, which means that they buy a lot of beautifully dyed fiber and it just sits in their stash, too loved to use. But color is easy if you let it be. Color is everywhere, all around you. If you can get dressed in the morning, you can work with color in spinning.

The key to not stressing about working with color is to make it as simple as possible. Don't use a color wheel; use the world around you. Don't get me wrong. If you want to study color and use a color wheel, by all means go for it, but if a color wheel and philosophies of color make you twitchy and keep you from spinning your colorful stash, start with the easy way. As soon as you start working with color without stress, you will start noticing color and color combinations everywhere.

HOW DYERS DYE

Remember that this book is all about commercially prepped and already-dyed fibers, so I'm not going to teach you to dye, but I do want to talk a little about how the dyers we love dye fiber. There are several ways that they do so; the most common are solid, semisolid, gradient, patterned, and random.

- In solid dyeing, a single color completely saturates the fiber.

- In semisolid dyeing, a single color doesn't saturate the fiber completely; it leaves lighter and darker areas of the single color.

- Progressive dyeing describes a multiple colorway, featuring long stretches of single colors that are each used only once along the length of the braid.

- In gradient or ombre dyeing, a single saturated color slowly fades to white along the length of the braid.

- In patterned, also called variegated or multicolored, dyeing, a fiber is dyed in a consistently repeating pattern, such as ABC, ABC, or ABC, CBA (where the letters represent specific colors).

- Random dyeing describes a multicolored fiber dyed without a repeating pattern. It doesn't necessarily have more colors than a patterned fiber; the colors are just applied randomly rather than in a repeated pattern.

WHAT AFFECTS COLOR ON FIBER

Many factors in addition to dye affect the color of a fiber, and just about everything in the spinning process can intensify or soften colors in your finished yarn. It's not magic. It mostly comes down to how close together the fibers are, because their density affects how much light and color they reflect. The denser and less airy a fiber is, the darker the color will be. The color itself doesn't change, and in fact, sometimes you can't even see a difference unless you look at the examples side by side. But when you're working with color, many little things taken together make a significant difference in the end result.

DIFFERENT FIBERS, DIFFERENT COLORS

The fiber you are using affects the color. Notice in the photos below how different undyed wool and silk are. The Corriedale fiber looks soft, and the bombyx silk is reflective and super shiny. When color is applied to them, look what happens. Each fiber was dyed a light blue, attempting to saturate the fibers completely. The color looks the same, but different: softer on the wool and brighter on the silk, yet it is the same exact color and dye.

Corriedale fiber (far left and far right) and silk fiber (center) undyed, then dyed with same dye color

The Color Wheel

Okay. I know some of you want the basics of a color wheel. I get the same questions over and over again when I teach: "How do I pick colors that go together?" "How do I keep my dyed fiber from turning to mud when I spin it?" Here are the basics and the answers to those two questions.

A color wheel is set up around the *primary colors*. You know those; all the way back to preschool we've been talking about them and mixing a few colors from them. They are blue, yellow, and red. They are usually set up like a peace sign on a color wheel that looks like a big pie.

In between the primary colors are three slices of color called the *secondary colors*, which are what you get when the two primaries on either side of a secondary color are combined. For example, the primary colors blue and yellow make the secondary color green. Flanking the secondary colors are the *tertiary colors*. A tertiary color is created by combining a secondary and a primary color. For example, lime green is a tertiary color made by mixing the secondary color green and the primary color yellow.

A *complementary color* is the color directly across the wheel from any color.

If you want to make sure your colors are not dull or muddy, work with colors and colorways that use three colors all in a row on the wheel, with maybe a single complementary for an accent. Yarn becomes muddy when you travel around the wheel, picking up too many colors that are spaced far apart or across from each other on the wheel. For example, if you blend red and purple from one side of the wheel with green and yellow from the other, you'll end up with a muddy brown.

Have you run out of a particular colorway on a particular breed and then filled in with the same colorway on a different breed only to discover something wasn't quite right? Even between wools there's a difference in color. The photos below show three different wools — Corriedale, Bluefaced Leicester (BFL), and Wensleydale —

all dyed with the same colorway. You may not notice a big difference at a casual glance, but put them side by side, and you can see that the Corriedale brings an almost matte quality to the colors, whereas the BFL is a deeper color with a hint of shine, and the Wensleydale, with its natural luster, makes the colors intense and glossy.

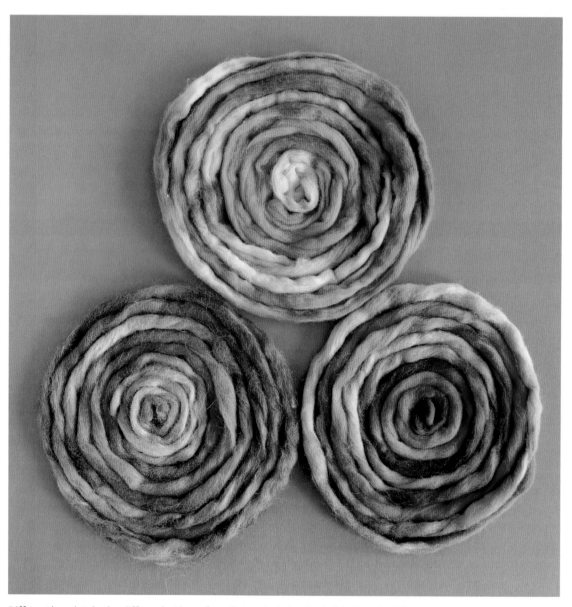

Different breeds take dye differently. *Shown from the top clockwise:* Corriedale, Wensleydale, and BFL.

WHY THE PREP MATTERS

How fiber is prepped affects the color, too. A combed preparation, like top, aligns and compacts the fiber, providing more surface to reflect the colors, so they look deeper. Going in the opposite direction, a woolen preparation, like roving, crisscrosses the fibers and adds air among them, providing less surface to reflect colors, so they tend to look lighter. The more woolen and airy the preparation, the lighter the colors look. Compare the examples of a roving, a rolag, and a batt (below): the color gets a smidgen lighter as the preparation gets airier. This characteristic gives you options; as a spinner, you're never stuck with a color. If you like a color you've bought as top but would like it to be a little lighter or softer hue, card it into rolags or batts.

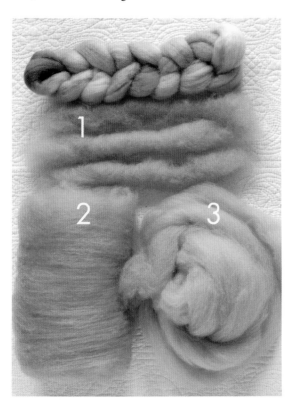

Different fiber preparations affect color. Note the color variation among these preps made from the same braided top: (1) rolag, (2) batt, (3) roving.

THE EFFECT OF DRAFTING ON COLOR

Another factor that affects color is whether your drafting method works for or against the way the fiber behaves because of its preparation. Spinning top with a worsted draft gives the most intense version of a color, whereas spinning top with a woolen draft lightens it a bit. The opposite is true when you're working with a carded preparation: spinning it with a woolen draft produces a softer version of a color than spinning the same preparation worsted.

ABOVE LEFT, Top spun woolen; ABOVE RIGHT, Top spun worsted

BELOW LEFT, Roving spun woolen; BELOW RIGHT, Roving spun worsted (long draw)

Yarn size affects color. Note the more vibrant color in the finer yarn on the right compared to the thicker yarn on the left spun from the same braid.

SIZE MATTERS

Size does matter! The finer the yarn, the deeper a color appears. Look at the two yarns above. They are the same colorway, fiber, preparation, and draft, and both are 2-ply. As a side note, this sample illustrates a case of when "I know better" leads to disappointment. I was sure my brain, hands, and feet would remember the size of yarn I was spinning. I spun one yarn, plied and finished it without saving even a ply-back sample — because I knew better. I was going to spin the second yarn right away. What could change so much, after all? As you can see, however, the second yarn is a great deal finer and denser, bad for the project I was going to knit but excellent as an example of how size can change a color. The color of the finer yarn is deeper and much more vibrant.

The spirals of yarn at the left were all spun from the same variegated braid, but the amount of each color was determined by how many times the braid was split (divided vertically). The bottom yarn was spun from a section of pink fiber without splitting the braid; the next one up was spun from the braid split in half; the second from the top was spun from one-quarter of the thickness of the braid; and the top yarn was spun with one-eighth of the thickness of the braid.

Size also matters when you're working with a variegated fiber and you want to control the length of a color run. I see spinners sit at their wheel with a fresh braid and instantly start stripping it vertically. When they begin to spin it, some ask what happened to the long color runs they thought they'd get from this fiber. Short answer: They stripped them away! The more a pattern-dyed fiber is stripped vertically, the shorter each color run becomes. Look at the example below. I spun all into approximately the same-size singles. Here, the orange is pulled out of each to compare the lengths of the color runs; look at the difference. If you want the longest possible color runs from a dyed fiber, strip it as little as possible.

The more plies in a yarn, the more saturated the colors appear to be. **FROM LEFT TO RIGHT**: singles, 2-ply, 3-ply

THE EFFECT OF THE NUMBER OF PLIES

The more plies, the more saturated a color looks. Adding plies condenses the yarn and adds more area with less space for light to get through. The more light reflects off a surface, the more intense a color looks. Compare the yarns in the photo above; they are the same fiber, prep, draft, and size of the singles. The difference is the number of plies: a singles, a 2-ply, and a 3-ply.

FINISHING TOUCHES

How you finish a yarn affects the surface structure, and if it affects the surface of a yarn, it affects the color. The more roughed up or fuzzy a yarn is, the less surface it has to reflect light and color. If you want to keep your color as intense as it is in your freshly spun yarn, finish it with as little disruption as possible: a soak and a snap. If you'd like to soften the look of the yarn and color, whack it not only to soften its look, but also to raise fuzz. (See chapter 7 for information on finishing.)

What Is Superwash and How Does It Affect Color?

Superwash is a chemical process that strips the scales from wool fiber and yarn. The scales on wool are what cause a fiber or yarn to felt when introduced to soap, agitation, and abrupt changes in temperature. The removal of the scales also creates a surface on yarn and fiber that dye loves. Dye strikes fast and intensely on superwash fiber and yarn. The same colorway can look completely different on a regular and a superwash fiber.

The superwash Merino top at the left took the same dye more intensely than the same Merino top untreated at the right.

DIGGING INTO YOUR STASH

All of this leads me to your fiber stash. Just how many braids of variegated fiber do you have in there? How many are in colorways that match? The variegated braid is both the joy and bane of a spinner's stash. We love to buy them, but we aren't sure how to use them.

I know my stash is 80 percent variegated braids, and probably less than 5 percent match the colorway of any other braid. I buy them as souvenirs now when I go on a trip. It used to be T-shirts, then it was spindles; for years now it's been braids of variegated fiber. If we toured my variegated braid stash, I could tell you where I bought each one, who was with me, and at least two funny stories from the trip. I take my stash very personally.

What can you do with a stash heavy in variegated braids in ones or twos of a particular colorway? If you're happy with the amount of fiber but spin your braids the same every time, just taking what you get and not even quite sure what that's going to be, you can keep the color flow exactly the same as the braid or learn to mix up the colorway within a single braid with some confidence. If you want to make something bigger than is possible with 4 to 8 ounces of fiber, you can learn to combine variegated fibers with solids, semi-solids, and other dyed fibers to create an almost infinite amount of fiber that all works together.

MAINTAINING THE BRAID'S COLOR SEQUENCE

The two easiest ways to maintain the sequence of colors in a fiber braid are to spin singles or to chain ply.

Singles for Knitting

Have you ever spun a singles, finished it, and knit with it, only to discover that the fabric leaned in one direction or the other? This is called *biasing,* something that makes spinning knitters crazy. I have a fix for this, and it has nothing to do with blocking or weighing your yarn. The fix for bias can be described in two words: less twist. When I spin a singles to keep as a singles, I use about 30 percent less twist than I would for a singles that will live its life as a plied yarn. Why? When you ply a yarn, you remove a portion of the twist in the singles. If you spin a singles as if it were going to be plied, but then finish it without plying it, the extra twist destined to be a lovely ply is now a singles with extra twist. That twist will go somewhere in your knitting; it will make your stitches lean. Your knitting will bias in one direction or another, depending on which way you spun your singles.

When I'm spinning a singles that I intend to use as singles, I still do a ply-back sample to help keep me on track as to size and twist (see page 69). A singles hanging on my wheel will just untwist, so I let it ply on itself and knot it to keep twist in the yarn. I usually use a control card, too.

The swatch at the left was knit with a loose-twist singles; the one on the right was knit with a tightly twisted singles, which caused biasing.

I keep ply-back and yarn samples on a control card nearby whenever I spin. The more loosely twisted yarn on the left would work better for knitting if used as singles.

Chain Plying for Color Consistency

A quick-and-easy way to ply for color consistency is to chain ply (also called Navajo ply, N-ply, and crochet ply; see How to Chain Ply, page 86). I like to call it chain ply because it is literally a way of plying that makes a continuous chain through looping — like crochet. I've had a hard time coming to love chain ply, but it's quick and easy, and since the technique uses only one or two bobbins it's perfect when I don't have enough bobbins free for a 2-ply or 3-ply. There are spinners, like Sarah Anderson, who adore the technique and make truly beautiful yarn with chain ply.

I use it sparingly, but I have become quite smitten with one aspect of it: it allows me to match up the colors of the singles as closely as I possibly can while plying. For a long time, when I chain plied I used the same-size loops. Once I got into a rhythm, I took the colors as they came,

even where the colors didn't match (marled parts — high-contrast colors plied together like a candy cane — and all). Here's a truth about handdyed fiber: it's dyed by a person, not a machine. Rarely are the lengths of color equal and even; sometimes the dyer even intentionally makes the lengths uneven and different. When I used the same-size loops to ply, there were more than a few marled spots, since I wasn't trying to keep same-color sections together as I plied.

When I'm chain plying, I particularly want to keep the colors clear and the same as the original fiber, with as little marling as possible. It was a revelation to me when I realized I could vary the size of the loops throughout the plying process in order to match up the color lengths. When there is a long stretch of a color, I use big loops; when the color span is short or I get close to the spot where the colors change, I switch to smaller loops to catch the changes in a shorter length, and therefore avoid marling.

I controlled the colors when plying on the yarn on the left to avoid marling; I allowed the colors to overlap when plying the yarn on the right.

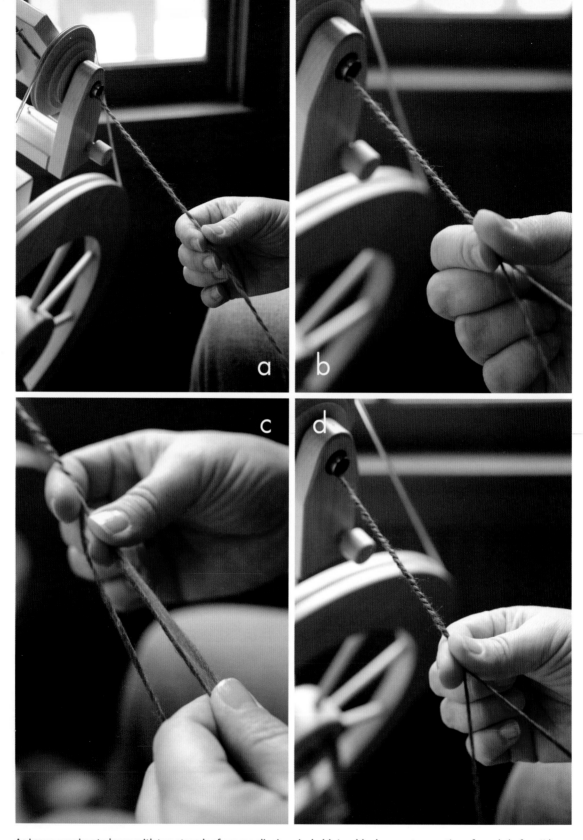

As I spun a variegated yarn with two strands of orange aligning nicely (a), I suddenly came to a section of purple before I'd used up the orange (b). To avoid marling, I broke off the orange at that point (c) and moved ahead to where the purple began in the second strand. I spliced in the new purple end and continued to ply with colors matching.

THE SECRET TO PLYING TO MATCH

Until very recently, I thought that achieving a color match between plies was just sorcery. I imagined there were just a few spinners talented enough to divide the fiber evenly enough and spin singles consistently enough to ply a perfect match colorwise. I tried measuring every aspect of this process in grams, twist angle, and grist (see page 137), but nothing ever worked for me; it was always hit or miss. Then I learned the trick: *break it to make it.* I divide and spin my singles as I always have, but when I ply, I change the way I approach it. Using a 2-ply as an example, I start plying and the colors match just fine, then the inevitable happens: a new color creeps in too soon. Instead of just giving up and letting it barber pole, what I do now is to break one of the plies and remove the too-soon or too-late color so that the plies match again. I then splice the new end to the old and keep plying, magically matching colors!

ANOTHER WAY TO MAINTAIN A MATCH: CORE SPINNING

Do you core spin? I use core spinning to keep my colors in line and, at the same time, create a unique yarn. The keys to successful core spinning are to use a core that won't become overtwisted too quickly, to draft at a 90-degree angle, and to use low to medium twist to create the yarn. There are whole books written on making textured and art yarns that teach all of the nuances of creating an excellent core-spun yarn.

When I core spin, I use either commercially spun wool yarn or unspun fiber as the core. I like wool because it's grabby, but other spinners use cotton, acrylic, and even wire as their cores. If I am using a commercial yarn for the core, I run it through my wheel in the opposite direction that I will be spinning my core spun. This helps avoid the overtwisting problem that most new core spinners have.

When you first try core spinning, slow way down, because you're dealing with more variables than when you're just drafting a regular yarn. Attach your core to your leader, and spin the core and the fiber that will wrap the core as a singles yarn together for a few inches before you start core spinning. Let the core rest lightly in the palm of your front hand; there is no need to manipulate the core yarn. Hold the fiber that will wrap the core in your fiber hand, and start the wheel spinning to the right (Z twist), letting the fiber wrap around the core at a 90-degree angle. Draft the fiber out by opening and closing the thumb and index finger of your front hand (like a lobster claw) to tension against. Draft on the wrapping fiber or yarn as thinly or thickly as you'd like, but make sure that it's secure and that it doesn't slide on the core.

MIXING IT UP WITHIN A BRAID

Many times when I sit down to spin, I spin a variegated braid just as it comes: I divide it to spin two singles and then ply it to a little overbalanced. That is my go-to yarn. But I love to have choices, especially when I have a project in mind and may not want lots of hard striping in it. I also want options when I'm trying to spin down my stash and come across colorways that need a little something or when I'm spinning a braid I don't really like any more. Sometimes the fiber just needs a bit of rearranging to look fresh again. My examples are all for a 2-ply yarn, but the idea can be used with 2, 3, 4, or more plies.

Example of yarn spun with flipped plies

DO A FLIP

An easy way to get different color combinations is to flip half of the fiber when spinning the singles. Split the fiber vertically to spin a 2-ply, and then spin one half as it comes, beginning to end. When it comes time to spin the other half, spin it from the opposite direction, starting at the other end. This just lines up the colors differently when they are plied, and it makes a nice change.

Here's a tip to keep track of which end to spin. Right after you split the fiber, place a loose overhand knot on the ends to spin from. This helps keep you from getting confused and spending extra nonspinning time trying to figure which end to start with for the second ply. (Ask me how I know.)

FRACTAL FUN

There has been a lot written about fractal spinning. The ultimate (and original) article is by Janel Laidman in the Summer 2007 issue of *Spin•off* magazine. I have a simple way of describing it that uses no math or science: it's all about combining long and short. When I discussed predrafting (see page 60), I pointed out that the

Spin from opposite ends of each strip of fiber to get the flip effect.

more a fiber is stripped vertically, the shorter the individual colors in a color run become. Fractal spinning takes advantage of that idea. For a 2-ply fractal, split your fiber once and spin one half of it so that you get long color runs. Split the remaining half again into halves, quarters, or even eighths, so that when you spin, you get shorter color runs. When the two singles are plied together, the short colors dart in and out of the long colors. Sometimes a whole colorway repeats on the short-run singles before the solid color changes on the long-run singles. The result is gorgeous, and it is mesmerizing to watch them ply together. When I divide my fiber for fractal spinning I take at least two steps between the sizes. I also keep in mind what size yarn I'm spinning, and I don't strip to a size that I can't draft. For example, I might ply the singles spun from half the length of the braid with singles spun from an eighth of the original braid.

What I notice about yarn spun fractally is that there are always more stretches of colors that match up than I expect. When the yarn is knit, there is still striping, but the stripes are softer and more undulating than the harder striping of a matched ply or even a random as-it-comes ply. Fractal is wonderful for bigger projects when minimal striping is desired.

PURE PROGRESSION

Yarns spun to create a progression are gorgeous to knit with, especially for lace. If you have a variegated braid and love the colors but don't

The yarn at the top is a 2-ply, fractal spun (a); the top swatch (c) was knit with this yarn. The bottom yarn (b) is a 2-ply, spun and plied as it comes, not trying to match colors; the bottom swatch (d) was knit with this yarn.

want the look of a variegated yarn, make it into a progression. Break the fiber apart by color. I am very aggressive about keeping my colors clear when I do this, picking out all secondary colors from each break. (In this context, "secondary colors" are those that occur where two dyes overlap to create a new color. They may not be true secondary color-wheel colors.) Then pile colors, like with like. Spin the colors one at a time in an order of your choice. You've given an old colorway new life!

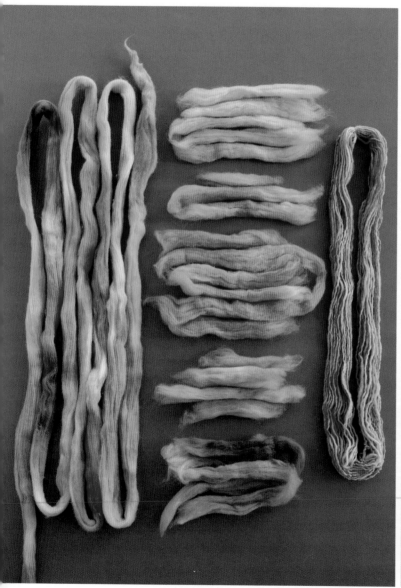

To spin a progression, break the fiber apart by color, then spin all of each color for a long, gradual shift in the colorway.

This lace swatch was knit with yarn that was spun progressively from top that was originally dyed in a variegated pattern.

CHUNK REMOVAL

Sometimes I find I have an issue with a particular color in a colorway. Maybe I used to love it but now I don't. Or I liked all of the other colors in the colorway so much that I was sure I'd come around to that particular shade of pastel yellow. My technique for solving this dilemma is quick, easy, and oh so satisfying: break apart the top or roving, and get rid of the color you dislike! It's up to you whether to remove just most of it or all traces of the offending color. You'll never miss it.

CREATE CONFETTI

I love this technique for no-longer-loved color-ways. I usually split the braid into fourths and then shred it into pieces between 2 and 4 inches long, not worrying if the breaks happen between or within a couple of colors. I toss all of the pieces into a bag or basket and then spin, pulling fiber randomly from the bag. I ply it on itself and almost always am delighted with the crazy confetti yarn I've made.

COMBINING AND DRAFTING TOGETHER

This is my 100 percent favorite thing to do with variegated fibers. It makes me feel like a mad color scientist, and it lets me stretch my stash to make something beyond scarves and socks. This technique is the one spinners in my classes are, at first, the most reluctant to try, but then they never want to leave the classroom, because they want to keep trying new combinations.

No color wheels will be used in the combining of colors for this portion, but why not? Because fiber dyers are color geniuses, and they really do all of the work for us, if we follow their lead. The quick-and-easy way to combine colors in a variegated roving is to get close to matching one color between two braids. That's it. It works out to be gorgeous a frighteningly high percentage of the time.

If you want to use fiber braids for a large project, such as a sweater, you can use variegated tops in succession without combining them in any

A basketful of chunks ready to spin into confetti yarn

These 2-ply yarns were made using a variegated top and a natural white top. The top swatch (a) was knit with the yarn on the left (b), spun by drafting the variegated and white at the same time, then plying together. The bottom swatch (c) was knit with the yarn on the right (d), a singles of white and a singles of variegated plied together.

way when you spin, but just letting them follow one after the other in your knitting. For instance, you might start with a yarn made from fiber that is grass green, light blue, and fuchsia, and then next knit with a yarn spun from light blue, lemon, and orange, and after that orange, purple, and red. This method works great for sweaters knit in the round, especially if you save some yarn for matching the sleeves. If you like to knit your sweaters in pieces and then assemble them, you will have to separate your yarns to get fronts, backs, and sleeves to match, or simply embrace the beauty of a patchwork look.

If you'd like your succession of braids to blend a little more, you can ply them together in a pattern. For instance, for a 2-ply, ply together two singles of the first colorway, one singles each of the first and second colorways, two singles of the second colorway, one singles each of the second and third colorways and two singles of the third colorway. I divide the fiber evenly before I spin and make sure to label it or tuck it into labeled plastic bags. Make sure to label your yarn as soon as it's on your niddy noddy, too. (No, you won't remember which is which after you're done!) If you want to get more color complexity with successions, add more braids and create more plies.

Variegated fibers can be mixed and blended with natural, solid, or semisolid fibers, which create a color veil, or cast, on the variegated colors. If you'd like your knitted fabric to have more contrast, ply the colors together, and if you'd like your fabric to look more washed by a color, blend the two together in the draft before you ply them together.

Blending Two Different Colors or Colorways while Drafting

Blending fiber while drafting takes a little bit of practice before you can watch TV while doing it, but I've got a few tips to make it go smoother from the start.

- **USE SMALLER STRIPS OF FIBER THAN YOU THINK YOU SHOULD.** I never use a strip wider than my finger, because I don't want to fight with the fiber. If I am drafting a natural, semisolid, or solid color with a variegated fiber, I strip that color to less than a finger's width. A single color is so strong visually that it can take over a variegated pretty quickly.

- **ATTENUATE SIMULTANEOUSLY.** Holding the two strips of fiber side by side and just barely touching, attenuate the length of the fiber. This helps loosen the fibers for easier drafting, especially if you are using two different fibers or blends and just getting the fibers to shake hands with each other.

- **DON'T WORRY IF YOU DROP ONE.** Don't bother to stop and undo and try to fix your singles if you drop one of the colors while drafting. Simply reattach it when you notice you've dropped it. So much is going on visually in blending while drafting that a stretch of single color isn't going to be noticed in the final yarn.

- **SIDE BY SIDE OR STACKED,** it's up to you. You can hold your fibers side by side or stack them on top of each other; both ways will blend the colors. I like to draft with the colors side by side so I can watch them combine, but however is easiest for you to draft is how you should do it.

- **MORE THAN TWO.** Yes! It's absolutely feasible to use more than two colors or colorways while drafting. I have a spinning friend who likes to use between three and five different colorways at a time. In this case, use narrower strips of fiber; the total size of fiber to draft should be about the width of two fingers.

Blending two different-colored fibers holding them side by side

Blending with fibers stacked

The two skeins of singles at the top were spun separately and then plied together to create the third skein.

The same colorways were blended together before spinning the two skeins of singles at the top and then plied together to create the third skein.

BFL 2-ply

Merino/Tencel 2-ply

Merino/Tencel and BFL drafted together, then plied

Merino/Tencel and BFL spun as separate plies, then plied together

COMBINING VARIEGATED COLORS

Working with variegated colorways is never-ending fun. I always get the same questions: which is easier, draft or ply, and how do the results differ? For me, both methods are equally easy, but they do give different, though similar, results in the finished yarn and fabric. They are different because there are different-size spots of color at play and multiple levels of combining; they are similar because the colors are the same.

When two colorways are spun as singles and plied together, they create a single marl. The colorways are mixed once, and the spots of color of each are bigger (relative to the size of the yarn you are spinning). When you draft two colorways

together before plying, the colorways are mixed together twice, once in the singles while drafting and then again when you ply. The two colorways marl together in the single and then again in the ply. The spots of color in this method are smaller, creating color speckles rather than dots, with more visual color blending. You can see in the finished yarns on the facing page that the overall look is different.

When these mixed and blended yarns are knit, the look is strikingly different. In the plied sample, the striping is more pronounced, with visible edges; and depending on the contrast between the colorways, the marl or barber pole is more apparent. With the swatch knit with drafted-then-plied yarn, the striping is diminished, and sometimes there are no edges to be seen. The overall colors are softened into speckle-y loveliness. The photos at the left and on page 109 show more swatches knit with plied-and-drafted yarns, compared to swatches knit with just plied yarns. The set on page 109 has a bonus: it was spun with a combination of different fiber blends, too.

Color blending isn't limited to 2-plies! These samples are all 3-ply yarns made with three different colorways. The top samples (a) are each colorway spun as a single and plied together and the bottom samples (b) are all three colorways drafted together and then plied together. Adding more plies and colorways creates intricate and rich combinations of colors.

WORKING WITH BATTS

One of the most beloved types of batt is the striped version. Whether large or small, the colors and textures can be intoxicating when you first buy it, but after a bit, it sometimes may not be your favorite anymore. Don't despair; there are ways to manipulate the colors within striped batts, too.

Most spinners strip their batts vertically, but the length of each color in the spun yarn is dependent on the width of your strip. You can strip each color individually and spin them in order for a gradated yarn, or you can strip each color multiple times and spin them in a repeating order of the original colors and make a variegated yarn. You can also try one of the techniques on the next four pages, including stacking, creating a fauxlag, chunking, or combining batts.

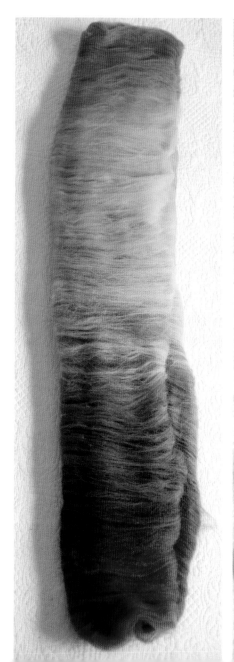

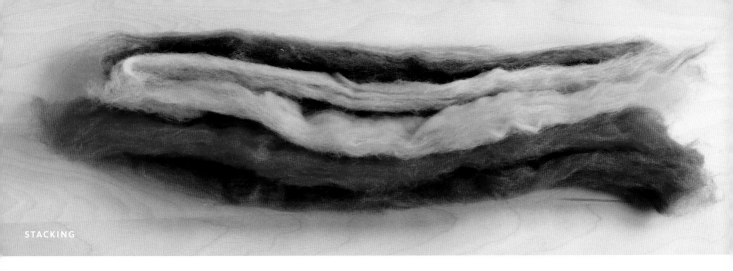

Stacking. Stacking is a great way to make a tweedy yarn from a batt. Strip the batt vertically, then stack the colors on top of each other, making lovely fiber layers. Attenuate your layers into roving and spin. Plied on itself, this method makes the stripes into speckles.

Batt with colors stripped one by one and spun in order for gradated yarn

Colors stripped
multiple times and
spun in repeating
order for a
variegated yarn

a

b

c

down my ruler on my color arrangement (a), then roll the fiber and ruler together two or three rotations (b), tearing away the rest of the batt as I go. I then tear the fauxlag free of the batt and spin it (c). (All of these samples are from the same batt.)

Chunking. To create a truly random yarn from a batt, use chunking. Strip your batt multiple times, and then tear each strip into pieces 2 or 3 inches long. Throw all of the pieces into a basket or bag and mix them up. Then pull from your fiber salad randomly to spin.

Combining. You can always combine batts, too, just as I described working with variegated braids (page 105): strip, stack, ply, or blend, keeping a color or two in common.

Fauxlags. Creating fauxlags from the batts results in smaller bursts of color and a loftier yarn. You decide whether to make them a single color or to include more than one color. I use a ruler or a dowel to create my fauxlags from batts. I lay

These examples of yarns and swatches illustrate the results of stacking (top), creating a fauxlag (middle) and combining fibers to make a gradient (bottom). The middle swatch has no red because of the length of the color repeats; similarly, *only* red came up to be used in the bottom swatch

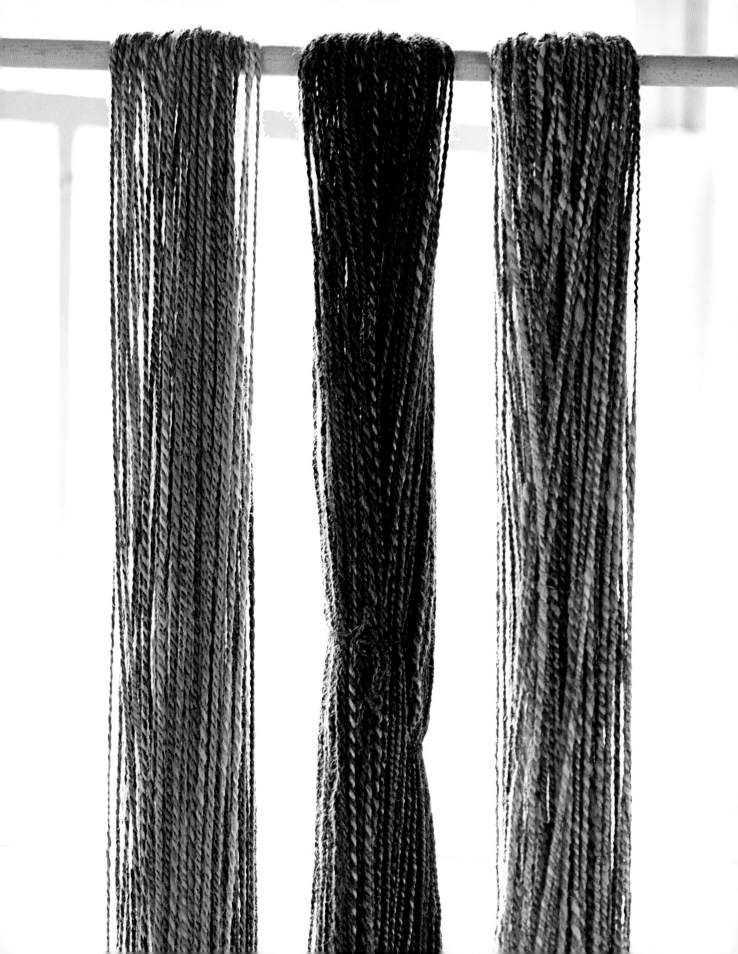

7 | the front door:
FINISHING

FINISHING IS ONE OF THE LAST THINGS done to yarn before knitting with it, but it's one of the first things people notice. Each method of finishing has a distinct effect on the look, and sometimes the feel, of the finished yarn as well as the knitted fabric. I have seven different ways of finishing my yarn, and, yes, I *always* finish my yarn. Why? Finishing helps the ply twist even out throughout the skein. I also think that the application of steam or hot water helps the yarn relax into itself, resulting in a yarn that's easier to knit. With each method of finishing, I hang my skeins to dry. Sometimes, if the weather cooperates, I hang them outside; other times, if I'm in a hurry, I hang them inside with a fan blowing on them.

STEAMING

I steam yarn in several ways. If I'm working with small samples, I use my electric kettle or a wide soup pot of boiling water. I hold the skein in the steam with a pair of plastic tongs, rather than use a steamer basket sitting inside the soup pot. (I find that using a steamer basket gets my yarn almost as wet as when I wet-finish it.) I use tongs to hold the yarn in the steam for about 20 seconds, remove it from the steam, rotate the yarn's placement in the tongs, and steam it again. I repeat this until I have completely rotated through the skein. For really big skeins or a large number of them, I use a garment steamer, following the same procedure as described for the kettle or pot of water. Or I sometimes steam the skeins flat on the floor by spreading them on towels and then slowly running the steaming nozzle over the circumference of each skein. I flip the skeins over and repeat.

Pro: This method is quick because there's almost no drying time.

Con: I don't think the fiber and twist move as much with steam as they do when submerged in soapy, hot water.

Good for: Tender yarns, art yarns with many things added in that might come off when soaked in hot water; any yarn that you feel needs only a light finish.

SOAKING

I soak yarn in warm to hot water and a no-rinse wool soap, such as Soak or Eucalan, for 10 to 15 minutes. Next, I remove the yarn from the water, lightly squeeze it, roll it into a towel, and compress the towel to get more water out. I then hang the yarn to dry.

Pro: Easy; the hot water relaxes the yarn and redistributes twist somewhat.

Con: Drying time; finding a place to hang the yarn, especially in a cold climate in the winter; doesn't redistribute ply twist much.

Good for: Low-twist yarns.

SNAPPING

Soak the yarn in hot water with wool wash, and roll it in a towel. Before hanging it up, snap it. To do this, put your hands inside the skein, like you're going to play cat's cradle, then move your hands apart quickly, and snap the yarn — not hard enough to break it, but hard enough to get some water sprayed in your face. Do this about four times, sliding the skein around your hands so that different areas of the yarn lie across the backs of your hands for each snap. I love how that little motion evens out the twist. This is the way I finish yarn most of the time.

Pro: Excellent redistribution of twist.

Con: Can break fine, low-twist yarns.

Good for: Almost all fibers.

CENTRIPETAL FORCE (LASSO)

This is a method I learned from my students. I follow all of the steps I do for soaking, but before hanging the skein to dry, I take it outside and twirl it above my head like a cowgirl with a lasso. It works! Do this three or four times, moving your hand to a different spot on the skein before

To give yarn a thorough soaking, immerse it in warm to hot water with a no-rinse wool soap for 10 to 15 minutes.

each swing. The centripetal force of the swinging forces the extra water out. Combining swinging with a berserk war whoop or a "yee-haw" makes this method entirely entertaining.

Pro: Scares the neighbors; really gets the extra water out; cuts down on drying time; fun.

Con: Scares the neighbors; needs nice weather.

Good for: Medium to strong or fine fibers spun and plied for durability.

WHACKING

Then there's whacking — a favorite of mine when I'm irritated at someone. I soak and roll as for the first methods, but before I hang the skein to dry, I beat the snot out of it. I literally hold one end of the skein and whack it against the floor, counter, deck, or table. I then move my hand to a new spot on the skein and do it again. This method abrades the surface of the yarn slightly. If a fiber or fiber blend is inclined to be fuzzy or puff, whacking will get it there fast. If you want a smooth-surfaced yarn, don't whack.

Pro: Redistributes the twist a lot; fun.

Con: Abrades the surface of the yarn slightly; depending on the fiber content, can make yarns fuzzy or even start to pill.

Good for: Unevenly plied yarns; yarns that want to be fuzzy.

FULLING

Fulling is the process of giving your yarn a slight felting, just a mere drawing in of fibers. For this, I use a bowl of water as hot as I can stand to put my hands in and a bowl of ice water; I add a drop or two of wool wash to the hot water. I soak the skein in the hot water, remove it from the water, barely squeeze it in my hands, and then soak it in the cold water, again barely squeezing it over

the cold water. I move the skein back and forth between hot and cold, letting the yarn soak up the water for a minute or two in each bowl, not agitating, just squeezing most of the water out between bowls. This fulls the yarn, giving it a light felting. It firms up the yarn and pulls the fibers together a little. It also evens out the twist and stabilizes the yarn. This is my favorite finishing for singles.

Pro: Stabilizes singles yarn; redistributes twist.

Con: Works for anything you want to be more durable and fluffier, but not anything labeled superwash.

Good for: Singles destined to be knit as is.

MENACING

My last finishing technique is the full-on menace: felting your skein. I learned an easy way to do this without burning your hands in spinning superstar Judith MacKenzie's class: use a sink plunger. I add a drop or two of wool wash to a bowl of really hot water from my teakettle and place it next to a bowl of ice water. I move the skein back and forth from hot to cold, but not gently. I menace that skein with a small sink plunger, like a sink backed up after a hair-dyeing slumber party. I've never taken it to hard, stiff felt, but I've gone to firm. The whole look and feel of the yarn changes, and it resists pilling. Judith recommends this method for downy undercoats, such as cashmere: they don't felt, and it makes them gorgeous and puffy.

Pro: Increases the durability of a yarn.

Con: Only works for wool and wool blends; can't undo; shortens yardage.

Good for: Downy undercoat fibers, such as cashmere, that don't felt; wool and wool blends.

Of Course, the Fiber Matters!

I've learned that for any question about spinning, particularly spinning to knit, the answer is always "Well, it depends." But everything depends on the fiber used, as well as the draft, the ply, and the finishing. Here are the seven finishing methods described in this chapter, on four different fibers. All seven are applied to top that has been drafted woolen, then spun into 2-ply to balance.

The Yarns

In each of these photos, the yarns are arranged in the following order, from left to right: Merino, Corriedale, Bluefaced Leicester, tussah silk.

UNFINISHED

STEAMED

SOAKED

SNAPPED

CENTRIPETAL FORCE

WHACKED

FULLED

MENACED

The Knitted Fabrics

Sometimes the differences between finishes don't show until a yarn is knitted. The knitted swatches are arranged in the following order, left to right: Merino, Corriedale, Blueface Leicester, and tussah silk.

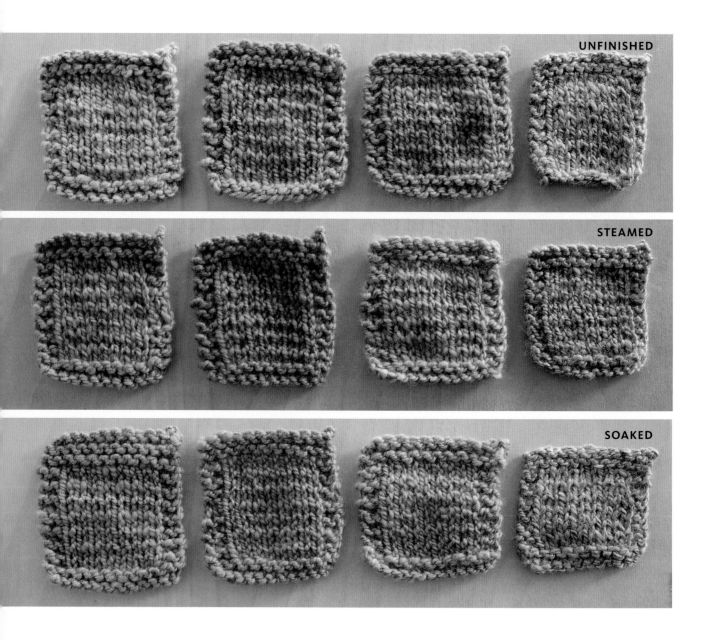

UNFINISHED

STEAMED

SOAKED

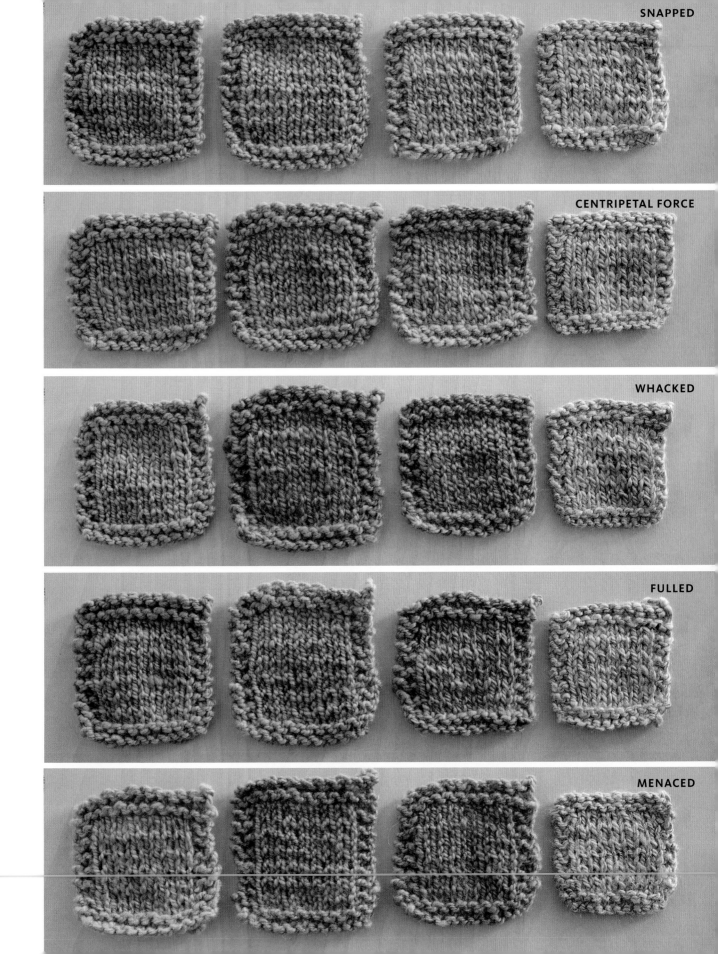

SNAPPED

CENTRIPETAL FORCE

WHACKED

FULLED

MENACED

Why Not Weight?

Some spinners set their yarn under tension by letting it dry with weight attached to it to take out the overtwist. There's a reason it's not a great idea to do this. I use my yarn mostly to knit, and when I weight or tension-set an overtwisted yarn and then knit with it, most of that overtwist comes back when I put the finished item in water to block it. Setting a yarn under tension is done by many spinners for effect, as well as for different fiber crafts than knitting, but when you're going to knit with it, it's only a temporary fix. Weighting a yarn takes all of the natural elasticity out of it, and weighted yarns therefore always seem a little limp (see the example on the facing page). You swatch and knit with it, and it looks lovely. You block your knitting — and *sproing*! The extra twist comes back. Even a fiercely pinned blocking can't get it all the way back to its stretched and tensioned state. Sometimes your knitting looks okay, but sometimes it's not quite right.

There are things to be done with overtwisted yarn that don't involve tension or weighting. The easiest one is to run it back through your wheel to take some of the twist out. Using the twist on purpose to give a piece visual motion in knitting is beautiful, as you can see if you check out master spinner Kathryn Alexander's work.

These swatches were both knit with the tension-set yarn above. The swatch on the left has not been blocked; at the right, compare what happened when the swatch was rewet.

KNITTING WITH YOUR HANDSPUN

THIS IS IT! This is why many of us spin. I know it's why I started spinning: I wanted to make yarn to knit, something I couldn't find in a store — a different fiber, a different color, something a little livelier feeling, a yarn as unique as my knitting. As I learned more about spinning and how to construct a yarn, I learned that draft and twist have so much to do with the yarns I like to knit, and that I could customize those aspects and many more when I spun my own yarn. I learned that it's all a process: every bit I learn about spinning allows me to make the yarn I want to knit.

With any yarn I look at now, I can see every step that went into it: the fiber, prep, draft, twist, ply, finish. I now can read yarn. I can put that knowledge to use while I'm spinning a yarn or when I'm evaluating a finished yarn to knit with.

It took me a long time of spinning and knitting (and respinning and reknitting) to figure out just how interrelated the processes are and how to make a yarn to use, instead of a mill-spun yarn, in a commercial pattern, or how to find a great pattern for my already-spun yarn.

The keys to all things related to spinning and knitting are these: sample, swatch, measure, and keep track. I can hear the moaning out there. But I will say I am not inclined to be overly technical or detail oriented. If I learned to sample, swatch, and keep track, it is in the bare minimum way. I do not make busy, fiddly, detaily work for fun.

A WORD ON MILL-SPUN YARNS

The main difference between mill-spun and handspun yarns lies in the two words *mill* and *hand*: one is made by machine and one by a person. One is made in large quantities (usually) to broad specifications; the other is made a skein at a time with a specific intention in mind.

Machines that make yarn put a lot of pressure on it. It's constantly under tension to get it to flow through the process, and that can leave the yarn looking and feeling a little exhausted. Mill-spun yarns tend to be less elastic, a little limp and lifeless. (Note that I'm speaking generally; there are some small-batch mill-spun yarns that make spinners sing.) Handspun yarns can be whatever you want them to be, for whatever you're making. They are usually bouncier and livelier than their mill-spun sisters.

When I knit, the difference between a handspun and a mill-spun yarn is huge for me. Even if the handspun yarn was not purpose-spun for a project, I find that I can knit handspun yarn at multiple gauges and it still works better than mill-spun yarn. I find that my gauge varies between a mill-spun and a handspun yarn, even if two yarns have the same wraps per inch (wpi; see page 130). Handspun yarns are rarely consistent throughout, so they vary in gauge within the same yarn.

Color and handspun yarn is another big win for me and my knitting. With some mill-spun yarns, especially variegated ones, the dye is applied after the yarn is spun. Some handspinners do this also, but most either dye their own fiber before spinning or buy their fiber already dyed. For solids and semisolids, the color has more depth and interesting characteristics if the unspun fiber has been dyed, rather than dyeing the yarn after it's spun. With variegated yarns, the depth of color is there, and you can also manipulate and blend colors when spinning (see chapter 6). Variegated mill-spun yarns are gorgeous, but a knitter is locked into a color flow, unless you alternate skeins.

COMBINING HANDSPUN AND MILL-SPUN YARNS

This is a great way to highlight your handspun! Make sure the yarns are in the same ballpark for wpi and gauge, and always swatch both yarns separately until you get gauges that work together.

In the sweater "Party Mix," designed by Julia Farwell-Clay for *Knittyspin*, the front and back of the sweater are knit with handspun; the sleeves and side panels are knit with Cascade 220.

You may not use the same size needle for both yarns. If knitting colorwork with a mill-spun and a handspun together, swatch them together in pattern. If using the two yarns in the same part of a project (a sweater front, for example), swatch big — at least 8 inches — and make sure to block it. (Of course, the same goes for any project where accurate gauge is paramount. You don't want any surprises when fit is an issue.)

Handspun takes plain mill-spun to another dimension, even when using it for edges and bits. Imagine a plain scarf edged with a highly textured handspun yarn or a super-big and lofty handspun. Or how about a sweater with a body knit with mill-spun yarn, but with handspun pockets or collar? One technique that I've not had much luck with is combining a variegated mill-spun yarn with a variegated handspun yarn. I always want my handspun to stand out as the focal point in a mill-spun pairing.

If you're using a mill-spun and handspun pairing for colorwork, the yarns should be as close as you can get them in gauge, grist, and hand, unless you're going for a particular effect. This is even more true when you're knitting a Fair Isle project than when you're working intarsia. The more the yarns snuggle next to each other, the closer in look and behavior you want them to be.

You don't have to match every characteristic of the mill-spun yarn. For instance, if I'm using a mill-spun wool yarn that is worsted spun and worsted in size, with six thin, loose plies, I might combine it with a handspun 2-ply, worsted- or woolen-drafted yarn made from top, with the same knitted gauge. A secret: In order to get the same gauge and hand, I frequently don't use the same-size needles for the mill-spun that I use for the handspun yarn.

HOW MUCH FIBER DO I NEED?

This is the number one question for all spinners: How much fiber do I need to make something? My flippant answer is "More"; the more useful answers are "What are you spinning for?" and "How important is it to get the exact yarn or fiber for the project?" For instance, if you are making a summer top with a drapey neckline, you need a yarn that will drape, not one that is stiff and made to show off cabling. Or if you're spinning and knitting for someone with a wool allergy, you wouldn't use even a small percentage of wool. The less wiggle room that you have in your yarn, the more fiber you need for sampling and for compensating if something goes not exactly to plan.

If something needs to be exact and I know I will do a lot of sampling to get it right, I buy an extra 2 ounces when I'm planning to use a middle weight like DK or worsted (not a chunky yarn, for instance). I then add another ounce or two for each element that might require extra testing, such as a variegated yarn, which requires color manipulation, or a heavily patterned project, as well as for a yarn that's not my default. It's always better to have too much rather than too little, as often you won't be able to find the same fiber again. If you end with the yarn you want and extra fiber, do a dance, and trade your fiber with a friend or hoard it for a rainy day.

If you know a project's yardage, the size of the yarn it calls for, and that yarn's wpi, it's easy to estimate. For example, say I want to make a woman's size-large sweater in a worsted-weight wool yarn. I consult a general pattern and see that a woman's large sweater uses 800 yards of worsted-weight yarn. I know that worsted-weight yarn has a ypp (yards per pound) of 900 to 1,200, so I know I would be safe buying a pound of fiber, plus more for sampling.

The table below lists the general commercial yarn size names and knitted gauges provided by the Craft Yarn Council, along with the wraps per inch and yards per pound of each yarn. The wpi and ypp numbers are compiled from various sources, as well as my own personal spinning. It is important to note that these numbers are most likely based on a middle-of-the-road fiber like Corriedale, so if you use a heavier wool fiber like Wensleydale or a lighter one like Merino or a wool blend, you must tinker with your numbers.

MEASURING HANDSPUN YARN

Feeling comfortable and confident about measuring your handspun is key to being happy while knitting with it. At first it feels like a lot of work and a lot of steps, but the more you do it, the easier and faster it gets. Plus, you'll learn where to cut corners and where your handspun is most variable. My handspun is most consistent in ply twist, but I have issues with consistent density and wpi in my singles, especially when I am spinning for a big project or if I'm rushing. In this section, I explain the basic measurements for handspun yarn, why the measurement matters to your knitted results, and how to do it. If you're already a knitter when you begin to learn to spin, you have a lot of knowledge about yarn already, but handspun yarn may surprise you in a few different ways.

WRAPS PER INCH (WPI)

Wraps per inch, or wpi, is so ubiquitous in spinning that I consider it the while-you-are-spinning equivalent of knitted gauge, not because they measure exactly the same thing, but because they are the most basic measurement. Wpi measures the width of the yarn, and it can be just as susceptible to lying as gauge (see sidebar on page 132).

Wpi and knitting. Wpi is important when you're spinning for a knitting project because it's the one measurement that will help you make a consistent yarn.

YARN NAME	KNITTING GAUGE (STITCHES PER 4")	WPI	YPP
Lace	33–40	>25	na
Fingering	27–32	20–25	1,800–2,400
Sport	23–26	17–20	1,300–1,800
DK	21–24	13–16	1,000–1,400
Worsted	16–20	9–12	900–1,200
Bulky	12–15	6–8	500–800

From the Craft Yarn Council Standard Yarn Weight System; wpi and ypp are compiled from various sources and personal spinning.

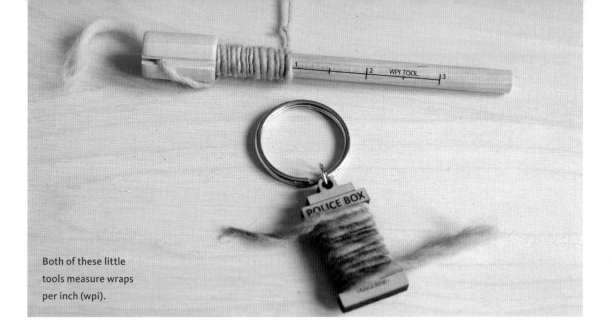

Both of these little tools measure wraps per inch (wpi).

How to measure wpi. The three ways I measure the width of a yarn are with a wpi tool, with a spinner's control card, and with a sample yarn. The first two of these measurements can vary a lot depending on how firmly I pull on the yarn while I'm measuring.

- **Wpi gauges.** I have a love/hate relationship with wpi gauges. I love them in their gorgeous variety, but I am terrible at consistently wrapping as I'm working on a project.

- **Spinner's control card.** I use my spinner's control card more often, especially while I'm spinning for consistency in my singles. I lay my yarn behind the card and visually gauge its width in the space between the black lines. I find it quicker than wrapping, and I can find a reasonable, repeatable tension. I usually measure the yarn just pulled straight from when it starts to ply back. Still, I can become excited or rushed and get varied results.

- **Sample yarn.** I always keep an index card with yarn samples of my project. On it I have an unfinished single, an unfinished plied yarn, and a finished plied yarn. I find I have less tendency to tug when wrapping singles on a control card. The quickest way to make sure that I am on track when I'm spinning is to measure my singles next to the singles sample on my index card. I hold them side by side and check them visually against one another.

If you need to adjust your wpi, do the following:

- **For a lower wpi,** you need a thicker yarn, so draft more fiber and twist less.

- **For a higher wpi,** you need a thinner yarn, so draft less fiber and twist more.

A spinner's control card provides printed gauge bands to compare your yarn against.

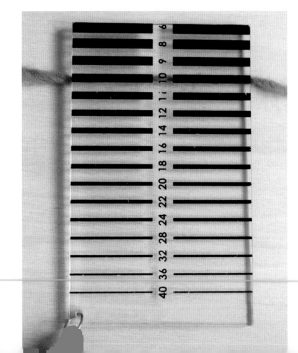

wpi: A Cautionary Tale

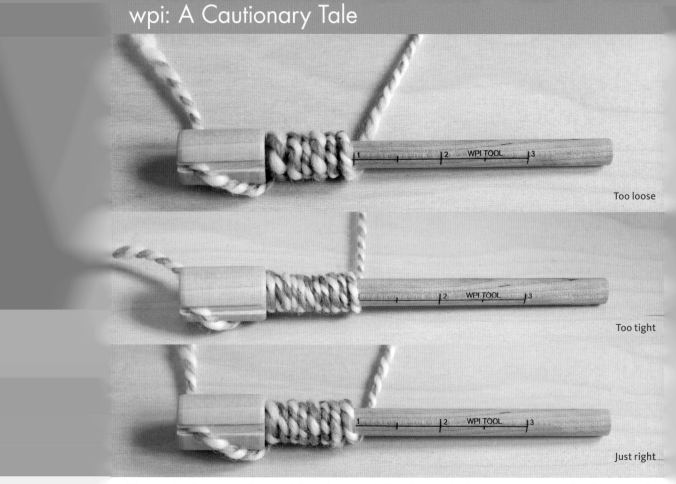

These photos demonstrate how easy it is to change a wpi. Note that exactly the same yarn was used for all three samples.

My wpi, like my knitting gauge, lies constantly. I use wpi as a guide to keep my yarn consistent when I'm spinning and to match a yarn I used in specific knitting projects. The problem is I can get my yarn to read at almost any wpi I want it to. It's the same as when I knit a gauge swatch: my hands can knit the perfect gauge with a particular yarn, but once the project starts and I relax into it, my true gauge appears, and it's often different.

It's easy to influence wpi, since it's based on tension. I think of measuring my wpi using a wpi gauge more like placing the yarn on the wpi gauge rather than wrapping it around it.

Pulling tightly gives a finer wpi; winding with no tension yields a bigger wpi. To find a happy medium, try rolling (turning the wpi gauge to feed on the yarn) instead of wrapping, and make sure the threads touch but aren't crowded.

The lesson I learn from these examples is that I need to measure several times and evaluate the results as a range of wpi. Also, I need to try not to make the yarn fit the measurement I'm looking for. I have to remind myself to let the yarn speak, or it won't work. As in all things spinning, I find that I can encourage the yarn, but if I try to bully it, it always gets the last laugh.

GAUGE

My biggest surprise was, and continues to be, knitting gauge when I'm working with handspun yarn. The gorgeous inconsistencies in handspun make the gauge a touch fluid. Be sure to check it and recheck it several times while you're knitting.

Gauge and knitting. Because it's spun by hand and not machine, it might like a bigger needle than you think. I've had the experience of holding a commercial yarn against a handspun yarn and thinking that they look and mostly feel the same. When I start to knit the yarns using the same size needle for both, however, I often find it squeezes the life out of the handspun yarn. Swatch often, and swatch big. Getting and maintaining gauge is all about the fit. If your gauge isn't right, whatever you knit won't come out the size you are expecting. I often recheck my gauge after I've been knitting on a project for a bit, because as I relax, my gauge changes.

How to measure gauge. If you can stand it, try for a 6- to 8-inch swatch rather than the standard 4 inches. If you are planning to knit a garment where fit is important, knit the bigger swatch even if you *can't* stand it. Using a ruler or a knitting gauge, measure at least four different places on the swatch and take an average of the results. Don't press down while you are measuring, especially if you are using lofty yarn, as this stretches the stitches and changes the gauge.

TWIST ANGLE

Without twist there would be no yarn. Yarn is just fiber and twist. I measure twist to keep the hand of my yarn (or the feel — for example, is it firm or supple?) consistent. The longer I spin on a project, the greater my tendency to put in more twist. The result is that a potentially lovely, soft, drapey yarn ends up hard and wiry. The higher the angle of twist in your yarn, the tighter the twist. Of course, all of the other aspects of the yarn you are spinning affect the twist angle, too. A thin yarn with less fiber needs more twist to hold together; a fat yarn with more fiber needs

Measure gauge on a knitted swatch that's large enough to give you a generous section in the center to count your stitches.

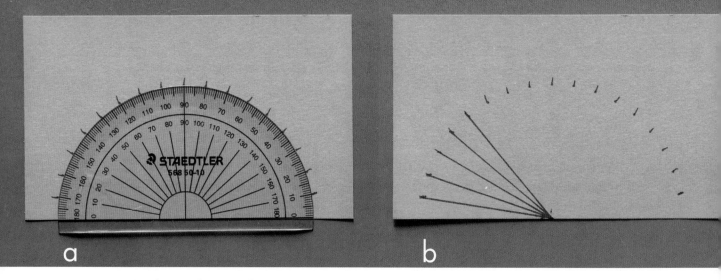

Creating a homemade twist-angle gauge

less twist to hold together. Lower-twist yarns are loftier yarns because there's room in the fiber for air. Higher-twist yarns are denser because the air is pushed out by the twist. If you find a twist angle you love for a particular yarn, it is unlikely to be the perfect twist angle for a different fiber or a different project.

Twist and knitting. Twist informs how your yarn will behave and how it will last. Twist contributes to the durability of a yarn and to the hand of a yarn. If you want to make sock yarn, you need a tighter twist than if you are making a lace shawl.

How to measure twist. You can purchase a twist-angle gauge or make one. Sometimes it's nice to create a twist-angle gauge especially for a project, marked with only the twist angles you're using for that particular project. To make one, you need a 3 × 5-inch index card and a protractor. Line up the long edge (the base) of the protractor with the long edge of the index card. Mark the card in 10-degree increments out from the center top in both directions (a). (Going in both directions allows you to measure both S and Z twists.) Then draw lines to connect these marks

to the point at the center bottom (b). Number the lines starting with 0° at the center top, increasing by 10s to 90° at the base on both left and right as shown in the drawing below (c).

To measure twist angle, lay your yarn across the card and match the twist to the closest twist-angle line. The things that I need to help me see my twist angles are strong light and a magnifying glass; a double-pointed needle or a tapestry needle help me follow the twist in the yarn.

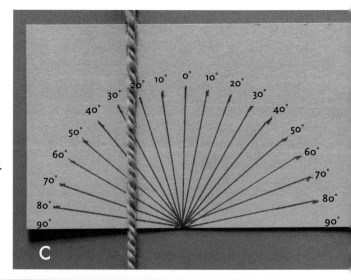

This yarn has a twist angle of 30°–40°.

TWISTS PER INCH (TPI)

I frequently measure my twists per inch (tpi) while I'm plying. It's a quick check to make sure I'm keeping my ply twist consistent.

Knitting and tpi. Perfect ply for a project is a wonderful thing; perfect consistent ply for a project is like winning the lottery.

How to measure tpi. All I use to check tpi is a ruler and a magnifying glass. (I need the magnifying glass only if I'm measuring singles or very fine yarn.) I lay the plied yarn next to a ruler and count ply bumps in an inch. I divide the number of bumps by the number of plies and get twists per inch. If I am measuring quickly on the fly while I'm plying, I measure just the ply bumps. Make sure to note whether you're measuring bumps per inch or twists per inch; they aren't interchangeable.

PLY-BACK

This is quickest way to check twist for consistency. This is the twist measure (or test) that no spinner can complain about doing. It takes less than a minute, and it barely disrupts your spinning.

Knitting and ply-back. This is the easiest way to check twist to ensure that you're spinning a consistent yarn, and a consistent yarn is a happy knitting yarn, with a gauge that doesn't change dramatically within a skein or a project.

The yarn has to be fresh, full of live energy for this technique to work. After you've been spinning for a bit, getting into a rhythm and making a yarn that visually pleases you, stop spinning and pull a length of singles from the bobbin. Fold it in half and let it twist (ply) onto itself. How does it look? It will approximate what it will look like as a balanced 2-ply yarn. You can untwist it a bit manually to see what it would look like if slightly

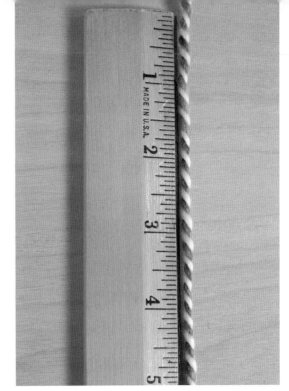

Measuring tpi, or bumps per inch, in your ply-back sample.

LEFT, 7 bumps per inch, or 3.5 tpi; RIGHT, 11 bumps per inch, or 5.5 tpi.

underplied, or give it more twist with your fingers to see what it would look like overplied. If this is the yarn you want, use it as your ply-back sample to periodically measure the rest of your yarn against as you spin. You can measure the bumps in an inch on your ply-back sample and record the number, or you can do a ply-back sample, knot it, and break it off. I usually keep the ply-back sample on my wheel somewhere, hanging from one of the knobs where it's easy to reach but where it won't be caught in the workings of the wheel or sucked into the orifice. If you choose the latter, make sure to write the bump count down somewhere; those little ply-back samples go missing easily.

LENGTH

How much yarn do you have? Is it enough? This is the fundamental measurement you need when you're going to be knitting with your yarn.

How to measure length. Use a niddy noddy or a swift to wind your yarn into a skein. For example, one wrapping path on my biggest niddy noddy is 2 yards. After I finish wrapping my yarn onto my niddy noddy, I count the individual threads and multiply by the 2-yard length, and I have the length of my skein. This way, you can pretty closely estimate the yardage when you're done. Be sure not to pull tightly or spin your swift too quickly; if there's any tugging at all, your yarn is being stretched. Keep in mind, also, that the way you choose to finish your yarn can change

A niddy noddy makes a convenient tool for measuring the length of your skein.

your yardage. If you aggressively finish (as you would with felting or menacing and fulling; see page 119), your yarn shrinks in the process, so remeasure the length after the yarn has been finished.

WEIGHT

I like to weigh my yarn as well as measure its length. I have an electronic scale that I use just for fiber, and it's one of the tools I use the most. If I have the length and weight of a skein of yarn, I can calculate the grist (the yarn density; for more information, see at right). I also use weight to make sure I'm splitting my fiber evenly, to evenly divide bobbins I'm rewinding, and to estimate how much yarn is left on a bobbin. As explained above, I can use weight to calculate the length of a skein, too.

Weight and knitting. When substituting a handspun yarn for a commercial yarn in a knitting project, weight is every bit as important as length. You don't want to make a 50-pound shawl!

How to weigh yarn. Buy a small kitchen scale, and hide it from everyone in your house. Make sure it can be set to both ounces and grams. Skein your yarn and weigh it, in either ounces or grams, whichever way you think best. Write the weight down on a tag or band fastened to the skein.

GRIST

When I need to be really exact in my spinning, especially when I'm trying to duplicate an already-spun yarn, I check its grist, or density, or, in other words, how much fiber is in a certain

How to Figure the Length of a Mystery Skein or a Partial Skein

Weigh it! To estimate how many yards your mystery skein contains, you can weigh it. First, weigh just a few yards, and then divide the yardage by its weight in ounces to find out how many yards there are in 1 ounce. I like to use 10 yards because it makes the math easy. For example, if 10 yards weighs 0.15 ounce,

divide 10 by 0.15 to get 66.6. Rounded up to 67, this is the length of my yarn per ounce. Next, I weigh the whole skein, which in this example weighs 3.5 ounces. I multiply the length per ounce (67) by the weight of the whole skein (3.5). My mystery skein is no mystery anymore: It has 234.5 yards.

Here's the formula:

(sample yardage) ÷ (sample yardage weight in ounces) = (length per ounce)

(length per ounce) × (total weight of skein) = (total length of skein)

These woolen-spun (top) and worsted-spun (bottom), DK-weight yarns may look similar, but the worsted-spun yarn is actually denser and heavier, with less yardage.

length of yarn. The grist of a yarn is expressed as a measurement of length to weight, usually how many yards are in a pound of yarn (ypp). The higher the yardage per pound, the thinner the yarn. Grist will surprise you. Sometimes I think two yarns are the same, the wpi and gauge are the same, but then my yarn runs out. What? If I had checked my grist, that wouldn't have happened. It's a little like how many miles per gallon your car gets. In this case, how far can you spin on a pound of yarn?

I've heard grist (and ypp) used interchangeably with wpi, but that just isn't right. I think that misconception comes from describing grist as the thickness of a yarn, whereas grist includes density or weight, not just the side-to-side yarn-width measurement.

Grist is an important measurement because it takes into account *both* width and weight. Notice the difference between two DK-weight yarns, one spun woolen and the other worsted. If I am trying to match a DK woolen-spun yarn with a yarn I drafted worsted with the same amount of fiber, my wpi could be exact, but even so, I would end up with shorter yardage and a denser, heavier yarn. Checking grist and making an adjustment, like spinning with a different, airier drafting style, would quickly fix that problem.

I find that knowing grist is good for specific things. Do I use it all the time? Nope. Plenty of times I just spin, but I use it more than I thought I would when I first figured out grist. Grist can be a powerful tool in the hands of a spinner. Making friends with grist helped me to become a more consistent spinner overall. It gives me deeper information about the yarn I've spun and more control over yarn that I will spin. It helped to answer questions I had about why the yarn in my hand didn't match the yarn I intended to spin.

Grist is key to matching yarns, using handspun for a pattern that was written for commercial yarns, replicating another handspun yarn, or making it easier for someone else to match a yarn that you've spun. Grist can also be used to solve one of the greatest yarn mysteries of all: the yardage of a mystery skein of yarn. (See sidebar, page 137 for more advice on this dilemma.) How many times have you found the perfect skein of yarn with no tags or labels? Of course, this is the yarn that must be used instantly, if only you could quickly figure out the length. If I am measuring grist to make sure my yarn is consistent while I spin, I check my singles at least once per bobbin.

Grist and knitting. Measuring grist can help you make yarn that is consistent from the start of a project to the end. It's easy to make a yarn that looks similar and even has the right wpi and knitted gauge, but if the grist isn't right, the project can go disastrously wrong. This area of spinning is where I've made my biggest mistakes when I'm spinning for a project and trying to match a commercial yarn. For example, when I'm spinning yarn for a sweater, I frequently start out drafting my usual worsted but end up with a weird, heavy worsted weight. It more or less looks the same, and the wpi is the same, but the yarn I'm spinning as I finish doesn't behave or drape like the yarn I spun when I was just starting out. What I found out by studying grist is that when I'm in a hurry, I add more twist because I'm treadling faster. When I check my wpi as I'm working, it measures the same as when I started, but because of the tighter twist I'm giving the yarn,

I'm adding more fiber into the same length of yarn. So the hurry-up yarn weighs more per yard and behaves differently in the end.

How to measure grist. There are two ways to measure grist: with a yarn balance and with a digital kitchen scale.

- **A digital kitchen scale** is one of my often-used fiber tools; it gives me a quick measure. Following the same procedure that you used to determine the length per ounce of your yarn (page 137), multiply the length of 1 ounce of your yarn by 16 ounces to get yards per pound. For example, if your yarn measures 50 yards per ounce, multiply by 16 and you'll find that your yarn has 800 yards per pound. As described for estimating the length of a skein, 10 yards is usually enough, but the more variation there is in your yarn, the bigger yarn sample you need. For instance, if you are figuring the grist of a thick-and-thin yarn, use 20 yards.

- **A yarn balance** is a little fiddly, but it's also accurate. Using a yarn balance (see photos on the next page) involves getting a length of finished yarn to balance over the arm of the scale, then measuring it and multiplying by 100. For example, if the length of the piece of yarn that balances the scale measures 8 inches, multiply by 100 to find that your yarn has 800 yards per pound. To do this, cut a length of yarn and lay it across the hook on the balance arm. The goal is to get the arm to balance, like the old-fashioned scales in your doctor's office. If the arm dips down, the length of yarn is too long. Snip small amounts of yarn from the ends until it balances. (Don't snip too much at a time, because if the balance arm tips up, you'll need to start again with a new, longer length of yarn.) Now measure the length of yarn that balanced with a ruler or tape measure. Lay the yarn and a ruler side by side on a table. Don't pull the yarn taut. I run my finger down the yarn lightly to smooth it against the ruler, but I never pull it tightly. Write down your yarn's measurement (no, you won't remember it), and multiply by 100. Voilà — yards per pound for your yarn.

If you'd like to use this information to find how much yardage you have in a particular skein of yarn, divide the ypp by 16 to find out the yardage in 1 ounce, weigh the skein in ounces, then multiply the yardage per ounce by the weight of your skein.

Once you have this measurement, you can calculate grist.

USING A YARN BALANCE

1. Lay a length of yarn over the balance arm of the scale.

2. Snip small pieces off the yarn ends until the arm balances.

3. Measure the length of yarn that balanced the arm and multiply by 100. This yarn has 325 yards in 1 pound.

The Gist of Grist

A lot of spinners don't measure grist and don't want to think about grist. Some don't even know what it is. Grist is the density of a yarn, how heavy a particular length of yarn is. It's measured in yards per pound (ypp). I find knowing the grist really useful for making consistent yarn.

Yes, there is math involved, and that's why some spinners won't tackle grist. But the math is really basic, no complex equations. I don't do any math I can't do on a calculator, so all I need is a calculator and the knowledge that there are 16 ounces in a pound. Divide the yardage of your sample by its weight in ounces to find out how many yards there are in 1 ounce. For example, if you've got 20 yards that weighs half an ounce, divide 20 by 0.5; the answer is 40, which means there are 40 yards in

1 ounce. Multiply by 16 for the per-pound yardage: 640 ypp. Another example: If you've got 20 yards that weigh 0.32 ounce, divide 20 by 0.32 to get 62.5 (see, I told you you'd need a calculator). There are 62.5 yards in an ounce of this example, so multiply by 16 to find that this yarn has exactly 1,000 yards in a pound. Here's the formula:

(sample yardage) ÷ (sample yardage weight in ounces) = (length per ounce)

(length per ounce) × (16 ounces) = (yards per pound)

The higher the ypp, the finer the yarn. For instance, the grist of a bulky yarn is 400 ypp; the grist of a laceweight yarn is 4,000 to 6,000 ypp. Below are three examples that demonstrate the wpi and ypp in commercial yarns.

Socks That Rock Lightweight: 18–20 wpi and 1,350 ypp

Helen's Lace from Lorna's Laces: 36–38 wpi and 5,000 ypp

Cascade 220: 10 wpi and 1,000 ypp

What Influences Grist?

Because I was really curious about what influences grist, I started sampling. I can't learn anything without sampling; it never sticks unless I make it happen with my hands. I found out that, like all things in spinning, grist comes down to fiber type, drafting style, and twist. Two yarns can look similar and even have the same wpi but have different grist. Or they may have the same grist and a very different wpi. The photos below show some examples of my experiments.

DRAFT. I spun some Bluefaced Leicester (BFL) top as a 2-ply. One sample is drafted woolen (b) and the other, worsted (a). Both samples hit a wpi between 9 and 10. But the woolen-spun yarn has 825 ypp while the worsted-spun yarn has 675 ypp. Spinning worsted-style put more fiber into the same amount of yarn through compression and twist. If I were subbing the same amount of worsted-spun yarn for the woolen-spun yarn in a knitting pattern, I would run out.

FIBER. I spun some Corriedale (c) and some 50% Merino/50% Tencel (d) 2-ply to a wpi of 9. I was curious about this one: The Corriedale is a not-too-heavy medium wool, an all-around average fiber. The Merino is crimpy and light, but the Tencel is heavy. Would they balance out? Nope. The Corriedale has 1,000 ypp, and the Merino/Tencel has 800 ypp.

SAME YPP, DIFFERENT WPI. This one may be my favorite. It showed me how wpi and grist need to work together for consistency; it's not about just one or the other. I spun two versions of BFL top, one spun worsted into a 3-ply (e), the other spun woolen into a 2-ply (f). Both are 750 ypp. The worsted has a wpi of 11; the woolen has a wpi of 6 — not very compatible.

TWIST. Lately, I've been plying my yarns with a little more twist than balanced. I like the look and the extra "sproing" it gives my yarn. To see what difference ply twist makes in ypp, I spun two singles, plied half to balanced or slightly under (h) and the other half overplied (g), even for me. The wpi for both ranged from 11 to 12; the balanced yarn has 1,325 ypp and the tighter ply has 1,050 ypp. I'm losing a few yards with my style of plying.

Altering Grist

If you are measuring grist to be consistent while you are spinning and finding your sample yarns don't match, you might ask yourself a few questions:

- Have I changed my drafting method? This often happens to me when I get in the zone. I should be spinning worsted for a project, but when I get into that sweet spot of spinning, I revert back to my regular draft, which is woolen.

- Have I changed the amount of twist going into my yarn?

- Am I spinning with the right whorl?

- Am I adding more twist by treadling faster?

If you are using grist to match an already-spun yarn but the ypp of the yarn you are spinning isn't the same as the ypp of the yarn you're trying to match, ask yourself these questions:

- What type(s) of fiber am I using? Lighter-than-air Cormo or a denser BFL, silk, mohair, or blend?

- What is the fiber preparation? Worsted preparation makes a denser yarn when all other things are the same.

- What is my drafting method? Compressed worsted or airy woolen?

- What are my singles and ply twists? More twist makes a yarn shorter and denser than a less twisty one.

- How many plies am I using?

How to Adjust to Correct Grist

You can choose a number of approaches in order to get the ypp you want. To make the right choice, however, each of these needs to be measured against the type of yarn you want to end up with.

Here's how to raise the ypp and make a finer or lighter yarn:

- Use a finer fiber.
- Use a woolen preparation.
- Draft less fiber for the same length of yarn.
- Draft woolen-style.
- Spin a lighter twist in your singles or ply or both.
- Use fewer plies.

To lower ypp to make a wider or denser yarn, follow these tips:

- Use a thicker, heavier fiber or blend.
- Use a worsted preparation.
- Draft more fiber in the same length of yarn.
- Draft worsted-style.
- Give more twist to your singles or ply or both.
- Use more plies.

SAMPLING AND KEEPING TRACK

Know yourself. You may think that entering all of your yarn information into a spreadsheet is a good idea, and you've seen it work for one of your most organized friends. If you are not inclined to be that detailed or use a computer to record things, however, you won't stick with it. Remember, spinning is supposed to relax you, to bring you joy. I always want to keep track on a spreadsheet; it would be so tidy and accessible, but it never works for me. I use tags, zip-top bags, and boxes if I need more storage room. I handwrite everything, too, including my yarn vision and all of my notes (see chapter 1). But because my writing isn't the neatest, I use the biggest labels, tags, and bands I can find.

WHAT YOU SHOULD KEEP TRACK OF

Yarn vision and goal yarn. Write it all down, and draw or include a picture if it helps to inspire you. Include a sketch or picture of the project if you are working toward one. Describe your yarn in words and figures. Spin your sample and take it all the way to knitting, including stockinette stitch as well as any pattern stitches that are prominent in your pattern. Keep an unfinished singles, unfinished ply, finished ply, and finished knitted swatch of all of your samples well labeled. I find myself going back to old samples as starting points for new projects. If you are working with color and doing any color manipulation, mixing, or blending, sample all the ways you think will work.

Yarn as you are spinning. Keep a length of the yarn you are spinning attached to the wheel if you can. You can make either a ply-back sample or a control-card sample, whichever you prefer. Note all of the measurements you might want to check while spinning, and don't forget to make a note of your wheel setup (and which wheel you're using!). Use the control card or a tag attached to your ply-back sample to write all this information down as ratios, or simply write something like "Lendrum, regular flyer head, second from largest groove in the whorl."

When you first start spinning, you'll check constantly, and then you'll think you know better and stop checking. Find a happy medium. I check two or three times per bobbin.

Listen to that little voice in the back of your head, listen to your hands, listen to your gut. I don't know how many times I've known something was wrong with my yarn, and yet I've just kept going, only to be disappointed in the end. I usually know something is not quite right when I start fiddling more with the yarn, trying to manipulate it a different way so that my hands get twitchy.

PLANNING KNITTING PROJECTS

There are two ways to approach planning a knitting project using handspun yarn: find a pattern for yarn you already have, or spin for a pattern that calls for a specific yarn (commercial or handspun).

WHEN YOU HAVE A PATTERN WRITTEN FOR A SPECIFIC YARN

1. Know the commercial yarn specified by the pattern. It's ideal if you can put your hands on the yarn but not 100 percent necessary.

   * Yardage

   * Plies

   * Wpi

   * Tpi

   * Ypp

   * Twist angle

   * Fiber content (This will tell you a lot about the yarn if you can't actually hold it in your hand.)

   * Alleged gauge from the ball band

2. Pick apart the pattern and how the yarn is used in it.

   * Stitches used

   * Gauge

   * Yardage for your size

   * Hand (Is it stiff, fluid?)

3. Ask yourself if you want to do any customization.

   * Will you make any changes to the pattern?

   * Will you make any changes to the yarn?

4. If you customize, what changes will you make, and how will you achieve them? Figure out how to spin a yarn to get a similar end result, or the result that you want. Plan each of the following:

   * Fiber

   * Plies

   * Wpi

   * Tpi

   * Twist angle

   * Ypp

   * Wheel and setup

5. Find the fiber and do a quick sample of the whole process: spinning, finishing the yarn, knitting a swatch, and blocking. Don't forget to make detailed notes.

6. Do you have a yarn that you think will work? Do a bigger sample, big enough to get a feel for the hand, or drape, of the fabric. Use all of the stitch patterns, colorwork, and other tricky bits in the pattern.

   Repeat steps 5 and 6 until you are satisfied with your yarn.

7. Spin and knit your project.

WHEN YOU ALREADY HAVE YOUR YARN

1. Know your yarn.
   - Yardage
   - Plies
   - Wpi
   - Tpi
   - Twist angle
   - Ypp
   - Fiber, colorway, and dyer if you have that information

2. Swatch your yarn, trying out different needle sizes and different stitch patterns. Then block your swatches, and label each one with all the information about it, including the type and size needles you used.

3. Fall in love with one of your swatches, or start again. This can go on for days!

4. Once you've decided on the swatch you want to use, measure the stitch and row gauge and write them down. If your swatch is just in a pattern stitch, knit another swatch in stockinette using the same needles.

5. Find a pattern, and swatch for the particular pattern and particular stitches.

6. Check that you have enough yarn.
   - If you do, start knitting.
   - If you don't, will you spin more or supplement with commercially spun yarn?

TWIST AND KNITTING STYLE

You may be surprised to discover that the way you knit will add or subtract twist from your yarn. If you throw your yarn (the right-handed method, known as English or American style), wrapping your yarn clockwise around the needle, you will lose twist in a yarn that has been plied S. If you pick your yarn (the left-handed method, known as continental or German style), wrapping your yarn counterclockwise around the needle, you will add twist to your yarn and make the stitches look and act differently.

You can use these characteristics for specific visual effects or added durability. On the other hand, you can avoid the issue by adding more or less ply twist in your yarn to counteract what's happening with the twist as you knit. You can also avoid it by spinning your yarn in the opposite direction.

What you decide really depends on what you're knitting, the stitch pattern you're using, and how much you mind the look. If you've been frustrated previously knitting with handspun, because you think the stitches always somehow look wrong, addressing this issue could be the answer to your problem. The swatches on the facing page are examples of how the method used for knitting affects three different stitch patterns.

When your stitches tighten as you knit, it can add firmness and durability to stockinette and help cable and texture stitches pop. For lace, tighter stitches mean holes will roll in and shrink, and decreases will be a visual focus.

When your stitches loosen as you knit, it can add drape to stockinette and make lace relax and open. For texture and cables looser stitches mean a softening of the stitches and an overall flatter look.

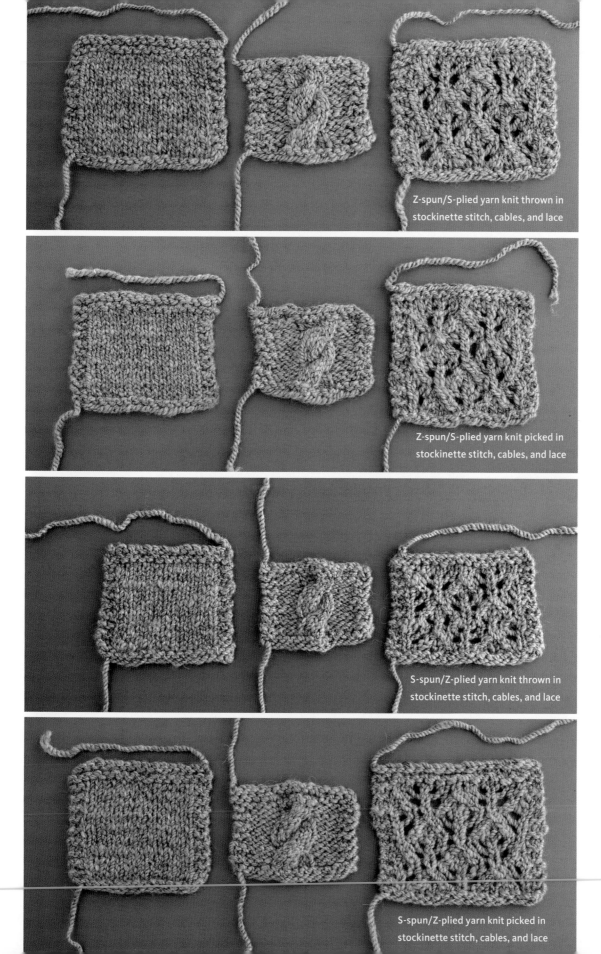

Z-spun/S-plied yarn knit thrown in stockinette stitch, cables, and lace

Z-spun/S-plied yarn knit picked in stockinette stitch, cables, and lace

S-spun/Z-plied yarn knit thrown in stockinette stitch, cables, and lace

S-spun/Z-plied yarn knit picked in stockinette stitch, cables, and lace

9 housewarming:

12 PATTERNS USING HANDSPUN YARN

SWEET OMEGA MÖBIUS
Designed by Lynne Vogel

This romantic Möbius wrap combines knitting and crochet for feather-light drape and face-framing grace. A central lace panel sports gently undulating stripes of color, while knitted surround and crocheted edging break colors up into random areas of solid and stripe.

FINISHED MEASUREMENTS

44" circumference × 22" long

FIBER

Three Waters Farm, 40% Merino/40% superwash Merino/20% tussah silk top, three 4 oz braids (12 oz), Ocean Light

YARN DESCRIPTION

- DK-weight singles
- Approximately 1,400 ypp
- 16 wpi
- Spun using short forward draw with minimal twist
- Washed and set in warm water with Eucalan, skein "walked" hand over hand under tension while still wet, 12 counts in each direction (not whacked); hung to dry without weight

YARN AMOUNT

Allow 600 yds; I spun 4 skeins. Here are the weights and lengths of each skein, in order of heaviest to finest:

Skein 1: 248 yds, 76 g, 3.25 yds per g

Skein 2: 210 yds, 64 g, 3.28 yds per g

Skein 3: 316 yds, 91 g, 3.47 yds per g

Skein 4: 244 yds, 69 g, 3.53 yds per g

YARDAGE FOR EACH SECTION OF PATTERN

Center Panel: 168 yds

Knitted Surround: 260 yds

Crocheted Edging: 160 yds

GAUGE

Knitting: 15 stitches and 26 rows = 4" × 4" in stockinette stitch

Crochet: 14 stitches and 16 rows = 4" × 4" in single crochet

NEEDLES/HOOKS

US 10 (6 mm) circular, 40" or longer, *or size needed to obtain correct gauge*

US I/9 (5.5 mm) crochet hook (See Knitting Notes on page 153 for advice about comparable needle and hook sizes.)

OTHER SUPPLIES

- One 2 yd niddy noddy
- Stitch markers in different colors
- Yarn needle

Spinning Notes

I used a Ladybug wheel with standard whorl on a larger setting. I spun from handpainted top, split lengthwise into eight equal sections. I was careful to keep the fibers of each color band aligned with each other so that the colors would come out crisp and clear; short forward draw helps to do this. I spun it fairly fast so that I didn't introduce much twist. I think, however, this pattern still would look great in a yarn with more twist, or even an active twist yarn. It would have a very different look, of course. I spun as much for feel as for looks. When knitted loosely on large needles, a singles yarn will hold its shape better than a plied one — at least mine does. I spun smooth, but allowed some natural irregularities to remain, as I like them. A minimal amount of twist helps with soft hand and drape, which this piece has in spades.

Because my spinning from bobbin to bobbin is not exactly the same, I weighed each skein and measured it for yardage. I divided the yardage by the weight in grams to give me yards per gram, which aided me in selecting the heavier skeins for the knitted portion and the finer skeins for crochet. The higher the number of yards per gram, the finer the yarn. There was an overall difference of 0.25 yards per gram — not a lot, but it's noticeable. Since crochet is heavier than knitting, I used the finer grist to crochet so that the Crocheted Edging would not be overly heavy. I had enough yarn that I didn't even have to touch the finest skein. I used the heaviest skein in the Knitted Surround and the second heaviest in the Center Panel.

Knitting Notes

This pattern is worked in three sections: Begin with a Center Panel worked flat with chain selvedge. Join the panel, end to end, with a Möbius twist (see Center Panel, page 155), and pick up and knit the continuous edge of the Center Panel to work a Knitted Surround followed by a crocheted edging. When it's time to bind off the Knitted Surround, use a single crochet bind off, which becomes the first round of crochet. It is a very flexible bind off and helps to make a seamless transition between the knitting and the crochet. The center panel is a nod to Rita Buchanan; the knitted surround, a nod to Cat Bordhi.

A few words about gauge in knitting and crochet: I knit to needle size, but I'm a loose crocheter, so I need to go down a hook size or two from the knitting needle I used. Your gauge could be very different from mine (for instance, you could be a loose knitter and a tight crocheter), so experiment. My crochet gauge gives a very slight flare to the edge of the Möbius, and this helps the wrap flow and drape. Getting the correct gauge for both the crochet and knitting is more important than matching the size of needle and hook listed in the pattern.

Pattern Stitches

Continuous Flow
(worked flat with a chain selvedge over 26 stitches)

Row 1: Slip 1 knitwise, k2, k2tog, k5, yo, k3, yo, k5, ssk, k6.

Row 2 (and all even-numbered rows through Row 12): Slip 1 purlwise, purl to end.

Row 3: Slip 1 knitwise, k1, k2tog, k5, yo, k5, yo, k5, ssk, k5.

Row 5: Slip 1 knitwise, k2tog, k5, yo, k7, yo, k5, ssk, k4.

Row 7: Slip 1 knitwise, k5, k2tog, k5, yo, k3, yo, k5, ssk, k3.

Row 9: Slip 1 knitwise, k4, k2tog, k5, yo, k5, yo, k5, ssk, k2.

Row 11: Slip 1 knitwise, k3, k2tog, k5, yo, k7, yo, k5, ssk k1.

Slanting Eyelet Pattern A (knit)

(worked in the round over a multiple of 5 stitches)

Rounds 1, 3, and 5: Yo, k2tog, k3.

Rounds 2, 4, and 6: Knit.

Slanting Eyelet Pattern B (purl)

(worked in the round over a multiple of 5 stitches)

Rounds 1, 3, and 5: Yo, ssp, p3.

Rounds 2, 4, and 6: Purl.

Single Crochet Bind Off

Using a crochet hook, pull a loop through the first stitch of the knitted round, sliding the stitch off the needle. Insert the hook into the next knit stitch, pull through a loop, and let the stitch slide off the needle. * Yarnover the crochet hook and pull a loop through both stitches. Repeat from * until 1 stitch remains. Join the round by working a slip stitch into the first crochet stitch of the round.

Continuous Flow Pattern

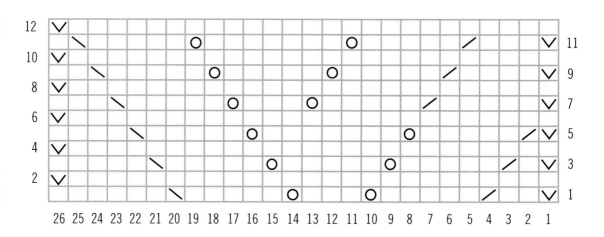

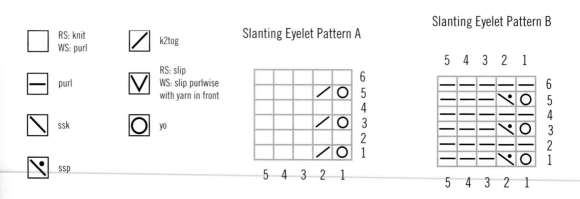

Slanting Eyelet Pattern A

Slanting Eyelet Pattern B

KNITTING THE SHAWL

CENTER PANEL

Cast on 26 stitches.

Following chart or written instructions, as you prefer, complete rows 1–12 of Continuous Flow pattern (see Pattern Stitches) a total of 18 times.

Bind off.

Join Center Panel into a Möbius strip by bringing the cast-on end to meet the bound-off end with right sides together, then flipping one end so that the wrong side is facing. Sew the seam the prettiest way you know how. I let the chains of the bound-off edge show as a reversible design element.

KNITTED SURROUND

Setup: Hold the Center Panel with right side facing. Beginning at the join, pick up and knit 1 stitch for every chain of the chain selvedge until you reach the join (108 stitches) You are now halfway around. Place marker B. Pick up and purl 1 stitch for every chain of the chain selvedge for the remainder of the round (108 stitches from marker B). Place marker A to mark the beginning of the round and join for working in the round. (216 stitches total, 108 between each marker)

Round 1: * M1, k3; repeat from * to marker B, * M1, p3; repeat from * to marker A. (288 stitches total in round)

Round 2: Purl to marker B, knit to marker A.

Round 3: Knit to marker B, purl to marker A.

Round 4: Knit to marker B, purl to marker A.

Round 5: Purl to marker B, knit to marker A.

Rounds 6–12: Knit to marker B, purl to marker A.

Round 13 (increase round): K1, M1, knit to marker B, p1, M1, purl to marker A. (290 stitches total in round)

Rounds 14–19: Following chart or written instructions, as you prefer, work Slanting Eyelet Pattern A knit version (see facing page) to marker B, and work Slanting Eyelet Pattern purl version B to marker A.

Rounds 20–22: Knit to marker B, purl to marker A.

Round 23: Purl to marker B, knit to marker A.

Round 24: Knit to marker B, purl to marker A.

Round 25: Purl to marker B, knit to marker A.

Round 26: Knit to marker B, purl to marker A.

Round 27 (decrease round): K2tog, knit to marker B, p2tog, purl to marker A. (288 stitches)

Rounds 28–33: * K6, p6; repeat from * around.

Round 34: * K3, yo, k3, p2, p2tog, p2; repeat from * around.

Rounds 35 and 36: * K7, p5; repeat from * around.

Round 37: Knit to marker B, purl to marker A.

Round 38: Purl all stitches.

Bind off all stitches using single crochet bind off. With crochet hook, join with slip stitch in first sc. Do not break yarn.

CROCHETING THE EDGING

Round 1: Ch 1, work 1 sc into each st. Join with slipstitch in first st. Turn. (288 stitches)

Round 2: Ch 1, * sc into next 8 sts, 3 sc into next st, sc into next 3 sts; repeat from * around. (*Note:* The 3 sc should be directly above the yarnover in the Knitted Surround.) Join round with slipstitch in first sc. (336 stitches) Turn.

Round 3: Ch 1, sc into first st, * skip 2 sts, 4 dc into first sc of 3 sc point, ch 3, skip 1 sc, 4 dc into 3rd sc of 3 sc point, skip 2 sc, sc into 3rd sc, ch 5, skip 5 sc, 1 sc into 6th sc; repeat from * around. On last multiple of round, work multiple through ch 5, join with slipstitch to first sc of round. Do not turn.

Round 4: Slipstitch into each of 4 dc, slipstitch into 3 ch-space, ch 3, 2 dc into 3 ch-space, ch 3, 3 dc into 3 ch-space, ch 1, 9 dc into 5 ch-space, * chain 1 (3 dc, chain 3, 3 dc into 3 ch-space), chain 1, 9 dc into 5 ch-space, slip 1; repeat from * around, join with slipstitch into first dc. Turn.

Round 5: Ch 1, *1 sc into each of 9 dc, 1 sc into space, 1 sc into each 3 dc, 1 sc, ch 3, sc into 3rd chain from hook to create a picot, 1 sc into 3 ch-space, 1 sc into each 3 dc, 1 sc into space; repeat from * around. Join with slipstitch into first sc. Break yarn and pull through final stitch to secure.

FINISHING

Block and weave in ends.

MAYA CARDIGAN
Designed by **Kirsten Kapur**

Worked in one piece from the bottom up, this romantic cardigan is knit loosely to take advantage of the drape of the soft fiber. When spinning for this project, keep in mind that heavier-weight yarns knit to the same gauge as finer yarns require more yardage. The hems and front edges feature a unique eyelet pattern that highlights handspun yarn without being fussy. An open neckline and three-quarter sleeves will take you from early spring to late fall, and work equally well with jeans and a T-shirt or a flirty dress.

SIZES
Woman S (M, L, 1X, 2X)

Sample is size S; choose a size with 1"–2" of positive ease.

FINISHED MEASUREMENTS
Chest: 33¾" (36¾", 41¼", 45¾", 48¾")

Length from shoulder: 22" (22", 24", 24", 26")

FIBER
Anzula Luxury Fibers, 50% Baby Camel/50% Tussah Silk top, 10 (11, 13, 15, 16) oz, color: Seabreeze

YARN DESCRIPTION
- 2-ply to balance
- 900 ypp
- 9-10 wpi
- Woolen drafted from the fold
- Cold soak and hang to finish

YARN AMOUNT
Approximately 650 (700; 825; 925; 1,025) yds

GAUGE
16 stitches and 24 rows = 4" × 4" in stockinette stitch

NEEDLES
One US 8 (5 mm) circular needle, 32" or longer, *or size needed to obtain correct gauge*

Set of four or five US 8 (5 mm) double-pointed needles, at least 5" long, *or size needed to obtain correct gauge*

OTHER SUPPLIES
- Two stitch markers of the same color (A) and four stitch markers of a different color (B)
- Scrap yarn
- Yarn needle
- Safety pins or locking stitch markers
- Sewing thread and sewing needle for attaching buttons
- 11 (11, 12, 12, 13) ½" buttons

Spinning Notes

From Carol Knox, spinner:

This was beautiful fiber but a challenge to spin. Silk is a long fiber and camel is very short, so I needed a drafting style that allowed for a good integration of each fiber, both to make sure they were secured in the yarn and to bring out the shine of silk and the downy softness of the camel. I tried a variety of worsted and woolen techniques to achieve a yarn that would meet the specifications. I finally settled on spinning it from the fold with a supported long draw, giving it a bit of a rustic look with a soft smooth hand. The fiber needed a lot of fluffing and preparation before spinning: I broke it into 4" to 6" lengths and fluffed and loosened the top.

Pattern Stitches

Cluster Stitch

K3, pass the first of the 3 stitches just knit over the next 2 stitches.

Eyelet Pattern Worked Flat

(multiple of 3 stitches plus 2)

Row 1 (RS): K3, *yo, Cluster Stitch; repeat from * to last 2 stitches, k2.

All WS Rows: Purl.

Row 3: K2, * Cluster Stitch, yo; repeat from * to last 3 stitches, k3.

Eyelet Pattern in the Round

(multiple of 3 stitches)

Round 1: *Yo, Cluster Stitch; repeat from * to end.

Rounds 2 and 4: Knit.

Round 3: K2, pass the last stitch of the previous round over the first 2 stitches of the round, yo, *Cluster Stitch, yo; repeat from * to end. Knit the first stitch of the next round, and transfer it to the end of the round. Mark new beginning of round.

KNITTING THE CARDIGAN

BOTTOM EDGE

With circular needle, cast on 131 (143, 161, 179, 191) stitches.

Working back and forth, work ribbing as follows:

Row 1 (RS): (K1, p1) to last stitch, k1.

Row 2 (WS): (P1, k1) to last stitch, p1.

Work rows 1 and 2 two more times. (6 rows total)

EYELET BORDER

Work rows 1–4 of Eyelet Pattern Worked Flat (see Pattern Stitches).

Work rows 1–3 once more.

Next row: P14, place marker A, purl 103 (115, 133, 151, 163) stitches, place marker A, p14.

BODY

Row 1 (RS): Work next row of Eyelet Pattern Worked Flat to first marker, knit to second marker; work Eyelet Pattern Worked Flat to end.

Row 2 (WS): Work next row of Eyelet Pattern Worked Flat to first marker, purl to second marker, work Eyelet Pattern Worked Flat to end.

Work body as established until piece measures 15" (14½", 16", 15½", 17") or to desired length from cast-on edge, ending with a wrong-side row.

SLEEVES

(MAKE 2)

Cast on 30 (36, 36, 42, 42) stitches onto the double-pointed needles. Divide stitches evenly among the needles. Join to work in the round, being careful not to twist stitches. Mark the beginning of the round.

Rounds 1–6: (K1, p1) to end of round.

Work rounds 1–4 of Eyelet Pattern in the Round (see Pattern Stitches) a total of two times.

Increase Round: K1, M1, knit to last stitch, M1, k1. (2 stitches increased)

Knit every round for 5 (7, 5, 5, 3) rounds (stockinette stitch).

Work the previous 6 (8, 6, 6, 4) rounds 6 (5, 8, 7, 10) more times. [44 (48, 54, 58, 64) stitches]

Continue to work in stockinette stitch until sleeve measures 13" (13", 13", 13½", 13½") from cast-on edge.

Final Sleeve Round: Work in stockinette to 3 (4, 4, 5, 6) stitches from end. Place the last 3 (4, 4, 5, 6) stitches of the round and the first 3 (4, 4, 5, 6) stitches of the next round onto a piece of scrap yarn. Place the remaining 38 (40, 46, 48, 52) sleeve stitches on a separate piece of scrap yarn.

Make the second sleeve in the same way as the first.

YOKE

Row 1 (RS): Work the first 30 (32, 36, 40, 42) stitches in Eyelet Pattern Worked Flat and stockinette stitch as established, and place marker B. Place the next 6 (8, 8, 10, 12) body stitches on a piece of scrap yarn. Place the 38 (40, 46, 48, 52) held stitches from the first sleeve on the left needle and work across the 38 (40, 46, 48, 52) sleeve stitches in stockinette stitch, place marker B. Work the next 59 (63, 73, 79, 83) body stitches in stockinette stitch, place marker B. Place the next 6 (8, 8, 10, 12) body stitches on a piece of scrap yarn. Place the 38 (40, 46, 48, 52) held stitches from the second sleeve back on the left needle, and work across the 38 (40, 46, 48, 52) sleeve stitches in stockinette stitch, place marker B. Work as established to end. [195 (207, 237, 255, 271) stitches on needles]

Row 2 (WS): Purl.

RAGLAN DECREASES

Decrease Row (RS): *Work as established to 3 stitches from B marker, k2tog, k1, k1, ssk; repeat from * three more times, work as established, to end. (8 stitches decreased)

Work 3 rows even in Eyelet Pattern Worked Flat and stockinette as established.

Work the previous 4 rows 7 (7, 6, 5, 5) more times. [131 (143, 181, 207, 223) stitches remain]

Work decrease row one more time. (8 stitches decreased)

Work 1 row in stockinette.

Work the previous 2 rows 4 (5, 9, 12, 14) more times. [91 (95, 101, 103, 103) stitches remain]

NECK

Row 1 (RS): (K1, p1) to last stitch, k1.

Row 2 (WS): (P1, k1) to last stitch, p1.

Work rows 1 and 2 two more times. (6 rows total)

Bind off in ribbing pattern.

BUTTON BANDS

LEFT FRONT

With right side facing, pick up and knit 89 (89, 97, 97, 105) stitches along the left front edge.

Row 1 (WS): (P1, k1) to last stitch, p1.

Row 2 (RS): (K1, p1) to last stitch, k1.

Work rows 1 and 2 two more times. (6 rows total)

Bind off in ribbing pattern.

RIGHT FRONT

With right side facing, pick up and knit 89 (89, 97, 97, 105) stitches along the right front edge.

Row 1 (WS): (P1, k1) to last stitch, p1.

Row 2 (RS): (K1, p1) to last stitch, k1.

Work row 1 one more time.

Row 4 (RS): Work 4 stitches in ribbing as established, *yo, p2tog, work 6 stitches in ribbing as established; work from * 10 (10, 11, 11, 12) more times, yo, p2tog, work 3 stitches in ribbing as established.

Work in ribbing for 2 more rows.

Bind off in ribbing pattern.

FINISHING

Place the held sleeve stitches at the underarm on a double-pointed needle, place the held body stitches at the underarm on a second double-pointed needle. Work Kitchener stitch to graft the underarm stitches.

Weave in all ends.

Block to measurements in schematic.

Using the buttonholes as a guide, mark the button placement with safety pins or locking stitch markers. Sew the buttons in place.

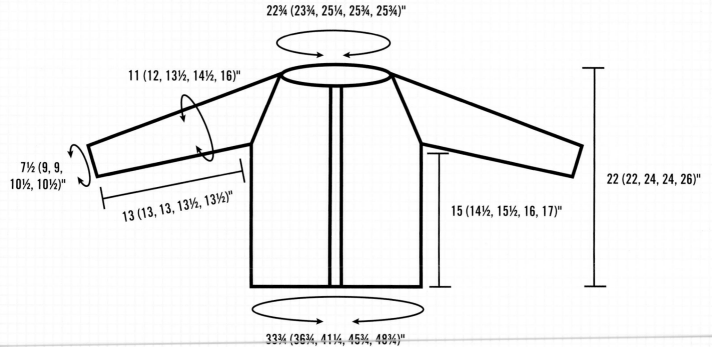

22¾ (23¾, 25¼, 25¾, 25¾)"

11 (12, 13½, 14½, 16)"

7½ (9, 9, 10½, 10½)"

13 (13, 13, 13½, 13½)"

15 (14½, 15½, 16, 17)"

22 (22, 24, 24, 26)"

33¾ (36¾, 41¼, 45¾, 48¾)"

JILLIAN SHAWL
Designed by **Rosemary (Romi) Hill**

This lovely crescent-shaped shawl is designed to show off the gorgeous variations in handdyed and handspun yarn. The simple garter stitch top lets your yarn shine, while the beautiful knit-on lace edging provides a sophisticated finish.

FINISHED MEASUREMENTS

72" wide from tip to tip; 17¼" from nape of neck to edge

FIBER

Hilltop Cloud, 65% Silk/34% Kid Mohair, 8.7 oz, color: Deep Red to Deep Pink

YARN DESCRIPTION

- 2-ply
- 1,072 ypp
- 14–15 wpi
- Worsted draft
- Finished by snapping

YARN AMOUNT

580 yds.

GAUGE

16 stitches and 24 rows = 4"× 4" in garter stitch

NEEDLE

US 5 (3.75 mm) circular needle, 24" or longer, *or size needed to obtain correct gauge*

OTHER SUPPLIES

- Yarn needle
- Wool wash
- T-pins
- Blocking wires
- Cornstarch

ABBREVIATIONS

cdd Slip next 2 stitches together knitwise, k1, pass 2 slipped stitches over stitch just knit

T2L Slip 1 stitch to cable needle, hold in front, p1, k1-tbl from cable needle

T2R Slip 1 stitch to cable needle, hold in back, k1-tbl, p1 from cable needle

Spinning Notes

The mohair/silk was lovely to spin. I used a short forward draw and lower twist because the yarn was for lace and I wanted it to be more drapey than mohair naturally is. I used a commercial fingering-weight yarn to give me an idea of wpi for this yarn.

KNITTING THE SHAWL

Setup: Loosely cast on 11 stitches using backwards loop cast on (see page 223).

Row 1: (K1-tbl, yo, k1) into first stitch, knit to 1 stitch before end, (k1-tbl, yo, k1) into last stitch. (15 stitches; 4 stitches increased)

Row 2 (and all even-numbered rows through Row 86: K1-tbl three times, knit to 3 stitches before end, k1-tbl three times.

Row 3: (K1-tbl, yo, k1) into first stitch, k2, * M1, k1; repeat from * to last 3 sts, M1, k2, (k1-tbl, yo, k1) into last stitch. (29 stitches after row 3)

Row 5: Repeat row 1. (33 stitches)

Row 7: Repeat row 3. (65 stitches)

Row 9 (and all odd-numbered rows through Row 27): Repeat row 1. (105 stitches after row 27)

Row 29 (increase row): (K1-tbl, yo, k1) into first stitch, k2, [M1, k5] nine times, M1, k9, [M1, k5] nine times, M1, k2, (k1-tbl, yo, k1) into last stitch. (129 stitches)

Odd-Numbered Rows 31–49: Repeat row 1. (169 stitches)

Row 51 (increase row): (K1-tbl, yo, k1) into first stitch, k2, (M1, k7) 11 times, M1, k9, (M1, k7) 11 times, M1, k2, (k1-tbl, yo, k1) into last stitch. (197 stitches)

Odd-Numbered Rows 53–69: Repeat row 1. (233 stitches)

Row 71 (increase row): (K1-tbl, yo, k1) into first stitch, k2, (M1, k9) 12 times, M1, k5, M1, k1, M1, k5, (M1, k9) 12 times, M1, k2, (k1-tbl, yo, k1) into last stitch. (265 stitches)

Odd-Numbered Rows 73–87: Repeat row 1. (297 stitches)

Row 88: K1-tbl three times, knit to 3 stitches before end, k1-tbl three times.

Do not break the yarn. Using the knitted cast on (see page 226) and the working yarn, cast on 18 stitches. (19 stitches)

THE EDGING

Follow the chart on page 171 or these written instructions for the edging pattern. Work edging pattern 36 times in full and work Rows 1–15 of a 37th repeat. Bind off loosely.

Row 1: K1-tbl twice, yo, k2tog, yo, k3tog, yo, T2L, k1-tbl, yo, ssk, k1, k2tog, yo, k1-tbl, T2R, p2tog-tbl (1 from edging and 1 from body of shawl), turn.

Row 2 (and all even-numbered rows through Row 16): Slip 1 knitwise wyif, purl to 2 stitches before end, k1-tbl twice.

Row 3: K1-tbl twice, yo, k2tog, yo, k1-tbl, k2tog, yo, T2L, yo, ssk, yo, cdd, yo, k2tog, yo, T2R, p2tog-tbl (1 from edging and 1 from body of shawl), turn.

Row 5: K1-tbl twice, yo, k2tog, yo, k1-tbl, k1, k2tog, yo, T2L, yo, cdd, yo, k1, yo, cdd, yo, T2R, p2tog-tbl (1 from edging and 1 from body of shawl), turn.

Row 7: K1-tbl twice, yo, k2tog, yo, k1-tbl, k2, k2tog, yo, T2L, yo, k2tog, k1-tbl, k1, k1-tbl, ssk, yo, T2R, p2tog-tbl (1 from edging and 1 from body of shawl), turn.

Row 9: K1-tbl, k2tog-tbl, yo, ssk, yo, k3, k2tog, yo, T2L, k1-tbl, yo, ssk, k1, k2tog, yo, k1-tbl, T2R, p2tog-tbl (1 from edging and 1 from body of shawl), turn.

Row 11: K1-tbl, k2tog-tbl, (yo, ssk) twice, k1, k2tog, yo, T2L, yo, ssk, yo, cdd, yo, k2tog, yo, T2R, p2tog-tbl (1 from edging and 1 from body of shawl), turn.

Row 13: K1-tbl, k2tog-tbl, (yo, ssk) twice, k2tog, yo, T2L, yo, cdd, yo, k1, yo, cdd, yo, T2R, p2tog-tbl (1 from edging and 1 from body of shawl), turn.

Row 15: K1-tbl, k2tog-tbl, yo, ssk, yo, k3tog, yo, T2L, yo, k2tog, k1-tbl, k1, k1-tbl, ssk, yo, T2R, p2tog-tbl (1 from edging and 1 from body of shawl), turn.

FINISHING

Weave in ends, and wash using wool wash. Remove excess water from shawl and block using T-pins and blocking wires. Stretch shawl tight, and pin each point of the edging. To assist the shawl in keeping its shape, dissolve a small amount of cornstarch in hot water (approximately ½ teaspoon of powder per quart of water) and use it to lightly spray the pinned shawl. (In humid climates, use commercial starch, rather than cornstarch.) When thoroughly dry, unpin and enjoy!

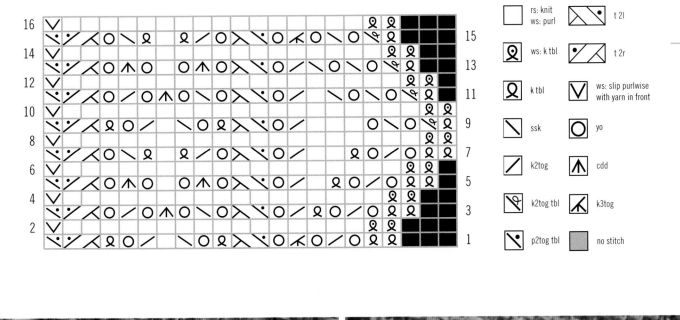

	rs: knit ws: purl		t 2l
	ws: k tbl		t 2r
	k tbl		ws: slip purlwise with yarn in front
	ssk		yo
	k2tog		cdd
	k2tog tbl		k3tog
	p2tog tbl		no stitch

LINA TOE-UP SOCKS
Designed by **Kate Atherley**

These toe-up socks in a simple pattern, interesting but not too interesting to knit, are suitable for a broad variety of colorways. The construction and patterning allow easy, on-the-go adjustments for variability in both yarn and feet. The sock has a reinforced gusset-and-flap heel for durability and improved fit.

SIZES

Adult XS (S, M, L, XL)

Sample is size S, with foot 9¼" long and leg 6½" long. Choose a size with about an inch of negative ease.

FINISHED MEASUREMENTS

Foot circumference: 7½" (8", 8½", 9", 9¾")

Foot and leg lengths are adjustable to fit.

FIBER

Porpoise Fur, Dorset Horn Top,
3.25 (3.5, 4, 4, 4.25) oz, color: Blue Coomassie

YARN DESCRIPTION

- 3 ply
- 1,575 ypp
- 14–16 wpi
- Woolen draft
- Hot soak, snap, and hang to finish

YARN AMOUNT

Approximately 325 (350, 375, 400, 425) yds

GAUGE

28 stitches and 40 rounds = 4" × 4" in stockinette stitch in the round. *Note:* Round gauge is less important than stitch gauge. If your round gauge doesn't match, the pattern can easily be adjusted. See Knitting Notes on the next page.

NEEDLES

US 1 (2.5 mm) needles for small circumference in the round (double-pointed needles, one long circular needle for Magic Loop, or two shorter circulars) *or size needed to obtain correct gauge*

OTHER SUPPLIES

- Two safety pins or removable stitch markers
- Two stitch markers (any style)
- Yarn needle

ABBREVIATIONS

C2L Skip next stitch and knit into the back of the 2nd stitch, leaving it on the needle; knit the first stitch and slip both off the needle

C2R Skip next stitch and knit into the front of the 2nd stitch, leaving it on the needle; knit the first stitch and slip both off the needle

w&t (wrap & turn) Slip the next stitch purlwise; move the yarn between the needles (if it's at the back, bring it to the front; if it's at the front, take it to the back); slip the stitch back to the left needle. Turn your work and bring the working yarn to working position for the next row.

Spinning Notes

From Carol Knox, spinner:

I had more trouble getting this to make a sock-weight yarn than I expected; it ended up being a little heavier than a standard sock yarn. Sometimes down fibers are like that, as they may have more second cuts or just shorter fiber over all. I always buy a little extra for sampling to get exactly the yarn I want. I spun it supported long draw from the end of the roving in a woolen style, letting the takeup on my wheel pull the fibers and allowing twist into the drafting triangle.

Knitting Notes

Working Wrapped Stitches Together with Their Wraps

When working a right-side row: With the tip of the right needle, scoop up the wrap from underneath, put the needle into the stitch, and knit the wrap and the stitch together. (Make sure you come back out through both the stitch and the wrap.)

When working a wrong-side row: Use the tip of the right needle to scoop up the wrap from underneath on the right side of the work (the opposite from the side you are facing), and bring the wrap up onto the needle; purl the wrap and the stitch together.

Cable Rib Motif

This motif is aligned differently on the left and right socks. Where only one set of instructions is given, it applies to both left and right socks.

The pattern is flexible, permitting easy adjustment for different gauges. If your round gauge doesn't match the gauge listed, you will need to calculate the length to work the foot before the heel and gusset, as follows:

- Length before starting gusset =
  Full foot length – heel and gusset length

- Heel and gusset length =
  38 (40, 44, 48, 50 rounds) ÷ number of rounds per inch

If, as you're working, you find that your stitch gauge doesn't match the pattern gauge (this isn't an excuse to skip checking it), you can adjust the stitch count in the plain sections of the sock. If you change the stitch count on the sole of the sock, you'll find it's easiest to stick close to the counts used by one of the sizes I've already calculated for you; just use those numbers instead. Once you're working the leg, you can change the stitch count as much as you need. For the ribbing, the plain section needs to be a multiple of 3 stitches plus 2: work increases or decreases as required to get to that stitch count in the final round of the leg.

Pattern Stitches

Cable Rib

(worked in the round over 12 stitches)

Round 1: P1, k2, p1, k4, p1, k2, p1.

Round 2: P1, k2, p1, c2R, c2L, p1, k2, p1.

Eye of Partridge

(worked flat over a multiple of 2 stitches)

Row 1 (RS): (Slip 1 purlwise, k1) across.

Rows 2 and 4 (WS): Purl.

Row 3 (RS): (K1, slip 1 purlwise) across.

KNITTING THE SOCKS

TOE

Setup: Using Judy's Magic Cast On (see page 224), cast on 16 (20, 20, 24, 24) stitches: 8 (10, 10, 12, 12) stitches each on two needles. Distribute stitches across needles as you prefer, and join for working in the round. Knit 1 round.

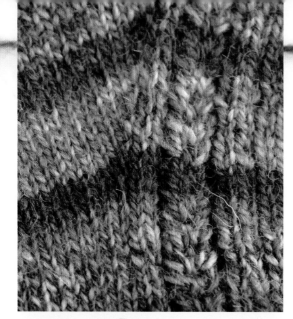

The following instructions refer to the start of the round and the center of the round; place removable stitch markers in the fabric or arrange your stitches on your needles so that you can identify them.

Round 1: Knit.

Round 2 (increase round): K1, M1, knit to 1 stitch before center of round, M1, k1; k1, M1, k to 1 stitch before end of round, M1, k1. (4 stitches increased)

Next Round: Knit.

Repeat the last 2 rounds 8 (8, 9, 9, 10) more times. (52 [56, 60, 64, 68] stitches)

FOOT

Round 1, Right Sock: K14 (16, 18, 20, 22), work Cable Rib pattern round 1, knit to end of round.

Round 1, Left Sock: Work Cable Rib pattern round 1, knit to end of round.

Pattern is now established. The first half of the round forms the instep; the second half is the sole.

Work even in pattern as established until foot measures 3¾" (4", 4½", 4¾", 5") short of the desired foot length (or length required to gusset). See Knitting Notes on page 174 for details on adjusting this if your round gauge doesn't match the pattern gauge.

GUSSET

Round 1 (place heel markers and start increases): Work across instep in pattern as established, M1R, place first heel marker, knit to end of round, place second heel marker, M1L. (54 [58, 62, 66, 70] stitches)

Round 2: Work even in pattern as established.

Round 3 (increase round): Work across instep in pattern as established, M1R, knit to end of round, M1L. (2 stitches increased)

Repeat the last 2 rounds 8 (9, 10, 11, 12) more times. (10 [11, 12, 13, 14] gusset stitches per side; 72 [78, 84, 90, 96] stitches total)

HEEL TURN

Row 1 (RS): Work in pattern as established to 1 stitch before second heel marker, w&t.

Row 2 (WS): Purl to 1 stitch before first heel marker, w&t.

Row 3: Knit to 1 stitch before previously wrapped stitch, w&t.

Row 4: Purl to 1 stitch before previously wrapped stitch, w&t.

Repeat the last 2 rows 7 (7, 8, 9, 9) more times, until 8 (10, 10, 10, 12) stitches remain unwrapped in the center, and there are 9 (9, 10, 11, 11) wrapped stitches on each side. The right side is now facing.

HEEL FLAP

Row 1 (RS): K8 (10, 10, 10, 12), knit the next 8 (8, 9, 10, 10) stitches together with their wraps, work ssk on the final wrapped stitch, its wrap, and the next stitch (the first of the gusset stitches) all together. Turn. (1 gusset stitch decreased)

Row 2 (WS): Slip 1 purlwise, p16 (18, 19, 20, 22), purl the next 8 (8, 9, 10, 10) stitches together with their wraps, work p2tog on the final wrapped stitch, its wrap, and the next stitch (the first of the gusset stitches) all together. Turn. (1 gusset stitch decreased)

Row 3 (RS): Slip 1 purlwise, work 24 (26, 28, 30, 32) stitches in Eye of Partridge pattern, ssk. Turn. (1 gusset stitch decreased)

Row 4 (WS): Slip 1 purlwise, work 24 (26, 28, 30, 32) stitches in Eye of Partridge pattern, p2tog. Turn. (1 gusset stitch decreased)

Repeat the last 2 rows 7 (8, 9, 10, 11) more times, until 1 gusset stitch remains on each side. (54 [58, 62, 66, 70] stitches total)

Next Round: Work final gusset decreases and reestablish round as follows: slip 1 purlwise, work 24 (26, 28, 30, 32) stitches in pattern as established, ssk; work across instep in pattern as established; k2tog, knit to end of sole/start of instep. This is the new start of round. [52 (56, 60, 64, 68) stitches]

Here you start the cable and rib patterning on the back-of-leg stitches. Start the pattern on the same round as you work on the instep.

Leg Round, Right Sock: [K14 (16, 18, 20, 22), work Cable Rib pattern] twice.

Leg Round, Left Sock: [Work Cable Rib pattern as established, k14 (16, 18, 20, 22)] twice.

Work even in pattern as established until leg measures 2" less than the desired full leg length.

Size XS and L only: Proceed to Ribbing.

Sizes S, M, and XL only: Adjust the stitch count for ribbing as follows:

Size S only (both socks): Work in pattern as established to end of instep, M1R, work in pattern as established to end of round, M1R. (58 stitches)

Size M, Right Sock only: (K8, k2tog, k8, work Cable Rib Pattern) twice. (58 stitches)

Size M, Left Sock only: (Work Cable Rib Pattern as established, k8, k2tog, k8) twice. (58 stitches)

Size XL, Right Sock only: (K2tog, k18, k2tog, work Cable Rib Pattern) twice. (64 stitches)

Size XL, Left Sock only: (Work Cable Rib Pattern as established, k2tog, k18, k2tog) twice. (64 stitches)

RIBBING

Ribbing Round, Right Sock: [(K2, p1) 4 (5, 5, 6, 6) times, k2, work Cable Rib pattern] twice.

Ribbing Round, Left Sock: [Work Cable Rib pattern as established, (k2, p1) 4 (5, 5, 6, 6) times times, k2] twice.

Work even in ribbing as established for 2" (or desired length), ending with round 2 of the Cable Rib pattern.

Bind off as follows: k1; *k1, insert the tip of the left needle into the fronts of these 2 stitches (as if to ssk), and knit them together; repeat from * until all stitches are bound off. Cut yarn and pull through final stitch to close.

FINISHING

Block and weave in ends.

BUMP IN THE NIGHT

Designed by **Amy King**

I love a thick-and-thin yarn, but many people get stuck wondering what to make out of it. This shawl is a funky, warm, and interesting way to use that wonderful, squishy singles yarn.

FINISHED MEASUREMENTS
60" long × 20" at its widest in the center

FIBER
Spunky Eclectic, Polwarth (Progression colorway),
    14 oz combed top, Snowdrop Inn

YARN DESCRIPTION
- Singles
- 440 ypp
- 5.5 wpi
- Short draw
- Thick-and-thin spun
- Lightly fulled

YARN AMOUNT
340 yds (*Note:* You can use less or more than this,
    as you divide your yarn in half before you begin
    knitting in order to maximize the amount of
    yarn and fiber you have. See Knitting Notes on
    the next page.)

GAUGE
8 stitches and 13 rows = 4" × 4" in stockinette stitch
    after blocking. Gauge is approximate due to thick-
    and-thin nature of the yarn.

NEEDLES
US 13 (9 mm) needles, straight or a 24" or longer cir-
    cular needle, *or size needed to obtain correct gauge*

OTHER SUPPLIES
- Stitch marker
- Cable needle
- Yarn needle

ABBREVIATIONS
C6L Slip next 3 stitches to cable needle and hold in
    front of work; k3, then k3 from cable needle

C6R Slip next 3 stitches to cable needle and hold in
    back of work; k3, then k3 from cable needle

Spinning Notes

Spinning thick and thin is a lot about spinning incorrectly. You make the best lumps and bumps by pulling too far back into your fiber supply. Just a little too far back, and it will make your spinning perfectly uneven.

Knitting Notes

This shawl is worked side to side, first increasing to the center and then decreasing to the other end. You can work it two different ways. I've given directions for specific sizes and stitch amounts for the increases. If you're worried about not having enough yarn, however, or if you know you have more than enough and would like a larger shawl, you can divide your yarn in half, and then use half to create the section of the shawl with the increases and the other half to decrease and finish the shawl, skipping the even section in the middle. Either way, you will have a lovely shawl in the end.

Pattern Stitches

Cable Edging
(worked flat over 11 stitches)

Row 1 (RS): P1, C6R, k3, p1.

Row 2 and all WS rows to Row 8: K1, p9, k1.

Row 3: P1, k9, p1.

Row 5: P1, k3, C6L, p1.

Row 7: K1, p1, k9.

Cable Edging

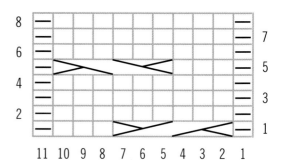

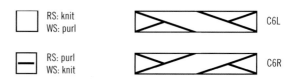

| | RS: knit WS: purl |
| | RS: purl WS: knit |

C6L

C6R

KNITTING THE SHAWL

FIRST SECTION

Setup: Cast on 18 stitches. Knit 2 rows.

Row 1 (RS): K2, yo, k2tog, kfb, place marker, work Cable Edging pattern (see Pattern Stitches), k2. (1 stitch increased)

Row 2 and all WS rows: K2, work Cable Edging pattern, purl to the last 2 stitches, k2.

Row 3: K2, yo, k2tog, knit to marker, work Cable Edging Pattern, k2.

Row 5: K2, yo, k2tog, knit to 1 stitch before marker, kfb, work Cable Edging Pattern, k2. (1 stitch increased)

Row 7: K2, yo, k2tog, knit to marker, work Cable Edging pattern, k2. *Note:* Every time you complete the 8-row repeat of Cable Edging pattern, you will have increased by 2 stitches.

Continue to work as established until you have increased to 38 stitches total, or if you've divided your yarn into two sections, work until the first half is almost done, ending with a wrong-side row.

SECOND SECTION

Next RS row: K2, yo, k2tog, knit to marker, work the appropriate row of the cable chart, k2.

All WS rows: K2, work appropriate row of Cable Edging pattern, purl to the last 2 stitches, k2.

Work in this manner for 16" or until you've used the first half of the yarn, ending with a wrong-side row. If you've separated your yarn into two equal portions, attach the second ball and continue, working the same number of rows even as you did in the first half of this section.

THIRD SECTION

Row 1 (RS): K2, yo, k2tog, knit to 2 stitches before the marker, ssk, work Cable Edging pattern, k2.

Row 2 and all WS rows: K2, work Cable Edging pattern, purl to the last 2 stitches, k2.

Row 3: K2, yo, k2tog, knit to marker, work Cable Edging pattern, k2.

Row 5: K2, yo, k2tog, knit to 2 stitches before the marker, ssk, work Cable Edging pattern, k2.

Row 7: K2, yo, k2tog, knit to marker, work Cable Edging pattern, k2.

Note: Every time you complete the 8-row repeat of the Cable Edging pattern, you will have decreased by 2 stitches.

Continue to work rows 1 and 2 until you have decreased to 18 stitches. Remove the marker.

Knit 2 rows. Bind off all stitches loosely.

FINISHING

Wet-block and pin to size. Weave in ends.

TETRIS PULLOVER
Designed by Julia Farwell-Clay

This slightly boxy drop-shoulder pullover uses a modular construction to highlight organically occurring color shifts from the random spinning of space-dyed roving.

SIZES
32" (36", 40", 44", 48", 52")

FINISHED MEASUREMENTS
38" (42", 46", 50", 54", 58") at bust, intended to be worn with 4"–6" of positive ease

FIBER
Into The Whirled, Romney top, 9 (10, 11, 12, 13, 14) oz Rhinebeck colorway

YARN DESCRIPTION
- 2-ply
- 1,600 ypp
- 13–14 wpi
- Worsted draft with short forward draw
- Finished by snapping

YARN AMOUNT
860 (970, 1,080, 1,180, 1,290, 1,400) yds

GAUGE
20 stitches and 30 rows = 4" × 4" in stockinette stitch on larger needles

NEEDLES
US 4 (3.5 mm) straight needles

US 4 (3.5 mm) double-pointed needles or 16" circular needle for finishing neck

US 5 (3.75 mm) straight needles *or size needed to obtain correct gauge*

OTHER SUPPLIES
- Extra needle in larger size
- Stitch markers, removable and ring style
- Stitch holders or scrap yarn
- Yarn needle

ABBREVIATIONS
cdd Slip next 2 stitches together knitwise, k1, pass 2 slipped stitches over stitch just knit

Spinning Notes

From Beth Smith, spinner:
For this yarn, I focused on what Julia wanted to happen with the colors, which was to have them as mixed up as possible. I spun a few yards from the full thickness of the top — short forward draw but with a light pinch — and sent her photos. We talked about color repeats and how long she wanted each color bit to be. We decided that I should strip the top in half so that the color lengths would be shorter and change more often. When plying there was some color matching, but the overlapping of different colors was desirable for this particular sweater.

I spun this yarn with a light pinch because Romney is a heavier wool and can make a dense yarn pretty easily. I didn't want to compress the yarn too much: I wanted a lighter and airier yarn without the woolen surface.

From Julia Farwell-Clay, designer:

When I originally spun the sample yarn for this sweater it was a DK-weight yarn with the colors as marled as possible. I ended up being pressed for time to both spin and design this sweater, so I asked my friend Beth Smith to spin the yarn for me. What Beth sent was a lighter-weight yarn than I would have spun for myself. This ended up being a wise decision on her part, as the Romney made for a lofty yet slightly crisp yarn.

After swatching, I decided to loosen up both the gauge and the profile of my original sweater idea, knitting the sport/fingering yarn closer to a gauge one might think better suited for a heavier yarn. The resulting fabric allowed the yarn to drape a little, which was suited to a slightly boxy, easy-to-wear shape. A fiber with a different character, like Merino or a silk blended with Bluefaced Leicester, for example, would be equally suitable for this project, so long as it is spun to a yarn that makes a pleasant knitted fabric at the recommended knitted gauge.

Knitting Notes

The sweater is worked flat and in front, back, and sleeve pieces. The front and back are worked modularly, then joined at the shoulder using a three-needle bind off. Hem and neck stitches are picked up after seaming and worked in the round. Sections are named according to their position on the sweater as it will be worn. In other words, a so-called Right section may appear on either the right or left of the working fabric, depending on if a right-side or wrong-side row is being worked, so sections will be referred to by their "as-if-being-worn" position.

KNITTING THE SWEATER

LOWER FRONT LEFT

Using the extra (larger needle and a long-tail cast on), cast on 50 (55, 60, 65, 70, 75) stitches and work in stockinette stitch until piece measures 11½" (12½", 12½", 13½", 13½", 14½"), or 4½" less than desired length to upper arm, ending with a wrong-side row.

Next Row (establish mitered section, RS): Knit to last stitch, M1R, place marker, k1. Keeping right side facing, pick up and knit along left edge at the rate of 2 stitches for every 3 rows, about 57 (62, 62, 67, 67, 72) stitches after marked stitch, but precise number doesn't matter. Turn.

Next Row (WS): P1, knit to last stitch, p1.

Next Row (RS): Knit to marker, M1R, slip marker, k1, knit to end of row. (2 stitches increased)

Repeat these 2 rows 16 times more, or until mitered section is 3" wide, ending with a right-side row. Do not cut yarn. With right side facing, slip all stitches up to marker onto stitch holder or length of scrap yarn and remove marker.

LOWER FRONT RIGHT

With wrong side facing, purl across live stitches.

Next Row (RS): Knit all stitches.

Continue in stockinette stitch until section measures 6½" (7½", 8½", 9½", 10½", 11½"), or until entire front measures 19" (21", 23", 25", 27", 29") across. Bind off all stitches.

With right side facing, return held stitches to working needle, starting at right edge of work.

UPPER FRONT LEFT

With right side facing, join new yarn at end of the held stitches (at mitered corner) and pick up and knit 2 stitches for every 3 rows along upper edge of Lower Front Right, about 32 (37, 42, 47, 52, 57) stitches.

Next Row (WS): Purl across all stitches (including the previously held ones) along the full width of the front.

Next Row (RS): Knit 36 (41, 46, 51, 56, 61) stitches. Place remaining stitches on holder and set aside.

Work these 36 (41, 46, 51, 56, 61) stitches in stockinette stitch as established until section measures 4" (4½", 5¼", 6", 6½", 7") or 14½" (15½", 15½", 16½", 16½", 17½") from initial cast on at lower hem.

FRONT NECK LEFT SHAPING

Next Row (RS): Knit.

Next Row (WS): Bind off as required until 36 (40, 45, 49, 53, 57) stitches remain. Purl to end of row.

Next Row (RS): Knit all stitches.

Next Row (WS): Bind off 3 stitches. Purl to end of row.

Bind off 1 stitch at neck edge every wrong-side row three times, or until 30 (34, 39, 43, 47, 51) stitches remain. Work until section measures 5½" (6", 6¾", 7½", 8", 8½"), or 21½" (23", 23¾", 25½", 26", 27½") total length from cast-on edge at lower hem. Place shoulder stitches on holder and set aside.

UPPER FRONT RIGHT

Setup Mitered Section: Return held stitches of Lower Front Right to needle.

With right side facing, join yarn at neck edge and pick up and knit 2 stitches for every 3 rows along Left

Front vertical edge, place removable stitch marker in the last stitch [about 20 (23, 26, 30, 33, 35) stitches total]. Continuing around the corner, work across stitches of the Lower Front Right.

Note: The following section is worked in garter stitch with purl selvedge.

Next Row (WS): P1, k to last stitch, p1.

Next Row (RS): Knit to last stitch before marked stitch, cdd, knit to end of row.

Repeat last 2 rows 16 more times, or until mitered section is 3" wide, ending with a right-side row. Move the stitch marker up onto the needle, to the left of the cdd stitch (when looked at from the right side).

From here you will work back and forth in stockinette on the stitches (the horizontally oriented stitches) to the left of marked stitch, decreasing away the stitches on the other side of the marked stitch.

Next Row (WS): Purl to marker, p2tog. Turn work.

Next Row (RS): Slip stitch from right needle to left needle, k2tog, knit to end of row.

Next Row (WS): Purl to marker, turn; *do not work a held stitch.*

Next Row (RS): Slip stitch from right needle to left needle, k2tog, knit to end of row.

Next Row (WS): Purl to marker, p2tog. Turn work.

Next Row (RS): K to marker, turn; do not work a held stitch.

Continue in this way, working held stitches together with first or last stitch in row 2 out of every 3 rows until all held stitches are worked. End having completed a wrong-side row.

FRONT NECK RIGHT SHAPING

Next Row (RS): Bind off as required until 36 (40, 45, 49, 53, 57) stitches remain. Knit to end of row.

Next Row (WS): Purl all stitches.

Next Row (RS): Bind off 3 stitches, knit remaining stitches.

Bind off 1 stitch at every right-side neck edge three times, or until 30 (34, 39, 43, 47, 51) stitches remain. Work until section measures 5½" (6", 6¾", 7½", 8", 8½") or 21½" (23", 23¾", 25½", 26", 27½") total length from cast-on edge at lower hem. Place shoulder stitches on holder and set aside.

LOWER BACK PANEL

This section is worked side to side.

Setup: With larger needle, cast on 75 (75, 80, 80, 85, 85) stitches.

Work in stockinette stitch until piece measures 8" (9", 10", 11", 12", 13"), ending with a wrong-side row.

Next Row (RS): Knit.

Next Row (WS): P1, k to last stitch, p1.

Continue piece in garter stitch with wrong-side purl selvedge as established for 3", ending with a wrong-side row.

Continue in stockinette stitch an additional 8" (9", 10", 11", 12", 13"), until Lower Back Panel measures 19" (21", 23", 25", 27", 29") across. Bind off all stitches.

UPPER BACK PANEL

Setup: With right side facing and starting at cast-on end, pick up along upper edge of Lower Back Panel as follows: 2 stitches for every 3 rows in stockinette sections and 1 stitch for every garter-stitch ridge. [about 95 (105, 115, 125, 135, 145) stitches]

Work in garter stitch for 3", ending with a wrong-side row.

Work in stockinette stitch with wrong-side purl selvedge as before until section measures 7" from pickup row, ending with a wrong-side row.

Place shoulder markers 30 (34, 39, 43, 47, 51) stitches from each end.

Work next row, bind off neck stitches between markers.

Join front to back shoulders using three-needle bind off (see page 229).

SLEEVES

(MAKE 2)

Setup: Using smaller needle, cast on 46 (46, 50, 50, 54, 54) stitches.

Work in garter stitch for 1½".

Switch to larger needle and work in stockinette stitch until sleeve measures 3" from cast-on edge, ending with a wrong-side row.

Increase Row (RS): K1, M1, knit to last stitch, M1, k1. (2 stitches increased)

Work this increase row every 12 (10, 8, 6, 6, 6) rows 7 (10, 12, 15, 16, 18) times altogether. [60 (66, 74, 80, 86, 90) stitches]

Continue until sleeve measures 17" (17", 18", 18", 19" 19") from cast-on edge. Bind off all stitches.

FINISHING

Wet-block all pieces to schematic measurements.

KNITTING THE NECK

Setup: Using smaller needle, join yarn at right shoulder seam with right side facing, pick up and knit 1 stitch in each shoulder seam and 1 stitch for every bound-off stitch across back neck for 38 (40, 40, 42, 44, 46) stitches, then 10 stitches down left front neck slope, 23 (25, 25, 27, 29, 31) stitches across front garter and bound-off edge, and 10 stitches up right front neck slope. [81 (85, 85, 89, 93, 97) stitches]

Work garter stitch in the round for 3 rounds (purl 1 round, knit 1 round, purl 1 round).

Bind off all stitches loosely.

Place markers on front and back pieces, 6" (6½", 7¼", 8", 8½", 9") down from shoulder seam. Sew sleeves to body between markers. Sew side seams.

HEM EDGE

With right side facing and using smaller needle, pick up approximately 190 (210, 230, 250, 270, 290) stitches along hem edge of piece by picking up 2 stitches for every 3 rows of stockinette stitch and 1 stitch for every garter-stitch ridge.

Work garter stitch in the round (purl 1 round, knit 1 round) until hem section measures 1½".

Bind off all stitches.

Weave in all ends.

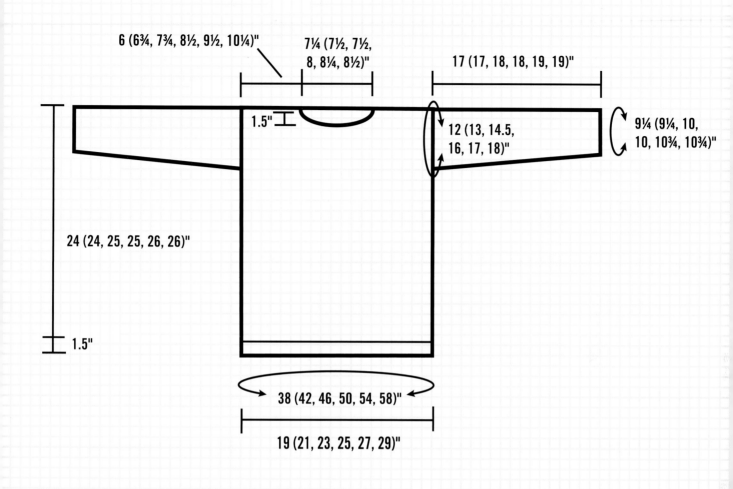

6 (6¾, 7¾, 8½, 9½, 10¼)"

7¼ (7½, 7½, 8, 8¼, 8½)"

17 (17, 18, 18, 19, 19)"

1.5"

12 (13, 14.5, 16, 17, 18)"

9¼ (9¼, 10, 10, 10¾, 10¾)"

24 (24, 25, 25, 26, 26)"

1.5"

38 (42, 46, 50, 54, 58)"

19 (21, 23, 25, 27, 29)"

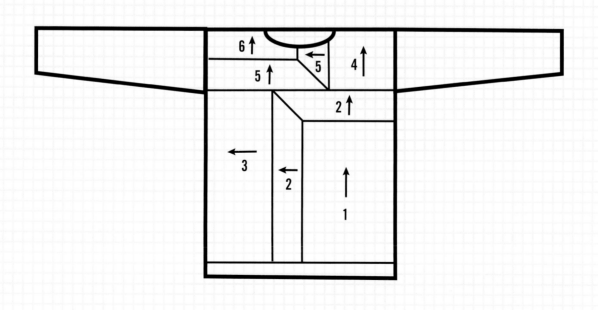

6

5

5

4

2

3

2

1

ORDER OF KNITTING

WENNY SHAWL
Designed by **Amy King**

Singles yarns come in all sizes. This shawl shows off the skinnier side of singles. Much like its thicker cousin (see Bump in the Night, page 179), this shawl has a single cable accenting the edge, this time with a bit more openness and toothiness.

FINISHED MEASUREMENTS
65" wide × 26" long at the center

FIBER
Spunky Eclectic, Wensleydale, 7 oz combed top, Lime Beginnings in the Progression colorway

YARN DESCRIPTION
- Singles yarn
- Fingering weight
- Worsted spun
- 1,200 ypp
- 24 wpi
- Drafted short draw
- Lightly fulled

YARN AMOUNT
560 yds, but more or less could be used (see Knitting Notes on next page)

GAUGE
18 stitches and 28 rows = 4" × 4" in stockinette stitch

NEEDLES
US 6 (4 mm) needles, straight or 24" or longer circular needle, *or size needed to obtain correct gauge*

OTHER SUPPLIES
- Stitch marker
- Cable needle
- Yarn needle

ABBREVIATIONS
C4R Slip next 2 stitches to cable needle and hold in back of work, k2, then k2 from cable needle

Spinning Notes

This fiber is a little tricky: you need to spin to the staple length. This is a great thing to remember. When you work with Wensleydale, pull out a bit and look at it. It's long! It really doesn't need a super lot of twist to hold together. Spinning this low twist for singles should be a dream. Set that wheel to pull in faster to help remind you to let go quicker than you would for other fibers.

Knitting Notes

This shawl is worked side to side, first by increasing to the center and then by decreasing to the other end. It can be worked two ways. I've given directions for specific sizes and stitch amounts to increase to, but if you're worried about the amount of yarn you have or you know you have more and want a larger shawl, you can divide your yarn in half. Use half to create the first (increase) part of the shawl, and then use the other half to create the second half of the shawl. Either way you will have a lovely shawl in the end.

Pattern Stitches

Shark Tooth

(worked flat over 3 stitches, increased to 8)

Row 1 (and all odd-numbered rows through row 11): Knit all stitches.

Row 2: Slip 1, yo, k2.

Row 4: Slip 1, yo, k3.

Row 6: Slip 1, yo, k4.

Row 8: Slip 1, yo, k5.

Row 10: Slip 1, yo, k6.

Row 12: Bind off 5 (1 stitch remains on right needle), k2.

Cable

(worked flat over 6 stitches)

Row 1 (RS): P1, k4, p1.

Row 2 (and all even-numbered rows through Row 6): K1, p4, k1.

Row 3: P1, C4R, p1.

Row 5: P1, k4, p1.

Shark Tooth

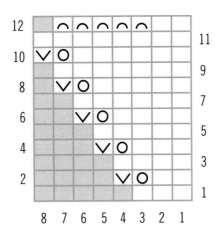

Cable Pattern

| | RS: knit WS: purl | | yo | | RS: slip WS: slip purlwise with yarn in front | | no stitch |
| | RS: purl WS: knit | | bind off | | C4R | | |

KNITTING THE SHAWL

Cast on 16 stitches.

Knit 4 rows.

INCREASE SECTION

Note: While the body of the shawl is gaining only 1 stitch per right-side row, sometimes the edging will be gaining a stitch as well and sometimes losing 5.

Row 1 (RS): K2, yo, k2tog, k1, yo, place marker, work Cable pattern (see facing page), yo, k2tog, work Shark Tooth. (1 body stitch increased)

Row 2 and all WS rows: Work Shark Tooth, p2, work Cable pattern, purl to the last 2 stitches, k2.

Row 3: K2, yo, k2tog, knit to the marker, yo, slip marker, work Cable pattern, yo, k2tog, work Shark Tooth.

Continue as established until you have completed 16 full repeats of the Shark Tooth edging. You will have 3 stitches for the tooth, and the rest of the shawl will have 109 stitches. (112 stitches total)

Note: If you are working this shawl with two balls of yarn instead, ensure you end this section close to the end of the first ball, ending after row 12 of Shark Tooth edging.

DECREASE SECTION

Row 1: K2, yo, k2tog, knit until 3 stitches before the marker, sk2p, yo, slip marker, work Cable pattern, yo, k2tog, work Shark Tooth.

Row 2 and all WS rows: Work Shark Tooth, p2, work Cable pattern, p to the last 2 stitches, k2.

Continue as established until you have decreased to 16 stitches.

Knit 4 rows.

FINISHING

Wet-block and pin to size. Be sure to pin out the points when blocking the shawl. Weave in ends.

LA CUERDA
Designed by Laura Nelkin

Knit jewelry is an excellent way to use up smaller bits of handspun. La Cuerda, a long sinuous rope, plays with a new technique Laura developed for working beaded I-cord. Beads are placed on stitches to create rings of sparkle around the entire I-cord strand. The beads are added individually on regular stitches and in sets of three on elongated stitches, creating a pattern of color and texture throughout the strand. It's incredibly addictive to experiment with the placement of color. Start to play, and see what you come up with — the possibilities are endless! La Cuerda is long enough to be worn wrapped two or three times around the neck and is easily adjusted to make it longer or shorter.

FINISHED MEASUREMENTS
1/2" wide × 60" long

FIBER
Blue Moon Fiber Arts 50% Merino/
   50% Yak top, 0.5 oz color: Cranberry Bogged

YARN DESCRIPTION
- 2-ply slightly more twisted than balanced
- 1250 ypp
- 12–14 wpi
- Worsted draft
- Hot soak and hang to finish

YARN AMOUNT
55 yds

GAUGE
21 stitches and 30 rows = 4" × 4" in stockinette stitch

NEEDLES
Two US 5 (3.75 mm) double-pointed needles
   or size needed to obtain correct gauge

OTHER SUPPLIES
- Hook-and-eye or toggle clasp
- 252 size 8° Miyuki Delica beads (approximately 10 g), Garnet Gold Luster (color A)
- 276 size 8° Miyuki Delica beads (approximately 11 g), Gunmetal (color B)
- US size 14 (0.75 mm), US size 12 (1 mm) steel crochet hook, or Verna-X Beadle Needle for placing beads
- Yarn needle

Spinning Notes

From Carol Knox, spinner

This was fantastic fiber to play with and a beautiful colorway. I spun this short forward draw, drafting back and forth across the top in a worsted style with no twist in the drafting triangle. It made a beautiful, smooth, yet very soft yarn — one of the nicest I've spun.

Knitting Notes

Working I-cord. I-cord needs to be worked on double-pointed needles, as follows:

- Knit 1 row, and *do not turn* your work.

- Slide your work to the other end of your double-pointed needle. The working yarn will be at the wrong end of your work.

- Pull the working yarn around the back of your work and knit the next row.

- Continue in this way, never turning your work but sliding the stitches at the end of every row. Easy!

Wrapping yarn. Insert the right needle into the next stitch on the left needle, wrap the yarn twice around the right needle at its widest circumference, and then knit the stitch. When you encounter these wrapped stitches on the next round, drop the extra wrap, creating an elongated stitch.

Placing beads. With super floss, crochet hook, or Beadle Needle, place bead onto next stitch on left needle, then knit the stitch. This will lock the bead into place. See the appendix, page 230, for more advice on how to do this.

KNITTING THE NECKLACE

Setup: Thread one end of clasp onto yarn. Using the long-tail cast on (see page 228), cast on 2 stitches, slide the clasp up, and then thread the tail of the yarn through the clasp as well. Cast on 2 more stitches. (4 stitches on needle)

Work I-cord throughout.

Rows 1–3: Knit.

Row 4: K1, M1, k2, M1, k1. (6 stitches on needle)

*****Next 12 Rows:** Knit.

Next Row: Place 1 color A bead six times, one on each stitch.

Next 2 Rows: Knit.

Next Row: Knit across, wrapping yarn twice for each stitch.

Next Row: Place 3 color B beads six times (3 beads on each stitch).

Repeat the last 4 rows once more.

Next 3 Rows. Knit.

Next Row: Place 1 color A bead six times, one on each stitch.

Next 12 Rows: Knit.

Next Row: Place 1 color B bead six times (3 beads on each stitch).

Next 2 Rows: Knit.

Next Row: Knit across, wrapping yarn twice for each stitch.

Next Row: Place 3 color A beads six times, as above.

Repeat the last 4 rows once more.

Next 3 Rows: Knit.

Next Row: Place 1 color B bead six times, as above.

Repeat from * four more times.

Next 12 rows: Knit.

Next Row. Place 1 color A bead six times, as above.

Next 2 Rows: Knit.

Next Row: Knit across, wrapping yarn twice for each stitch.

Next Row: Place 3 color B beads six times, as above.

Repeat the last 4 rows once more.

Next 3 Rows: Knit.

Next Row: Place 1 color A bead six times, as above.

Next 12 rows: Knit.

Next Row: K1, k2tog twice, k1. (4 stitches on needle)

Next 2 Rows. Knit.

Cut yarn, leaving an 8" tail.

K2, thread the second half of the clasp onto yarn, slide it up so that it is touching last stitch worked on the right needle, k2.

Bind off 1 stitch, slide the cut end of yarn through clasp again, bind off the remaining stitches.

FINISHING

Weave in all ends, making sure to thread the ends through the clasps a few times to secure them. Block if desired.

WINTER LIBRARY SHAWL

Designed by **Jillian Moreno**

I do a lot of my work at my public library, and in the winter there is a bit of a breeze that flows through the spot I like best. This is my favorite shawl to wear at the library. The quarter-moon shape and the weight of the fiber and gauge help it stay on my shoulders without slipping, and the bit of flowered embroidery brings a little spring to my winter work.

FINISHED MEASUREMENTS

81" long × 18" at its widest point

FIBER

Sweet Georgia Yarns, Bluefaced Leicester top, 10 oz, Ultraviolet (MC)

Sweet Georgia Yarns, 50% Merino/50% silk top, ½ oz each in the following colors: Glacier (CA), Raspberry (CB), Dutch (CC), Melon (CD), Basil (CE), and Wisteria (CF)

YARN DESCRIPTION

- **MC:** 2-ply
- 600 ypp
- 8–9 wpi
- Woolen draft
- Soak and snap finishing
- **CC:** 2-ply
- 775 ypp
- 12 wpi
- Woolen draft
- Soak and snap finishing

YARN AMOUNT

Ultraviolet (MC): 365 yds; 25 yards for each of the following:

- Glacier (CA)
- Raspberry (CB)
- Dutch (CC)
- Melon (CD)
- Basil (CE)
- Wisteria (CF)

(*Note:* These fiber amounts do not include fiber for sampling or swatching.)

GAUGE

12 stitches and 18 rows = 4" × 4" in stockinette stitch, after blocking

NEEDLES

One US 7 (4.5 mm) circular needle, 32" or longer, *or size needed to obtain correct gauge*

OTHER SUPPLIES

- Stitch markers (optional; removable are recommended)
- Yarn needle
- Tapestry or crewel needle for embroidery

Spinning Notes

I spun the embroidery yarns woolen and plied each to balance, looser than you might think you want for stitching. I did it this way because I want my stitches to spread softly on the knitted surface.

Pattern Stitch

Moss Stitch

(worked flat on an even number of stitches)

Row 1: *K1, p1; repeat from * to end of row.

Row 2: *P1, k1; repeat from * to end of row.

KNITTING THE SHAWL

Setup: Using MC, cast on 244 stitches. Do not join; the shawl is worked back and forth in rows.

Work Moss Stitch (see Pattern Stitch) for 4 rows.

SET UP SHORT ROWS

Row 1 (RS): K127, turn.

Row 2 (WS): P10, turn.

You now have two obvious gaps where you turned. If you wish, place removable markers in the gaps to help you navigate. If you are using markers, remove them before you work the decrease, and then replace them on the right needle before you turn at the end of a row.

SHAPE SHAWL BODY

Row 1: Knit to 1 stitch before gap, ssk, k2, turn work.

Row 2: Purl to 1 stitch before gap, p2tog, p2, turn work.

Repeat these 2 rows until all stitches have been worked, ending with a wrong-side row. (166 stitches)

Work in Moss Stitch for 4 rows. Bind off.

FINISHING

Wet-block the shawl to the finished measurements. Weave in ends. Embroider flower motif as shown in diagram or in your own design.

RIGBY CARDIGAN

Designed by **Bristol Ivy**

One of my favorite reasons for knitting with handspun is its texture, which I wanted to accentuate in this sweater. My goal was a project that felt textured and cozy, and that took advantage of the wonderful zeal and vibrancy handspun yarn has. The first step toward this was choosing to make rolags from the handdyed sliver and spinning it into an open, fluffy, woolen-spun 2-ply with a little bit of extra ply twist. The yarn is bouncy, lofty, and full of life, with the irregularities and toothiness inherent in carded fiber. From there, I picked a simple stitch pattern that would further accentuate that texture — a variation on Fisherman's Rib called English Rib. Typically, any stitch that compresses the row gauge could lead to a heavy, sagging fabric, but the open and airy woolen-spun yarn construction counteracted that. The cardigan that resulted is simple, clean, and wearable, with hints of architecture in the waist shaping in the back; ribs trail together and branch off to create a structured and flattering shape.

SIZES
Woman XS (S, M, L, XL, 2XL, 3XL, 4XL)

FINISHED MEASUREMENTS
33½" (37½", 41½", 45½", 48¾", 52¾", 56¾", 60¾") bust circumference, with fronts overlapping 3" (3", 3", 3", 3¾", 3¾", 3¾", 3¾")

FIBER
PortFiber, 100% domestic Rambouillet, 14½ (16¼, 18, 19¾, 21¼, 23, 24¾, 26½) oz (15% buffer added), Fields of Gold colorway (combed sliver), carded into rolags

YARN DESCRIPTION
- 2-ply
- Approximately 1,400 ypp
- 13⅓ wpi
- Assisted long draw drafting
- Finished by soaking, spinning out excess water, and whacking

YARN AMOUNT
Approximately 1,270 (1,420, 1,575, 1,730, 1,860, 2,015, 2,165, 2,320) yds

GAUGE
20 stitches and 40 rows = 4" × 4" in English Rib, after blocking, on size A needles

26 stitches and 40 rows = 4" × 4" in stockinette stitch, after blocking, on size B needles

NEEDLES

Size A: US 6 (4 mm) circular needle for English Rib, 32" or longer, *or size needed to obtain correct gauge*

Size B: set of four or five US 5 (3.75 mm) double-pointed needles, at least 4" long, *or size needed to obtain correct gauge*

Size C: set of four or five US 4 (3.5 mm) double-pointed needles, at least 4" long

Size D: US 7 (4.5 mm) circular needle, 32" or longer for 1x1 ribbing on body

OTHER SUPPLIES

- Stitch markers
- Cable needle
- Stitch holders or scrap yarn
- Yarn needle

ABBREVIATIONS

CD-L (cabled decrease left) Slip next 2 stitches to cable needle and hold in front, insert needle as if to purl through first stitch on left needle and first stitch on cable needle, purl these stitches together. Insert needle as if to knit through next stitch on cable needle and next stitch on left needle, knit these stitches together (2 stitches decreased; leans left)

CD-R (cabled decrease right) Slip next 2 stitches to cable needle and hold in back, insert needle as if to knit through first stitch on left needle and first stitch on cable needle, knit these stitches together. Insert needle as if to purl through next stitch on cable needle and next stitch on left needle, purl these stitches together (2 stitches decreased; leans right)

Pattern Stitches

English Rib
(worked flat over a multiple of 2 stitches plus 1)

Row 1 (RS): Slip 1, *p1, k1; repeat from * to end.

Row 2 (WS): Slip 1, p1, *k1 below, p1; repeat from * to end.

KNITTING THE SLEEVES

THE SLEEVES

(MAKE 2)

With size C needles and using long-tail cast on (see page 228), cast on 48 (48, 52, 52, 54, 54, 58, 58) stitches. Distribute across needles as you prefer, and join to work in the round.

Ribbing Round: *K1, p1; repeat from * to end.

Work in 1x1 ribbing as established until work measures 2" from cast on.

Change to size B needles.

Work even in stockinette stitch for 13 (11, 9, 9, 7, 5, 5, 5) rounds.

Next Round (increase round): K1, M1L, knit to 1 stitch before end, M1R, k1. (2 stitches increased; 50 [50, 54, 54, 56, 56, 60, 60] stitches)

Repeat this increase round every 14 (12, 10, 10, 8, 6, 6, 6) rounds 5 (1, 13, 1, 13, 24, 24, 16) more time(s), then every 12 (10, 8, 8, 6, 4, 4, 4) rounds 5 (12, 1, 16, 7, 1, 2, 14) time(s). [70 (76, 82, 88, 96, 106, 112, 120) stitches]

Work even in stockinette stitch until sleeve measures 19" (19", 19½", 19½", 20", 20", 20½", 20½"), ending final round 3 (4, 4, 5, 6, 7, 8, 9) stitches before end.

Next Round: Bind off next 6 (8, 8, 10, 12, 14, 16, 18) stitches, work in stockinette stitch as established to end. You will now work flat. [64 (68, 74, 78, 84, 92, 96, 102) stitches]

Next Row (WS): Purl.

Sizes XS and S only: Work 2 rows even in stockinette stitch.

All sizes:

Next Row (decrease row, RS): K1, ssk, knit to 3 stitches before end, k2tog, k1. [2 stitches decreased; 62 (66, 72, 76, 82, 90, 94, 100) stitches remain]

Repeat this decrease row every other row 29 (31, 34, 36, 38, 40, 43, 45) more times. (4 [4, 4, 4, 6, 10, 8, 10] stitches remain)

Bind off all stitches and set aside.

BODY

- With size D needle and using long-tail cast on, cast on 191 (211, 231, 251, 271, 291, 311, 331) stitches. Do not join.

Next row (WS): P1, *k1, p1; repeat from * to end.

Next row (RS): K1, *p1, k1; repeat from * to end.

Work even in 1x1 rib as established until work measures 2" from cast-on edge, ending after a wrong-side row.

Next Row (RS): Work 50 (55, 60, 68, 75, 80, 85, 90) stitches in rib as established, place marker for side, work 17 (19, 21, 23, 23, 25, 27, 29) stitches in rib as established, place marker, work 18 (20, 22, 24, 24, 26, 28, 30) stitches in rib as established, place marker, work 21 (23, 25, 21, 27, 29, 31, 33) stitches in rib as established, place marker, work 18 (20, 22, 24, 24, 26, 28, 30) stitches in rib as established, place marker, work 17 (19, 21, 23, 23, 25, 27, 29) stitches in rib as established, place marker, work 50 (55, 60, 68, 75, 80, 85, 90) stitches in rib as established to end. New markers placed will be referred to as shaping markers.

Next Row (WS): Work row 2 of English Rib.

Work even in English Rib for 22 more rows.

Next row (decrease row, RS): Work in English Rib as established to side marker, slip marker, (work in English Rib as established to 4 stitches before shaping marker, CD-R, slip marker) twice, work in English Rib as established to marker, slip marker, (CD-L, work in English Rib as established to marker, slip marker) twice, work in English Rib as established to end. (8 stitches decreased)

Repeat this decrease row every 24th row once more, then every 22nd row twice, ending with a decrease row. [159 (179, 199, 219, 239, 259, 279, 299) stitches remain]

Work even in English Rib for 1", ending after a wrong-side row.

Next row (increase row, RS): Work English Rib as established to side marker, slip marker, (work in English Rib as established to 2 stitches before shaping marker, k1-yo-k1 into next stitch, p1, slip marker) twice, work in English Rib as established to marker, slip marker, (p1, k1-yo-k1 into next stitch, work in English Rib as established to marker, slip marker) twice, work in English Rib as established to end. (8 stitches increased)

Repeat this increase row every 12 (12, 14, 14, 14, 14, 14) rows 2 (2, 1, 1, 1, 3, 3, 3) more time(s), then every 10 (10, 12, 12, 12, 0, 0, 0) rows 1 (1, 2, 2, 2, 0, 0, 0) time(s), ending with an increase row. [191 (211, 231, 251, 271, 291, 311, 331) stitches]

Work even in English Rib for 10 (10, 12, 12, 12, 14, 14, 14) rows.

Next Row (RS): Work in English Rib as established to 5 (6, 7, 9, 10, 11, 14, 15) stitches before side marker, bind off next 5 (6, 7, 9, 10, 11, 14, 15) stitches knitwise, remove marker, work in English Rib as established to next side marker, removing shaping markers as you go, remove side marker, bind off next 5 (6, 7, 9, 10, 11, 14, 15) stitches knitwise, work in English Rib as established to end. Do not break yarn. Place Back stitches and Right Front stitches on holders or waste yarn. [45 (49, 53, 59, 65, 69, 71, 75) stitches on needle]

Left Front

Work even in English Rib as established for 5 rows.

Next Row (decrease row, RS): Work 3 stitches in English Rib as established, CD-L, work in English Rib as established to end. (2 stitches decreased)

Repeat this decrease row every 6th row 11 (10, 9, 5, 6, 5, 6, 5) more times, then every 4th row 3 (6, 9, 16, 16, 19, 19, 22) times. [28 (32, 36, 42, 44, 48, 50, 54) stitches decreased; 15 (15, 15, 15, 19, 19, 19, 19) stitches remain]

Work even in English Rib as established until work measures 2¼" (2½", 2¾", 2", 2", 2¼", 2¾", 3") from final decrease, slightly stretched. Place all stitches on holder or waste yarn. Break yarn.

Back

Replace stitches on needle and rejoin yarn ready to work a wrong-side row. [91 (101, 111, 115, 121, 131, 141, 151) stitches on needle]

Work even in English Rib as established for 5 rows.

Next Row (decrease row, RS): Work 3 stitches in English Rib as established, CD-L, work in English Rib as established to 7 stitches before end, CD-R, work 3 stitches in English Rib to end. [4 stitches decreased; 87 (97, 107, 111, 117, 127, 137, 147) stitches remain]

Repeat this decrease row every 6th row 11 (10, 9, 5, 6, 5, 6, 5) more times, then every 4th row 3 (6, 9, 16, 16, 19, 19, 22) times. [56 (64, 72, 84, 88, 96, 100, 108) stitches decreased; 31 (33, 35, 27, 29, 31, 37, 39) stitches remain]

Work 1 wrong-side row even.

Bind off all stitches using a sewn (see page 229) or stretchy bind off to match English Rib gauge.

Right Front

Replace stitches on needle and rejoin yarn ready to work a wrong-side row. [45 (49, 53, 59, 65, 69, 71, 75) stitches on needle]

Work even in English Rib as established for 5 rows.

Next Row (decrease row, RS): Work in English Rib as established to 7 stitches before end, CD-R, work 3 stitches in English Rib as established to end. (2 stitches decreased)

Repeat this decrease row every 6th row 11 (10, 9, 5, 6, 5, 6, 5) more times, then every 4th row 3 (6, 9, 16, 16, 19, 19, 22) times. [28 (32, 36, 42, 44, 48, 50, 54) stitches decreased; 15 (15, 15, 15, 19, 19, 19, 19) stitches remain]

Work even in English Rib as established until work measures 2¼" (2½", 2¾", 2", 2", 2¼", 2¾", 3") from final decrease, slightly stretched. Place all stitches on holder or waste yarn. *Do not break yarn.*

FINISHING

Seam sleeves into place and seam underarms. Note that due to differences in gauge, the ratio of rows in the raglan seams and stitches in the underarm seams will not be 1:1; however, the lengths should be equal if gauge was accurate.

Replace front stitches on needles, and join using a three-needle bind off (see page 229). Be careful not to twist either of the pieces. Stretching slightly so that the three-needle bind off is at the center back, seam into place.

Weave in all ends, and block to measurements.

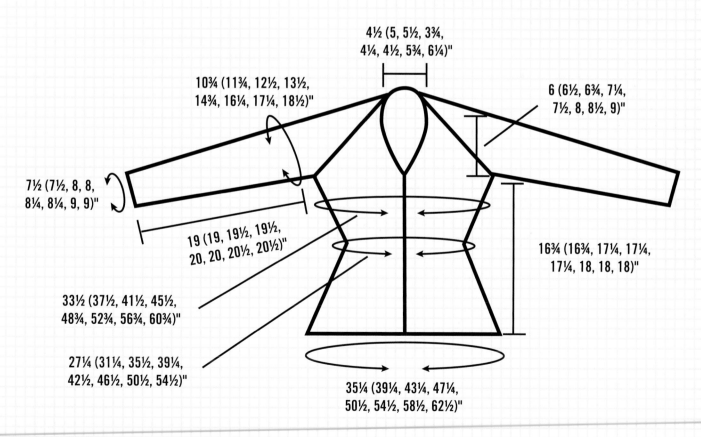

4½ (5, 5½, 3¾, 4¼, 4½, 5¾, 6¼)"

10¾ (11¾, 12½, 13½, 14¾, 16¼, 17¼, 18½)"

6 (6½, 6¾, 7¼, 7½, 8, 8½, 9)"

7½ (7½, 8, 8, 8¼, 8¼, 9, 9)"

19 (19, 19½, 19½, 20, 20, 20½, 20½)"

16¾ (16¾, 17¼, 17¼, 17¼, 18, 18, 18)"

33½ (37½, 41½, 45½, 48¾, 52¾, 56¾, 60¾)"

27¼ (31¼, 35½, 39¼, 42½, 46½, 50½, 54½)"

35¼ (39¼, 43¼, 47¼, 50½, 54½, 58½, 62½)"

HIVE MIND
Designed by Adrian Bizilia

The cellular patterning and deep, dark honey color of these mittens remind me of a beehive. These are a simple knit with peasant thumbs and a bold graphic stitch pattern that is easy to memorize. A contrasting color outline sharply defines the mitten edge. These mittens will look great in two semisolids or a semisolid and a striped yarn.

SIZES
Adult S (M, L)

FINISHED MEASUREMENTS
8¼" (9", 9¾") circumference; 9¾" (10½", 11¼") length

FIBER
MC: Hello Yarn, handdyed Corriedale wool, 2 oz (2.25 oz, 2.5 oz), Treacle semisolid

CC: Hello Yarn, handdyed Corriedale wool, 1.5 oz (1.75 oz, 2 oz), Frost handpaint

YARN DESCRIPTION
- 2-ply
- 1,000 ypp
- 12 wpi
- Worsted spun
- Soaked and hung to dry

YARN AMOUNT
MC: Treacle, 120 (140, 160) yds

CC: Frost, 100 (110, 120) yds

GAUGE
27 (25, 23) stitches and 32 (30, 28) rounds = 4" × 4" in colorwork pattern, after blocking

NEEDLES
The pattern is sized by gauge; use the needle size needed to obtain correct gauge. I've suggested needle sizes for each garment size:

- *Small:* US 3 (3.25 mm)
- *Medium:* US 4 (3.5 mm)
- *Large:* US 5 (3.75 mm)

You may use any of the following for working a small circumference in the round:

- A set of four or five double-pointed needles, at least 5" long
- Two circular needles, 16" or longer
- One circular needle, 32" or longer (for Magic Loop)

OTHER SUPPLIES
- Smooth scrap yarn for cast on and holding thumb stitches
- Bit of contrasting fiber for separating skeins
- Yarn needle
- Stitch marker
- Cable needle

Spinning Notes

For these mittens, I wanted a springy, balanced, 2-ply sport-weight yarn, so here's what I aimed for:

- 24 wpi singles
- 12 wpi plied
- 6 tpi singles
- 3 tpi plied

Both fibers are combed tops that I spun using the worsted short-draw method. I wanted a hard-wearing yarn for these mittens, so I flattened the fibers as I spun the singles, taming them and creating a smooth yarn that would also show the patterning better.

For the MC (Treacle semisolid fiber). Break the wool into two equal lengths and spin each from the end onto its own bobbin, then ply from the bobbins.

For the CC (Frost handpainted fiber). You want the colors to line up, but not perfectly, so that there is a bit of overlap and therefore soft transitioning between colors. Split the length of fiber into four equal pieces lengthwise. Roll them into little balls with the same color on the outside of each ball. Split the contrasting color fiber into two equal lengths. On one bobbin, spin piece 1, starting at the outside end. Spin in a piece of scrap fiber (something that's a different color from your project fiber), just so you'll know when plying that you've come to the end of the first skein, followed by piece 2, starting at the outside end. On a second bobbin, spin piece 3, starting at the outside end. Spin in the piece of contrasting fiber, then piece 4, starting at the outside end. Ply your handpainted singles, allowing some overlap where the colors

change. Depending on the dye job and evenness of spinning, you might want to do a little surgery and remove some of one singles to help the colors meet up the way you want. When you get to your contrasting-color sections, remove those and tie a knot. That's the separation of your two — hopefully matching! — skeins, one for each mitten.

Finishing. Soak your yarn in warm water and shampoo or wool wash, rinse, and hang to dry.

Knitting Notes

When working with the handpainted skeins, be sure to start at the same end of each ball for each mitten so that your colors will match. Tying a knot in the same end of both skeins will help you find the matching ends later. These mittens are knit in the round from the bottom up.

Charts are for stranded knitting with all knit stitches (stockinette) and are read from right to left on all rounds.

I did not catch the floating yarn at all in the body of the mitten, but I did twist the yarns together at each side of every thumb round to keep them from pulling across the inside of the thumb.

Tubular Cast On for 2x2 Ribbing
METHOD 1

Cast on 26 stitches in scrap yarn. Do not join. Switch to MC.

Round 1: (K1, yo) across. Distribute stitches across needles as you prefer, and join for working in the round. (52 stitches)

METHOD 2

Crochet a chain of 26 stitches with scrap yarn. Switch to MC.

Round 1: (K1 into bump at back of crochet chain, yo) across. Distribute stitches across needles as you prefer, and join for working in the round. (52 stitches)

FOR BOTH CAST-ON TECHNIQUES

Round 2: *Wyib, slip the knit stitch purlwise; purl the yo; repeat from * around.

Round 3: *K1; wyif, slip the purl stitch purlwise; repeat from * around.

Round 4: *Wyib, slip the knit purlwise, p1; repeat from * around.

Round 5: *K1, slip 2nd stitch onto cable needle and hold to back, k1, p1 from cable needle, p1; repeat from * around. Remove scrap yarn.

KNITTING THE MITTENS

(MAKE 2)

With MC, cast on 52 stitches with Tubular Cast On for 2x2 Ribbing.

Ribbing Round: *K2, p2; repeat from * around.

Work 8 rounds in ribbing as established.

THE HANDS

Work Mitten Chart (page 215) twice around, joining CC when required. Work as established until round 23 is complete. On the next round, you will place scrap yarn for the thumb position, as follows: Work in pattern as established on the back of the hand; begin the second repeat of the pattern on the palm side of the hand. When you get to the insertion point marked on the chart, knit the 11 marked stitches and place them on scrap yarn. *Note:* The insertion mark for the right mitten is red; the insertion mark for the left mitten is green.

Return stitches to left needle, and complete round per chart.

Continue as established until chart is complete. Cut both yarns, leaving 6" tails. Thread both tails onto yarn needle and pull through final stitches to close mitten top.

THE THUMBS

Without removing scrap yarn, place upper 11 and lower 11 thumb stitches onto your needles. Remove scrap yarn.

Thumb setup: Starting at stitches at lower side (cuff side of mitten), rejoin yarns and following appropriate Thumb Chart (Right or Left, as required), work the first 11 stitches per chart, pick up and knit a stitch with MC, and work it together with the following chart stitch; work in pattern to end of chart, and pick up and knit another stitch with MC at the end of the round, and slip it to the first needle of the round.

Next round: K2tog in color as indicated by chart, and complete round in pattern.

Continue as established until chart is complete. Cut both yarns, leaving 6" tails. Thread both tails onto yarn needle and pull through final stitches to close thumb top.

FINISHING

Wash and block mittens. Weave in ends.

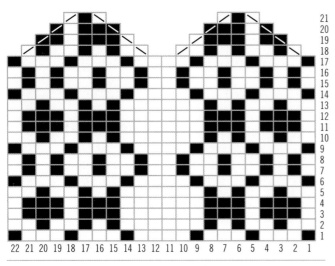

Left Thumb

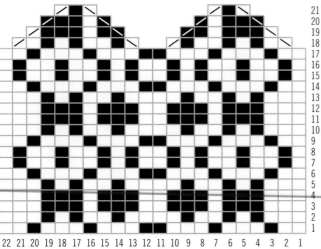

Right Thumb

5⅝" (6", 6⅜")

9¾" (10½", 11¼")

4⅛" (4½", 4⅞")

8¼" (9", 9¾")

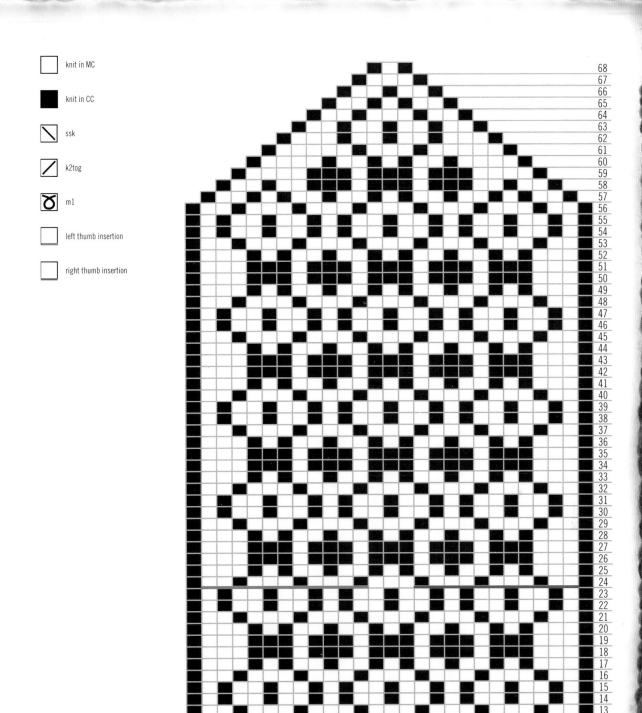

knit in MC

knit in CC

ssk

k2tog

m1

left thumb insertion

right thumb insertion

**Work this chart
twice around for
52 stitches.**

DYE GODDESS PULLOVER
Designed by Jillian Moreno

When I saw the sweater Lisa Souza was wearing at the New York State Sheep and Wool Festival in Rhinebeck — a pullover knit from spiral-ply yarn — I fell instantly in love. It looked like the exact sweater I want to wear on blustery fall days — it's the knitting equivalent of a big bowl of comforting soup. I asked Lisa to choose and dye the fiber for my version, and she presented me with deep, rich greens in matte Merino for the thick-and-thin ply and a bright acid green in lustrous Merino/silk for the core ply, which is so shiny it flashes like sparks over the sweater.

SIZES
Woman S (M, L, XL, 2XL)

FINISHED MEASUREMENTS
Chest: 35" (41", 44", 46½", 49½")
This sweater is loose and easy Kaanapali; recom-
mended ease for this sweater is at least 3".

FIBER
Thick-and-thin: Lisa Souza Knitwear and Dyeworks,
Merino, top, Kaanapali, 17 (19, 20, 21, 22) ounces
Core: Lisa Souza Knitwear and Dyeworks, 50%
Merino 50%/50% silk, top, Gween, 7½ (8, 8½, 9½,
10) ounces

YARN DESCRIPTION
Spiral-ply yarn is made up of two plies. One ply is
used as a core yarn and one ply (the thick-and-thin
yarn) is wrapped around the core by plying with
uneven tension. The spiral-ply and core yarns were
spun with a worsted draft; the thick-and-thin yarn
was spun with a woolen draft.
Spiral-ply yarn: 7.5 wpi; 500 ypp
Core yarn: 28 wpi; 1,600 ypp
Thick-and-thin yarn: 6.5 wpi; 900 ypp

YARN AMOUNT
750 (800, 850, 920, 960) yds spiral-ply yarn
(*Note:* This amount does not include fiber for
sampling and swatching.)

GAUGE
11 stitches and 16 rows = 4" × 4" in stockinette stitch
using the larger needles, after blocking

NEEDLES
- US 7 (4.5 mm) needles for working flat
  or size needed to obtain correct gauge
- US 6 (4.0 mm) needles for working flat
- One US 6 (4.0 mm) 16" circular needle

OTHER SUPPLIES
- Yarn needle
- Stitch marker

Spinning Notes

Your core-ply yarn should be heavily twisted — more than what you'd use for a regular 2-ply yarn. I used a twist angle of 60 degrees.

Spinning thick-and-thin yarn takes practice. Sarah Anderson has great instructions in her book *The Spinner's Book of Yarn Designs*.

Knitting Notes

This sweater is knit in pieces from the bottom up.

When swatching your spiral-ply yarn, use a needle size between what you would use for the thickest and for the thinnest parts of the yarn. This yarn is knit a bit looser than you might think necessary to give the thick parts room to puff!

Pattern Stitch

2x2 Rib

(multiple of 4 stitches)

All Rows: *K2, p2; repeat from * to the end.

KNITTING THE BACK

Setup: Using larger needles, cast on 48 (56, 60, 64, 68) stitches.

Work 2x2 Rib (see Pattern Stitch) for 2".

Work in stockinette stitch until piece measures 13" (14", 15", 15", 15"), ending with a wrong-side row.

ARMHOLE SHAPING

At the beginning of the next 2 rows, bind off 4 (4, 5, 5, 6) stitches. [40 (48, 50, 54, 56) stitches remain]

Work even in stockinette stitch until armhole measures 9" (10", 11", 12", 13"), ending with a wrong-side row. Your piece will measure 22" (24", 26", 27", 28") from the cast-on edge. Bind off all stitches.

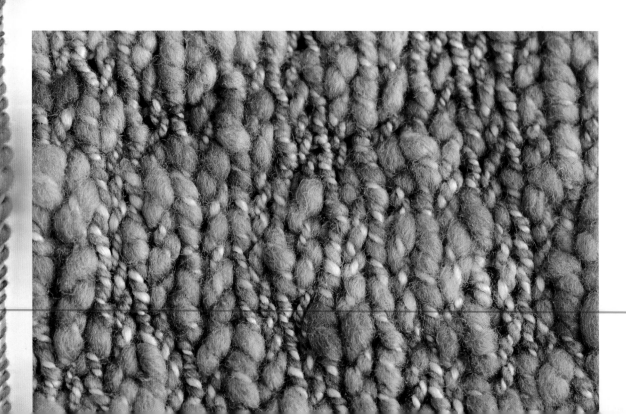

KNITTING THE FRONT

Work as for Knitting the Back to start of Armhole Shaping.

ARMHOLE SHAPING

At the beginning of the next 2 rows, bind off 4 (4, 5, 5, 6) stitches. You now have 40 (48, 50, 54, 56) stitches on your needles. Work in stockinette stitch for 6" (7", 8", 9", 10"), ending with a wrong-side row.

FRONT NECK SHAPING

Next Row (divide for neck, RS): K16 (19, 20, 22, 23). Join a second ball of yarn and bind off 8 (10, 10, 10, 10) stitches, knit to end of row.

Working both sides at the same time, k2tog at neck edge on each side every right-side row 4 (5, 4, 6, 6) times. (12 [14, 16, 16, 17] stitches remain on each side)

Continue even in stockinette stitch until armhole measures 9" (10", 11", 12", 13"), ending with a wrong-side row. *Your piece now measures* 22" (24", 26", 27", 28").

Bind off all stitches.

KNITTING THE SLEEVES

(MAKE 2)

Setup: Using smaller needles, cast on 24 (28, 28, 32, 32) stitches.

Work 2x2 Rib for 2", ending with a wrong-side row.

Change to larger gauge needles and work in stockinette stitch for 1", ending with a wrong-side row.

SLEEVE SHAPING

Next Row (increase row, RS): K2, M1, knit to last 2 stitches, M1, k2. (2 stitches increased)

Work 3 rows even in stockinette stitch.

Repeat the last 4 rows 7 (5, 12, 13, 18) more times.

Work an increase row followed by 5 even rows 5 (7, 3, 3, 0) times. [50 (54, 60, 66, 70) stitches]

Continue even in stockinette as required until sleeve measures 19" (20", 21", 21", 22"), ending with a wrong-side row.

Bind off.

FINISHING

Block pieces to measurements. Assemble sweater by sewing shoulders together first, then set sleeves into shoulders. Sew sleeves from wrist to armhole, and body seams from bottom to armhole.

Note: If you find you have trouble seaming with the spiral-ply yarn, change to a commercial yarn in a similar color and weight.

KNITTING THE NECK

Setup: Starting at left shoulder seam, and using the smaller circular needle, pick up and knit 52 (52, 56, 56, 60) stitches around neck edge.

Place marker, and join for working in the round.

Work 2x2 Rib for 2".

Bind off.

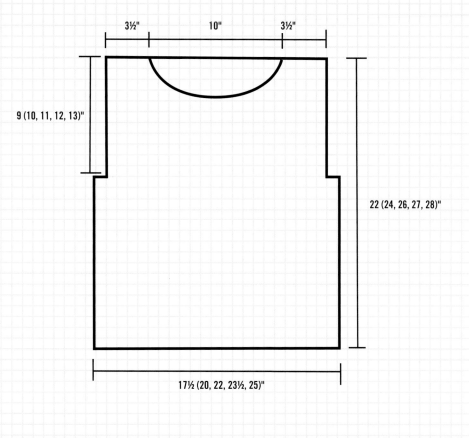

3½"   10"   3½"

9 (10, 11, 12, 13)"

22 (24, 26, 27, 28)"

17½ (20, 22, 23½, 25)"

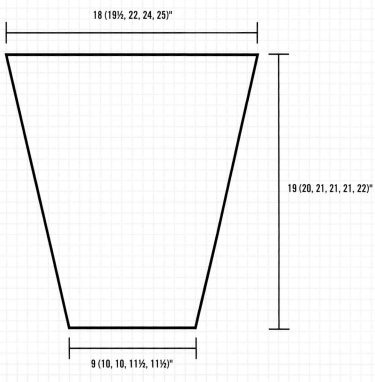

18 (19½, 22, 24, 25)"

19 (20, 21, 21, 21, 22)"

9 (10, 10, 11½, 11½)"

Suggested Reading

Amos, Alden. *The Alden Amos Big Book of Handspinning*. Interweave Press, 2001.

Anderson, Enid. *The Spinner's Encyclopedia*. Sterling Publishing, 1987.

Anderson, Sarah. *The Spinner's Book of Yarn Designs: Techniques for Creating 80 Yarns*. Storey Publishing, 2012.

Casey, Maggie. *Start Spinning: Everything You Need to Know to Make Great Yarn*. Interweave Press, 2008.

Fannin, Allen. *Handspinning: Art & Technique*. van Nostrand Reinhold, 1981.

Field, Anne. *Spinning Wool: Beyond the Basics*, rev ed. Trafalgar Square, 2010.

Fournier, Nola, and Elisabeth Fournier. *In Sheep's Clothing: A Handspinner's Guide to Wool*. Interweave Press, 1995.

Franquemont, Abby. *Respect the Spindle: Spin Infinite Yarns with One Amazing Tool*. Interweave Press, 2009.

King, Amy. *Spin Control: Techniques for Spinning the Yarn You Want*. Interweave Press, 2009.

Larsen, Kate. *The Practical Spinner's Guide: Wool*. Interweave Press, 2015.

McCuin, Judith MacKenzie. *The Intentional Spinner: A Holistic Approach to Making Yarn*. Interweave Press, 2009.

Menz, Deb. *Color in Spinning*. Interweave Press, 1998.

Parkes, Clara. *The Knitter's Book of Wool: The Ultimate Guide to Understanding, Using, and Loving this Most Fabulous Fiber*. Potter Craft, 2009.

———. *The Knitter's Book of Yarn: The Ultimate Guide to Choosing, Using, and Enjoying Yarn*. Potter Craft, 2007.

Robson, Deborah, and Carol Ekarius. *The Fleece & Fiber Sourcebook: More Than 200 Fibers from Animal to Spun Yarn*. Storey Publishing, 2011.

Ross, Mabel. *The Encyclopedia of Hand Spinning*. Interweave Press, 1988.

———. *The Essentials of Yarn Design for Handspinner*s. Rev. ed. Mabel Ross, 1986.

Smith, Beth. *The Spinner's Book of Fleece: A Breed-by-Breed Guide to Choosing and Spinning the Perfect Fiber for Every Purpose*. Storey Publishing, 2014.

Stove, Margaret. *Merino: Handspinning, Dyeing, and Working with Merino and Superfine Wools*. Interweave Press, 1991.

Vogel, Lynne. *The Twisted Sisters Knit Sweaters*. Interweave Press, 2007.

———. *The Twisted Sisters Sock Workbook*. Interweave Press, 2002.

BACKWARDS LOOP CAST ON

You can use this method of casting on in a variety of situations, but it's especially useful when you need to cast on in the middle or end of a row. Use only one needle for this cast on. Here's how to do it:

Make a slipknot in the yarn and place it on the needle. This is the needle that will receive the cast-on stitches. Holding it in your right hand, wrap the yarn counterclockwise around your left forefinger or thumb so that it creates a loop. The working end should be *over* the end that's attached to the stitch already on the needle. Next, insert the needle through the loop as though you were knitting, and slide the loop onto the needle. Repeat until you have cast on the required number of stitches. (*Note:* If you are using this method to cast on starting from scratch, you need to begin by placing a slip knot on the needle.)

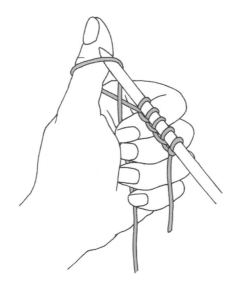

JUDY'S MAGIC CAST ON

Judy's Magic Cast On was first published in Knitty online, in the spring 2006 issue (http://knitty.com/ISSUEspring06/FEATmagiccaston.html). The version documented below differs from the original published version in two small ways; this update was also developed by Judy herself and makes the process a little easier.

Setup, Step 1: You'll need a tail, about a half inch per stitch for the total cast-on number, and two needles. Hold the two needles parallel in your right hand, with the tips pointing left. Loop the yarn over the topmost of the two needles.The stitch goes on the right-most needle.

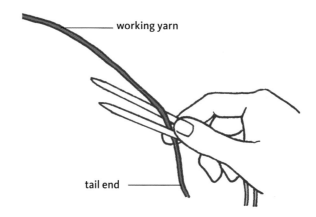

Setup, Step 2: Set up the tail and working ends of the yarn in your left hand as you would for the Long-Tail Cast On (see page 228), but with the yarn tail on your finger and the working yarn on your thumb.

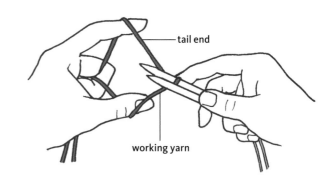

Creating Stitches, Step 1:
You work in pairs, and it's a game of opposites. The left/lower needle needs a stitch, so we take the yarn on the index finger and drape it over the needle from the outside, down into the middle.

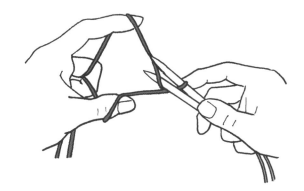

Creating Stitches, Step 2:
We have a pair of stitches. The right/upper needle now needs a stitch, so we take the yarn on the thumb, and bring it up between the tips of the needles and over the top of the right/upper needle.

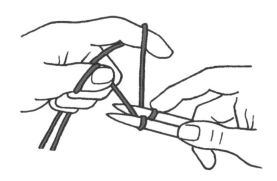

Repeat Steps 2 and 3 until you have the total number of stitches you need, half on each needle.

To knit, turn the work so that the working yarn and the tail end are on the right-hand side of the needle. Using the working yarn, knit the first stitch on the top needle. You'll see that the stitch isn't fully formed; you have to twist the yarns around each other for that first stitch.

The rest of that needle's stitches are well formed and stable. Knit to the end of that needle, and then turn the work around to knit the other needle's stitches. (Stay on the same side of the developing fabric to keep a smooth stockinette look.) Once you've knitted both needle's stitches, your first round is complete.

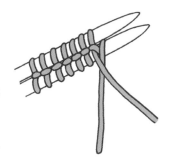

KNITTED CAST ON

Make a slipknot and place it on your left-hand needle. Knit into this loop as normal, but do not drop the stitch or the loop off the needles. Insert the left-hand needle into the front of the newly created loop from right to left, and place the new stitch onto the left-hand needle. Continue by knitting into the first stitch on the left-hand needle and placing the resulting stitch on the left-hand needle until you have cast on the required number of stitches.

KITCHENER STITCH

Also called "grafting," this way of joining two sections of knitting is done on "live" stitches. To set up for it, place half the stitches to be joined on one needle and the other half on another needle. Arrange the needles with their points facing in the same direction and with the wrong sides of the fabric facing each other. Thread a yarn needle with the working yarn. Note that some instructions have a setup step: the end result of this version is not significantly different, and it's a little easier to work.

1. Insert the yarn needle into the first stitch on the front needle from left to right (as if you were going to knit with it). Draw the yarn through the stitch, and slip it off the needle.

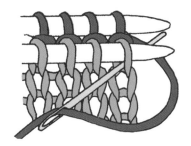

2. Insert the needle into the next stitch on the front needle from right to left (as if you were going to purl it), draw the yarn through, but leave the stitch on the needle.

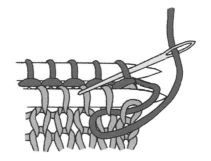

3. Insert the needle through the first stitch on the back needle from right to left (as if you were going to purl it). Draw the yarn through the stitch, and slip it off the needle.

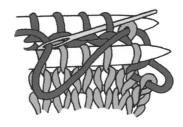

4. Insert the needle through the next stitch on the back needle from left to right (as if you were going to knit it). Draw the yarn through the stitch, but leave the stitch on the needle.

Repeat steps 1–4 until all of the stitches have been joined. Cut yarn and fasten off.

LONG-TAIL CAST ON

Estimate the length of yarn you will need for the cast on by wrapping the yarn around the needle as many times as the number of required stitches; add a few inches extra to be sure you have enough. Make a slipknot at that point and place it on the needle.

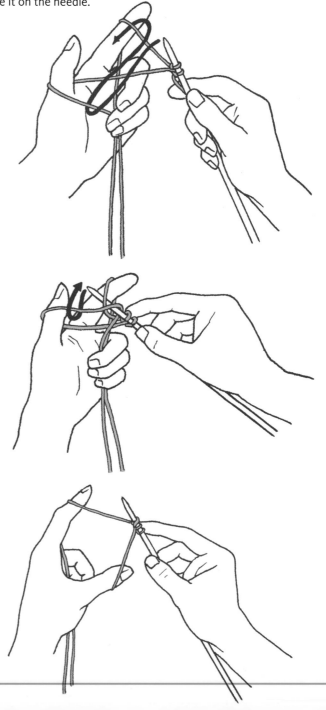

1. Hold the needle in your right hand, and arrange the yarns so that the tail comes from the slipknot to lie over your thumb to the outside and the working yarn comes from the slipknot to lie over your forefinger to the outside; use your other fingers to secure both yarns in your palm, and use your right forefinger to keep the slipknot from sliding off the needle. Take the tip of the needle under the yarn tail on the outside of the thumb, then over the working yarn on the inside of the forefinger.

2. Use the tip of the needle to draw this strand through the loop on your thumb.

3. Let the yarn tail slip off your thumb so that you can draw the yarn tail and working yarn snug to form a new stitch. Try to maintain an even tension for each stitch, but ensure that the stitches have a little bit of space between them on the needle. If they are too close together the edge will be too tight.

SEWN BIND OFF

This bind off is also called stretchy bind off. Cut your working yarn, leaving a tail three times as long as the length of stitches you're binding off. Thread a yarn needle with the tail.

1. Insert the needle from right to left (as if to purl) through the first two stitches on the needle, and draw the yarn through.

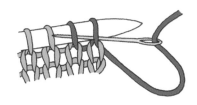

2. Insert the needle through the first stitch from left to right (as if to knit), and drop that stitch off the needle.

Repeat steps 1 and 2 until one stitch remains. Draw the yarn through that stitch, fasten off, and weave in the tail.

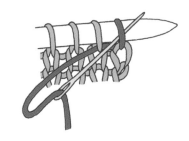

THREE-NEEDLE BIND OFF

As with Kitchener Stitch, this way of joining two sections of knitting is done on "live" stitches. To set up for it, place half the stitches to be joined on one needle and the other half on another needle. Arrange the needles with their points facing in the same direction and with the right sides of the fabric facing each other. Insert a third needle into the first stitch on each of the other needles. Knit these two stitches together. Insert the third needle into the first stitch on each of the other needles and knit them together. Draw the stitch already on the right-hand needle over the new stitch, just as you do in a "normal" bind off. Repeat this process until you have bound off all (or the required number) of the stitches.

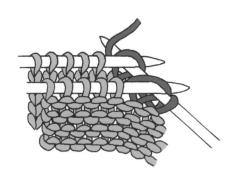

ADDING BEADS TO YOUR KNITTING

Choose a crochet hook small enough to fit through the holes in the beads you are using. When you come to the stitch where you want to place a bead, insert your hook through the bead and then into the next stitch on the left needle (a). Draw the stitch through the hole in the bead, then replace the stitch on the left needle (b). Knit the stitch as usual. (You can also use super floss or a Beadle Needle to thread the bead onto the stitch.)

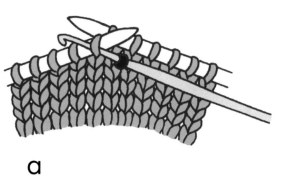

a

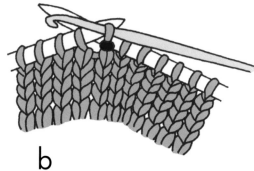

b

METRIC CONVERSION CHART

WHEN THE MEASUREMENT GIVEN IS	TO CONVERT IT TO	MULTIPLY IT BY
inches	centimeters	2.54
yards	meters	0.91
ounces	grams	28.4
pounds	kilograms	0.454
°F	°C	°F − 32 × 5/9

Abbreviations

[ ] Work instructions within brackets as many times as directed

( ) Work instructions within parentheses in the place directed

* Repeat instructions following the single asterisk as directed

** Repeat instructions between asterisks as many times as directed

CC Contrasting color

cdd Slip next 2 sts together knitwise, k1, pass 2 slipped stitches over stitch just knit

ch Chain stitch (crochet)

dc Double crochet

k Knit

k2tog Knit 2 stitches together: 1 stitch decreased

k2tog tbl Knit 2 stitches together through back loop: 1 stitch decreased

k3tog Knit 3 stitches together: 2 stitches decreased

kfb Knit into the front and back of the same stitch: 1 stitch increased to 2

kfbf Knit into the front, back, and front of the same stitch: 1 stitch increased to 3

M1 (Make 1), backward loop method Make a backward loop (yarn is wrapped counter-clockwise) and place it on your right needle: 1 stitch increased

M1L, lifted method Insert left needle, from front to back, under the horizontal strand that lies between the stitch just knit and the following stitch; then knit into the back of this loop: 1 stitch increased

M1R, lifted method Insert left needle from back to front under the horizontal strand that lies between the stitch just knit and the following stitch, then knit into the front of this loop: 1 stitch increased

MC Main color

p Purl

p2tog Purl 2 stitches together

pm Place marker

psso Pass slipped stitch over

RS Right side

sc Single crochet

skp Slip 1 stitch knitwise, knit next stitch, pass slipped stitch over: 1 stitch decreased

sk2p Slip 1 stitch knitwise, knit 2 stitches together, pass slipped stitch over the knit 2 together: 2 stitches decreased

sl1p Slip 1 purlwise

ssk Slip 2 stitches knitwise, one by one; return these 2 stitches to the left needle, and knit them together through the back loop: 1 stitch decreased

ssp Slip 2 stitches knitwise, one by one; return these 2 stitches to the left needle, and purl them together through the back loop: 1 stitch decreased

sssk Slip 3 stitches knitwise, one by one; return these 3 stitches to the left needle, and knit them together through the back loop: 2 stitches decreased

tbl Through the back loop

WS Wrong side

w&t, wrap and turn Slip the next stitch purlwise; move the yarn between the needles (if it's at the back, bring it to the front; if it's at the front, take it to the back); slip the stitch back to the left needle. Turn your work and bring the working yarn to working position for the next row

wyib With yarn in back

wyif With yarn in front

yo Yarnover

Fiber Companies

A Verb for Keeping Warm
averbforkeepingwarm.com

Abstract Fiber
abstractfiber.com

Anzula Luxury Fibers
http://anzula.com

Ashford Wheels & Looms
ashford.co.nz

Blue Moon Fiber Arts
bluemoonfiberarts.com

Bricolage Studios
bricolagestudios.bigcartel.com

cjkoho Designs
etsy.com/shop/cjkoho

Enchanted Knoll Farm
etsy.com/shop/enchantedknoll

Fiber Optic Yarns
kimberbaldwindesigns.com

Fiberstory
etsy.com/shop/fiberstory

Happy Fuzzy Yarn
http://happyfuzzyyarn.com

Hilltop Cloud
hilltopcloud.co.uk

Into the Whirled
shop.intothewhirled.com

Jazzturtle Creations
http://jazzturtle.com

Lisa Souza Knitwear and Dyeworks
lisaknit.com

Lorna's Laces
lornaslaces.net

Louet North America
louet.com

Mountain Colors
http://mountaincolors.com

The Natural Fibre Company
thenaturalfibre.co.uk

Porpoise Fur
porpoisefur.com

PortFiber
etsy.com/shop/portfiber

Sheepspot
sheepspot.com

Southern Cross Fibre
http://shop.southerncrossfibre.com

Spunky Eclectic
spunkyeclectic.com

Strathearn Fleece & Fibre
http://strathearnfleeceandfibre.co.uk

SweetGeorgia Yarns
http://sweetgeorgiayarns.com

Three Waters Farm
threewatersfarm.com

Treenway Silks
treenwaysilks.com

woolgatherings
etsy.com/shop/woolgatherings

Wheels and Tools

Camaj Fiber Arts
camajfiberarts.com
Twist angle gauge

HansenCrafts
http://hansencrafts.com
miniSpinner

Lendrum
lendrum.ca
Wheels

Louet North America
louet.com
Wheels

Nancy's Knit Knacks
nancysknitknacks.com
Lazy kates, wpi gauge

Schacht Spindle Company
http://schachtspindle.com
Wheels, lazy kate, bobbin winder, niddy noddy

Tangerine Designs
etsy.com/shop/Tangerine8?ref=l2-shopheader-name
wpi gauges

TravelKate
http://travelkate.com
Lazy kate

Other Online Shops

These resources have a variety of wheels, tools, and fiber.

Spunky Eclectic
spunkyeclectic.com

The Woolery
woolery.com

Acknowledgments

This book would never have been written and published without the help, love, and support of many, many people. My heartfelt thanks go out to the people listed below and to the people I've met in the fiber community who sparked an idea in passing or just simply understood my passion.

To my family I love you. Thank you for dealing with my crabby moods and my mess, for knowing the difference between a goat and a sheep, for pretending you understand what I'm always talking about, and for having fiber stuck to every piece of clothing you own and not minding too much.

To the people who literally touched this book in one way or another. I am grateful beyond measure.

The folks at Storey Publishing Gwen Steege, for believing in this book, for your encouragement, kindness, respect, and for holding all of the threads through the whole process.

Deborah Balmuth, for giving this book the green light and for treating your reps so well.

Carolyn Eckert, for your unique and beautiful vision for my book and for the shared love of texture.

John Polak, for making my book come alive with the most detailed and exquisite fiber photography.

Alee Moncy and Sarah Armour, for telling the world about my book.

Beth Smith, for giving this book your spinning stamp of approval and arguing about only one thing.

Kate Atherley, for being the greatest, most relentless tech editor any book or designer could have.

My designers Kate Atherley, Adrian Bizilia, Julia Farwell-Clay, Romi Hill, Bristol Ivy, Kirsten Kapur, Amy King, Laura Nelkin, and Lynne Vogel, who honored this book with their talent. Thank you for saying yes when this fan girl asked.

The dyers, for inspiring me with luscious color, for featuring prominently in my personal stash and supporting me with fiber for my samples (and more):

Christine Eschbach and James Shapiro, Carla Kohoyda-Inglis, Amy King, Sarah Freitas, Tina Newton, David Schulz, Adrian Bizilia, Riin Gill, Sasha Torres, Lisa Souza, Beth Casey, Kate Sitzman, Emily Wohlscheid, Esther Rogers, Josette McWilliams, Rachel Brown, Katie Weston, Felicia Lo, Mary Ann Pagano, and Casey Ryder.

To my spinners Carol Knox and Beth Smith, thanks for your steady hands, consistent drafting, and perfect yarns.

To The Porches for letting us shoot most of the book in your wonderfully eclectic hotel.

A big fuzzy hug to the people who kept me going, who answered my questions, who applied kindness and a foot to my butt in equal measure — this book would never have happened without you.

To my flock of friends, fiber and otherwise, who cheered me on, thank you for listening, always asking, "How's the book?," reminding me that I know how to spin, and believing in me and this book.

Kat Christensen, Greg Cotton, Kate Jackman, Amy King, Kirsten Mowrey, Sasha Torres.

The Women of BLAR: Alice, Beth, Carla, Dynese, Erica, Katherine, and Sarah — thank you for the years of fiber get-aways, the thousands of hours of movies, spinning, alcohol, and rude humor.

Carla Kohoyda-Inglis, for all the years of shared fiber obsession.

Jane Patrick (not the weaver), for letting me say whatever is in my head no matter how awful it is.

Amy Singer, for encouraging me to follow whatever dreams I have and helping to make them happen with *Knitty*.

Beth Smith, for teaching me so many things and for being my friend even though I don't like spinning white fiber.

I've encountered a lot of wickedly smart and creative women on my personal spinning journey. These women are my light; they keep me inspired, keep me going back to the wheel, the classroom, and the keyboard. I am indebted.

Jacey Boggs, for going your own way and thriving.

Maggie Casey, for teaching me that there is not just one way to spin.

Linda Ligon, for opening the door to the world of fiber publishing and giving me a chance when you didn't really want to. For planting the seeds for our spinning community from which so much has bloomed.

Judith MacKenzie, for keeping and sharing the stories and for the words of encouragement.

Clara Parkes, for leading by thoughtful example.

Jane Patrick, for creating the most beautiful spinning tools and adapting so well to a changing market.

Deb Robson, for never giving up, ever.

Sarah Swett, for showing how to be dedicated to your craft.

Lynne Vogel, for color and creativity and for starting me on this path.

Saving the best for last, my thanks to the spinners I have sat beside and talked to over the years — thank you for so generously sharing with me what you know and what you think.

To my students, for showing up, always asking the best questions, teaching me new things, and not minding when I sing or dance in class.

To you, for buying this book — thank you and happy spinning.

Index

bold = chart

A

Alexander, Kathryn, 124
alpaca, 36–37, 42
Andean ply, 88–89
angora, 42
    goat, 36–38
    rabbit, 35–36
Atherley, Kate, 173, 233
attenuating fiber, 56, 61–63, 107, 112

B

balanced yarn, 78–79, **80**
bamboo fibers, 39
batts, 44–45
    why prep matters, 95
    working with striped colors, 111–15
bison, 36–38
Bizilia, Adrian, 211, 233
Bluefaced Leicester (BFL), 31–33, 94, 120, 142
    blend, 72, 109, 185
    characteristics, 35
    project with, 199
Boggs, Jacey, 10, 233
bombyx silk, 37–39, 72, 92
braids
    braided top (worsted preparation), 42
    fiber preparations from braids, 40, 95
    maintaining color sequence, 98
    mixing up the colors, 101–6
    one braid spun five ways, 17
    packaged and unbraided, 60
Bump in the Night, 178–81
    stitch chart, **180**

C

camel, 36, 42, 45
    project with, 159
Camelids, 36
    alpaca, 36–37, 42
    camel, 36, 42, 45, 159–60
    llama, 36
carding machines, 43–44
casein fibers, 39
cashgora, 38
cashmere, 36–38, 42, 45, 56
    finishing, 119
center-pull ball, 79, 88
centripetal force, 118–19, 121, 123
chain plying
    for color consistency, 99
    how-to, 86–87
chunking from striped batts, 114–15
cloud, 43, 45, 47
color. *See also* variegated yarn
    blending two different colors while drafting, 107
    chain plying for consistency, 99
    core spinning to match colors, 101
    effect of drafting, 95
    effect of number of plies, 97
    effect of yarn size, 96
    how dyers dye, 91
    maintaining braid color sequence, 98
    marling, how to avoid, 100
    plying to match colors, 100–101
    why prep matters, 95
    working with striped batts, 111–15
color mixing in braids
    chunk removal, 105
    combining and drafting together, 105–6
    create confetti, 105
    doing a flip, 102
    fractal fun, 102–3
    pure progression, 103–4
color wheel, 93
Columbia wool, 35
combing, 35, 38–39, 41–43
commercially processed fiber, 15–16, 32, 49

control
  controlling yarn size while drafting, 59
  options when spinning, 16–19
  spinning from the fold, 57, 59
  worsted drafting, 50
control card, 77, 98–99, 131, 144
core spinning to match colors, 101
Cormo, 143
  characteristics, 32, 35
Corriedale, 35, 92, 94, 120, 142
  project with, 211
  staple lengths, 56
  swatches, 52, 55, 122
counting treadles, 67–68, 79
crimp, 32, 35–36

D

double-drive system, 64–67
drafting. *See also* predrafting
  consistency, 68
  controlling yarn size, 59
  effect of drafting on color, 91
  fiber blends, 56
  spinning from the fold, 57
  triangle, 50
  against type, 55
  woolen style, 53
  worsted style, 50–51
drive systems, 64–67
Dye Goddess Pullover, 216–21
  schematic, 221
dyeing. *See also* handdyed fibers and yarn
  different fibers, 92, 94
  how dyers dye, 91
  silk, 92
  why prep matters, 95

E

elasticity, 32
  spinning from the fold to add elasticity, 57
estimating fiber needs, 129–30

F

Falkland wool, 35
Farwell-Clay, Julia, 128, 183, 185
fauxlags, 45, 111
  creating from striped batts, 114–15
fiber festivals, 15, 31, 217
finishing
  centripetal force, 118–19, 121
  fulling, 119, 121
  knitted samples from different finishes, 122–23
  menacing, 119, 121
  snapping, 118, 120
  soaking, 117–18, 120
  steaming, 117, 120
  weight, why not to use, 124–25
  whacking, 119, 121
fluffing, 56, 61–62
fulling, 119, 121, 123

G

gauge
  homemade twist-angle, 134
  knitting, 128–29, **130**, 133
  wpi, 131
goat
  angora, 36–38, 42
  cashgora, 38
  cashmere, 36–38, 42, 45, 56, 119
  pygora, 37–38, 45
grist (ypp), **130**, 137–40
  altering, 143
  the gist of grist, 141
  how to adjust and correct, 143
  how to measure, 139–40
  keeping track, 26
  what influences grist, 142

H

handdyed fibers and yarn, 15
    color and handspun yarn, 128
    how dyers dye, 91
    questions to ask, 19
handspun yarn
    combining with mill-spun, 128–29
    gauge, 133
    measuring, **130**, 130–32
    vs. mill-spun, 128
    why to knit with, 16–17
HansenCrafts, 66
Hill, Rosemary (Romi), 167, 233
Hive Mind, 210–15
    stitch charts, **214–15**
how much fiber do you need?, 129–30

I

Irish tension, 64–67
Ivy, Bristol, 203, 233

J

Jillian Shawl, 166–71
    stitch chart, **171**
joining
    woolen-style, 54
    worsted-style, 52

K

Kapur, Kirsten, 159, 233
keeping track
    when you knit, 144
    of your spinning, 26
King, Amy, 179, 191, 222, 233
knitting
    how ply affects knitting, 81
    how twist affects knitting, 79–80, 146
Knox, Carol, 160, 174, 196, 233

L

La Cuerda, 194–97
lazy kate, 77–78, 88
leaders, 50
Lendrum spinning wheel, 66
Lina Toe-Up Socks, 172–77
llama, 36
Louet spinning wheel, 66

M

marling
    combining variegated colors, 109–10
    how to avoid, 100
    plying yarn, 99
    spinning variegated yarn, 83
Maya Cardigan, 158–65
    schematic, 165
measuring handspun yarn, **130**, 130–32
    how to check grist, 137–40
    how to figure length of mystery or partial skein, 137
    how to measure length, 136–37
    how to weight, 137
menacing, 119, 121, 123
Merino, 31, 120, 122
    blends, 39, 72–73, 109, 142
    characteristics, 32–33, 35
    projects with, 151, 195, 199, 217
    staple lengths, 56
    superwash, 97
mill-spun yarns, 16, 28, 127–29
MiniSpinner, 66
Moreno, Jillian, 199, 217
motivation, 27–28
musk ox, 36–37

N

Nelkin, Laura, 195, 233
nylon, 35, 39, 53

P

Parkes, Clara, 6, 13, 16, 222, 233
pilling
  fiber characteristics, 32, 35
  finishing methods, 119
  plied yarns, 72, 84
  singles, 81
  woolen-style drafting, 53
  worsted-style drafting, 50
planning knitting projects, 145–46
ply and plying. *See also* singles
  Andean ply, 88–89
  chain ply how-to, 86–87
  equipment needed, 76–77
  how ply affects knitting, 81
  how to ply, 77–79
  mistakes, how to fix, 87–89
  sampling 2-ply yarns, 82–83
  sampling 3-ply yarns, 84–84
  spit splice, 87
  templates, 77
  what it is and what it does, 71–74
ply-back sample, 99
  how to make one, 69
ply-back to check for twist, 135–36
Polwarth, 32, 56
  project with, 179
predrafting, 60–63
  attenuating, 62–63
  fluffing, 61
  stripping, 62
preparations
  batts, 44
  cloud, 45
  commercial vs. hand-prepared, 41
  fauxlags, 45
  fiber preparations from braids, 40, 95
  puni, 45
  rolags, 45
  roving, 44
  silk, 47
  sliver, 43

  wool locks, 46–47
  woolen vs. worsted, 41–42
  worsted top, 42–43
pulleys (whorls), 59, 63–64
puni, 43, 45
pygora, 37–38, 45

Q

qiviut, 37–38

R

Rambouillet
  characteristics, 32, 35
  project with, 203
ratios, 63–64
rayon fibers, 39, 42
Rigby Cardigan, 202–209
  schematic, 23, 209
Robson, Deborah, 16, 222, 233
rolags, 40, 45, 95
Romney, 35, 56
  project with, 183

S

sample yarn and index cards, 131
sampling, 22, 26, 28–29, 144
  control cards, 98–99
  for drafting consistency, 68
  ply-back sample, 69, 135–36
  sampling 2-ply yarns, 82–83
  sampling 3-ply yarns, 84–84
  sampling singles, 81
  sampling twist in plied yarns, **80**
scale for weighing yarn, 137, 139
Schacht spinning wheel, 66
schematic example, 23
Scotch tension, 64–67
semi-worsted or semi-woolen, 68
shine, 32, 36, 39, 44, 57

silk, 31, 35–36, 38–39
blends, 53, 56, 72–74
bombyx, 37–39, 72, 92
dyeing, 92
hankies, 38, 47
preparations, 47
preserving shine, 57
projects with, 151, 159, 167, 199, 217
tussah, 39, 120, 122
singles
compared to plied, 71–72, 75
for knitting, 98
resting and rewinding, 79
singles to stay singles, 75
sliver, 43–44
Smith, Beth, 16, 183, 185, 222, 233, 240
snapping, 118, 120, 123
soaking, 117–18, 120, 122
soy fibers, 39
spinner's control card, 131
spinning from the fold, 57, 59
silk, 39
spit splice, 87
stacking colors from a bat, 112–13, 115
staple length, 32, 56–57
stash, digging into your, 98–99
steaming, 117, 120, 122
stripping, 60, 62, 96
superwash yarn, 87, 97, 119
Sweet Omega Möbius, 150–57
stitch chart, **154**

T

Targhee, 33
Teeswater, 32, 35, 56
Tencel, 39, 42
blends, 72–73, 109, 142
Tetris Pullover, 182–89
schematic, 189
treadling speed, 54, 59, 63, 66–67
counting treadles, 67–68, 79

tussah silk, 39, 120, 122
projects with, 151
twist, 49
angle, 26, 133–34
controlling thickness, 59
direction, 26
how twist affects knitting, 79–80, 146–47
per inch (tpi), 26, 135
ratios and whorls, 63–64
sampling twist in plied yarns, **80**
tension, 67
woolen-style drafting, 53–54
worsted-style drafting, 51
Tyvek wristbands, 26

V

variegated yarn
braids, 98, 101, 103
chain-plying, 86–87
combining variegated colors, 109–10
how dyers dye, 91
how ply affects knitting, 81, 83, 85
how yarn size affects color, 96
maintaining color sequence, 98–99
plied samples, 73
stripping to control color, 62
working with striped batts, 111–15
vocabulary, 26
Vogel, Lynne, 151, 222, 233

W

Wenny Shawl, 190–93
stitch chart, 192
Wensleydale, 35, 56, 94, 130
project with, 191
whacking, 119, 121, 123
wheels
double-drive system, 64–67
evaluating your wheel, 27
Irish tension, 64–67
MiniSpinner, 66

Scotch tension, 64–67
    working together, 60
whorls (pulleys), 59, 63–64
why spin?, 25
Winter Library Shawl, 198–201
wool. *See also wools by breed name*
    backbone of spinning, 31–32
    characteristics of fiber, 32
    fine wools, 32, 35
    longwools, 35
    medium wools, 35
woolen preparations
    batts, 44
    cloud, 45, 47
    fauxlags, 45
    puni, 45
    rolags, 45
    sliver, 44
    wool locks, 46–47
    vs. worsted, 41–42
woolen style
    drafting, 53
    joining, 54

worsted style
    drafting, 50
    joining, 50
    preparations, 42–43
    vs. woolen, 41–42
wraps per inch (wpi), 26–27, 128–32
    A Cautionary Tale, 132
    gauges, 131
    how to measure, 130–31

Y

yak, 36–38, 42, 45
    project with, 195
    staple length, 56
yards per pound (ypp). *See* grist
yarn balance, 139–40

Z

zip-top bags, 26, 144

MORE STOREY BOOKS
to Help You Spin a Beautiful Yarn

Margaret Radcliffe

Say "Yikes!" to stripes no more! These in-depth, full-color instructions for multicolor knitting methods such as intarsia, entrelac, Fair Isle — and yes, stripes — will give you confidence in your colorwork.

Margaret Radcliffe

Make every project a success with this comprehensive guide to the whys and hows behind every knitting technique. This definitive resource will help knitters of all levels produce better-fitting garments.

Beth Smith

This essential companion for spinners of all levels is a sheep-by-sheep guide to 21 breeds and the characteristics of their wool. Learn the best washing, prepping, and spinning methods for each kind of fleece.

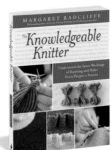

Sarah Anderson

Discover the fun and satisfaction of creating your own specialty yarns, from basic 2-ply to spirals, bouclés, crepes, and novelty styles. Step-by-step instructions and photographs feature 80 distinctive yarns.

These and other books from Storey Publishing are available wherever quality books are sold or by calling 800-441-5700. Visit us at storey.com or sign up for our newsletter at storey.com/signup.

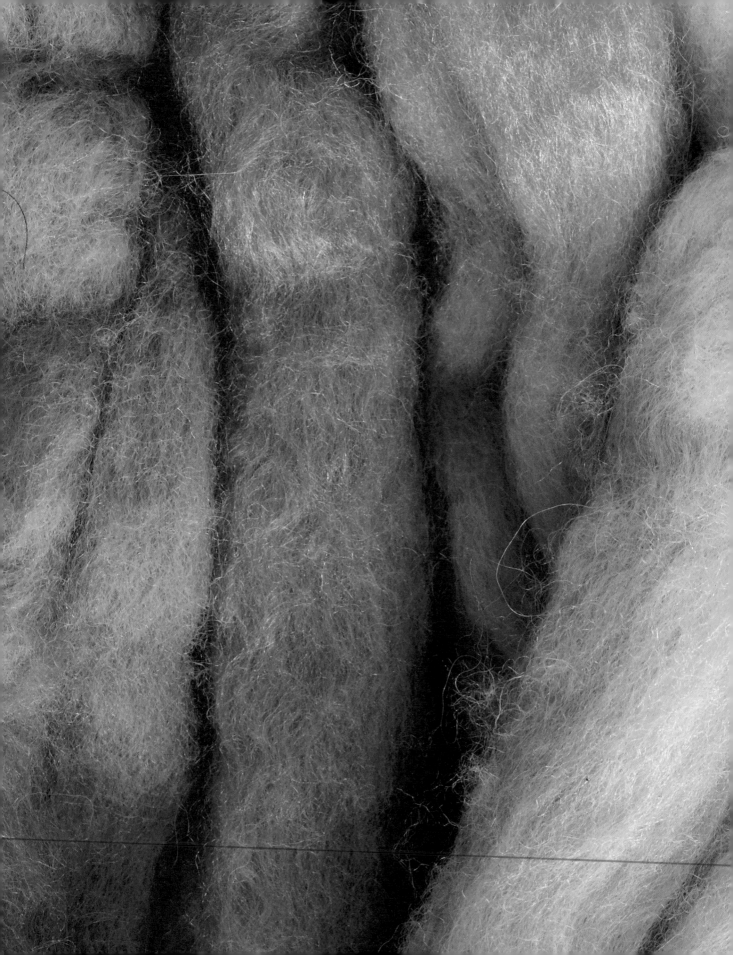